*Towards a New Paradigm in Monetary Economics* presents a fundamentally new approach to monetary economics, derived from the authors' pioneering work in the Economics of Information, for which one of the authors was awarded the Nobel Prize in 2001. Unlike the prevailing theory, it focuses not on the role of money in facilitating transactions but on the role of credit in facilitating economic activities more broadly. The "new paradigm" emphasizes the demand and supply of loanable funds, which in turn requires an understanding of how banks and other institutions in the economy process information to evaluate creditworthiness. It explains the factors which determine the willingness and ability of banks to provide credit, explores the consequences of credit interlinkages within the economy, describes the implications of the new paradigm for the conduct of policy, and analyzes how changes in the structure of the economy, such as those associated with the New Economy, are likely to impact the effectiveness of monetary policy, and thereby the stability of the economy. The book identifies the circumstances in which monetary policy alone is likely to be ineffective in restoring the economy to full employment, and suggests that those circumstances are likely to be more prevalent in the future.

The book consists of two parts. The first develops the basic theory, using a portfolio approach to explain how banks decide on how much to lend, and how changes in regulations as well as economic circumstances, both the balance sheets of banks and firms and perceptions of risks within the economy, affect the supply of credit. The second part is dedicated to the policy implications. It argues that the new paradigm provides a far better guide for addressing issues that range from financial market liberalization to how to handle the East Asia crisis than does the standard theory.

JOSEPH STIGLITZ is Professor of Economics and Finance at Columbia University, holding a joint appointment in the Graduate School of Business, the School of International and Public Affairs, and the Economics Department. In 2001 he was awarded the Nobel Prize in Economics for his work in the Economics of Information. Earlier, he was awarded the John Bates Clark Award, awarded biennially by the American Economic Association for the economist under 40 who has made the most significant contribution to economics. Formerly, he was Chairman of the President's Council of Economic Advisers and a member of President Clinton's cabinet, and Senior Vice President for Development Economics and Chief Economist of the World Bank.

BRUCE GREENWALD is Robert Heilbrunn Professor of Finance and Asset Management at Columbia Business School. Professor Greenwald has done pioneering work in the Economics of Information, especially the consequences of asymmetries of information for equity and labor markets. His recent co-authored work on value investing is already on its way to becoming a new classic in the field.

THE RAFFAELE MATTIOLI LECTURE SERIES

# Towards a New Paradigm in Monetary Economics

Joseph Stiglitz
and
Bruce Greenwald

PUBLISHED BY THE PRESS SYNDICATE OF THE UNIVERSITY OF CAMBRIDGE
The Pitt Building, Trumpington Street, Cambridge, United Kingdom

CAMBRIDGE UNIVERSITY PRESS
The Edinburgh Building, Cambridge CB2 2RU, UK
40 West 20th Street, New York NY 10011 – 4211, USA
477 Williamstown Road, Port Melbourne, VIC 3207, Australia
Ruiz de Alarcón 13, 28014 Madrid, Spain
Dock House, The Waterfront, Cape Town 8001, South Africa

http://www.cambridge.org

First published 2003

Printed in the United Kingdom at the University Press, Cambridge

*Typeface* Utopia 9.5/13 pt      *System* Quark Xpress    [TB]

*A catalogue record for this book is available from the British Library*


ISBN 0 521 810345 (hb)
ISBN 0 521 008050 (pb)

# Contents

# Figures and table

# The Raffaele Mattioli Lectures

The Raffaele Mattioli Lectures, in which many prominent economists have taken part, were established in 1976 by Banca Commerciale Italiana in association with Università Commerciale Luigi Bocconi as a memorial to the cultural legacy left by Raffaele Mattioli, for many years chairman of the bank.

The aim of the new series of Lectures, which was not only promoted by the then Banca Commerciale Italiana and Università Commerciale Luigi Bocconi but also supported by Università Cattolica del "Sacro Cuore" (Milan), Università degli Studi di Milano and Politecnico di Milano, was to create an opportunity for reflection and debate on topics of particular current interest, thus providing stimuli and ideas for the increasing challenges of a continually changing worldwide economic scenario.

The present initiative is therefore dedicated to the analysis of the effects of important changes which are now taking place in the world economy: the globalization of markets, the continuous evolution in the field of information, technology and communications and the convergence of economics and international relations.

It is evident that these changes, coupled with the European Monetary Union, provide many complex subjects that will be best dealt with from an interdisciplinary perspective.

Distinguished academics and researchers of all nationalities concerned with all kinds of economic problems will be invited to take part in this enterprise, with the intention of contributing to the debate interconnecting economic theory with practical policy.

# Preface

These lectures were presented in Milan in abbreviated form on November 9, 1999 at Banca Commerciale Italiana and on November 10, 1999 at Bocconi University as the biannual Raffaele Mattioli Lecture. We are grateful to the staff at BCI and Bocconi, and for the useful comments from the discussants: Patrick Artus, Giovanni Barone-Adesi, Giampio Bracchi, Marco Pagano, Luigi Spaventa, Mario Saranelli, and Gianni Toniolo. In addition we would like to acknowledge the contribution of Barbara Rindi from the Scientific Committee of Bocconi University. We used the occasion to try to summarize a line of research that we had been pursuing for the past fifteen years. Our theoretical work in this area was interrupted by Stightz going to Washington, as a member and then Chairman of the President's Council of Economic Advisers, and then as Chief Economist of the World Bank and its Senior Vice President for Development. While the seven years in Washington had interrupted our formal research program, the events surrounding that tumultuous period provided what could not have been a better testing ground for the ideas that we had been developing. We became increasingly convinced not only that our ideas were right, but that they were important and relevant: that had the perspectives on monetary policy that we had been developing been widely adopted, for instance, the IMF might well have managed the global financial crisis of 1997–1999 far better.

We have attempted to present these ideas here simply, with words, diagrams, and simple mathematics, illustrated by examples drawn from recent experiences.

In developing these ideas, we are indebted to a large number of co-authors, who have participated with us actively at various stages in our research program. The ideas of one of our longest-term collaborators, Andy Weiss, with whom we developed the theory of credit rationing, and one of our youngest collaborators, Jason Furman, with whom we analyzed the East Asia crisis, will be especially apparent. We should also like to thank Barry Nalebuff, Carl Shapiro, Arik Levinson, Michael Salinger, Meir Kohn, Amar Bhattarcharya, Alan Blinder, Michael Rothschild, Mark Gersovitz, Jonathan Eaton, Marcus Miller, Marilou Uy, Raj Sah, Yingi Qian, Steve Salop, Ian Gale, Dwight Jaffee, Kevin Murdoch, Thomas Hellman, Andreas Rodriguez, Richard Arnott, and Giovanni Ferri, who co-authored one or more of the papers that provided the backdrop to the results reported here. The notion that capital markets were imperfect, and that cash flows might therefore limit investment, was a conventional assumption in much of macro economics before neo-classical models came to predominate. Such an assumption played an important role in some of Stiglitz's earlier work in macro economics, some of which was done with Robert Solow, George Akerlof, Hirofumi Uzawa, and Peter Neary.

We have discussed the ideas presented in this book at universities and central banks throughout the world, and the innumerable comments and criticisms have been invaluable – and though too numerous to mention by name, whether friendly or hostile, they have helped improve the book immensely.

Research assistantship in preparing the manuscript was provided by Monica Fuentes, Noémi Giszpenc, Niny Khor, Anton Korinek, Nadia Roumani, Ravi Singh, Marco Sorge, Maya Tudor, Kelly Wang, and to all of these we are greatly indebted.

At various stages, the research on which this book is based has been supported by the National Science Foundation, the Ford Foundation, the Rockefeller Foundation, Bell Labs (now part of Lucent), Princeton University, Oxford University, and the World Bank. We are particularly indebted to Stanford University and

Columbia University for their support during the period in which this book was written.

The usual disclaimer that the ideas presented here are those solely of the authors, and not of the institutions with which they are currently or were previously affiliated, applies with particular force. We would be remiss not to acknowledge the vibrant intellectual atmosphere inside the World Bank, in which the ideas presented here were debated, challenged, and adopted and adapted as we confronted the most dramatic set of economic events of the last half of the twentieth century – the global financial crisis; but we would also be remiss if we did not express our sense of frustration at the attempts by the US Treasury and the IMF to suppress open discussion of these ideas. What was at stake was more than issues of intellectual freedom or professional integrity, but what we mean by meaningful democracy. There cannot be meaningful democracy without transparency and without open public discourse of vital issues that affect the lives and livelihoods of the citizens. The ideas presented here do represent a major change in thinking about certain aspects of policy, and as such they represent a challenge to the established orthodoxy. The policy implications are important – not only for the aggregate performance of the economy but for specific groups within our societies. It is our hope that in presenting these ideas, in an imperfect form as they are at the current state of development, they will stimulate debate and discussion, and that on the basis of these ideas alternative policies will be formulated which will spare those facing crises in the future from the policies that so ravaged the countries of East Asia.

The publisher has used its best endeavors to ensure that the URLs for external websites referred to in this book are correct and active at the time of going to press. However, the publisher has no responsibility for the websites and can make no guarantee that a site will remain live or that the content is or will remain appropriate.

Joseph Stiglitz, Columbia University, New York
Bruce Greenwald, Columbia University, New York

# PART ONE

# The principles of the new paradigm

Money has long played a central role in popular conceptions of economics – and life more generally. "Money makes the world go around" and "money is the root of all evil" are but two aphorisms that come to mind.

Professional economists give money an equally mixed review. The monetarists – whose enormous popularity in the early 1980s seems subsequently to have waned – place money as a central determinant of economic activity. By contrast, in the classical dichotomy, money has no *real* effects, a view which has been revived in real business cycle theory.[1] Monetary economics has thus been a curious branch of economics: At times, its central

---

These lectures are based on our joint research over the past decade, parts of which are reported in Greenwald (1998), Greenwald and Stiglitz (1987a, 1987b, 1987c, 1988a, 1988b, 1988c, 1988d, 1989a, 1989b, 1990a, 1990b, 1991a, 1991b, 1991c, 1991d, 1992, 1993a, 1993b, 1993c, 1995); Greenwald, Kohn and Stiglitz (1990); Greenwald, Levinson and Stiglitz (1993); Greenwald, Salinger and Stiglitz (1991); Greenwald, Stiglitz and Weiss (1984) and Clay, Greenwald and Stiglitz (1990). In parts of these lectures, we have also drawn upon joint work with Thomas Hellmann and Kevin Murdoch (especially in the discussions concerning bank regulation) reported in Hellmann, Murdoch and Stiglitz (2000) and in Hellmann and Stiglitz (2000). The analysis of the East Asia crisis in part II draws heavily upon joint work with Jason Furman, published in Furman and Stiglitz (1998). The views expressed here are solely those of the authors and do not necessarily represent those of any organization with which they are or have been affiliated.
[1] See Kydland and Prescott (1990) and Kydland and Cooley (1995).

tenet seems to be that it is a subject of no interest to anyone interested in real economics; at other times, it moves front and center.

While for long periods of time the view that money does not matter has held sway in monetary theory, this does not appear to be the view of the world, which hangs on anxiously, wondering whether the Federal Reserve will raise or lower interest rates by as little as twenty-five basis points. As our starting point for this book, we recognize there is some validity in the view that money matters, at least in the short run. We take it that the task of monetary economics is to explain why, and in doing so, provide better guidance to policymakers attempting to use monetary policy to enhance the overall economic performance – allowing expansion of the economy, at least to the point where such expansion does not lead to an increase in the rate of inflation.

The central thesis of this chapter is that the traditional approach to monetary economics, based on the transactions demand for money, is seriously flawed; it does not provide a persuasive explanation for why – or how – money matters. Rather, we argue that the key to understanding monetary economics is the demand and supply of loanable funds, which in turn is contingent on understanding the importance, and consequences, of imperfections of information and the role of banks. We argue, in particular, that one should not think of the market for loans as identical to the market for ordinary commodities, an auction market in which the interest rate[2] is set simply to equate the demand and supply of funds. T-bill rates do matter, but they affect economic activity largely indirectly, through their effect on banks. Banks provide vital certification, monitoring, and enforcement services, ascertaining who is likely to fulfill their promises to repay, ensuring that money lent is spent in the way promised, and collecting money at the due date.

---

[2] For most of part I, we assume that the inflation rate is fixed, so that the interest rates can be viewed as either nominal or real (since changes in nominal translate immediately into changes in real). Since traditional economic analysis has stressed that what matters is real variables, including real interest rates, it will be convenient to think of the interest rates as inflation adjusted real interest rates. In those chapters of the book where we focus on the effects of nominal interest rates as well as real ones, we will use subscripts to denote nominals.

That some loans are not repaid is central. A theory of monetary policy which pays no attention to bankruptcy and default is like *Hamlet* without the Prince of Denmark, and is likely to – and in the East Asia crisis, did – lead to drastically erroneous policies. Thus, a central function of banks is to determine who is likely to default, and in doing so, banks determine the supply of loans. Providing these certification, monitoring, and enforcement services is in some ways like any other business; there is risk, and thus the key to understanding the behavior of banks is understanding limitations on their ability to absorb these risks, and how their ability and willingness to do so can change with changes in economic circumstances and in government regulations. A closer look at these determinants of bank behavior reveals why it is that economic activity may depend on the nominal interest rate as well as the real interest rate, thus providing an explanation of one of the more disturbing anomalies in economics.[3]

While banks are at the center of the credit system, they are also part of a broader credit "general equilibrium" – a general equilibrium whose interdependencies are as important as those that have traditionally been discussed in goods and services markets. However, their interdependencies, until now largely unexplored, are markedly different – and are affected differently both by economic events and policies.

This book can be viewed as a contribution to the new institutional economics, which has emphasized the importance of institutions in any economy. In Walrasian economics, attention focused on equilibrium outcomes, determined by the underlying "fundamentals" of the economy – preferences and technology, which determined the demand and supply curves. Neo-classical economists argued that one should see through the superficial institutions to the underlying fundamentals. Monetary economics was easily incorporated into this framework, simply by postulating a demand function for money – and a supply determined by the government. The new institutional economics argues that there is much more to economic analysis – institutions

---

[3] As we shall comment below, standard economic theory argues that investment should depend just on real interest rates, not nominal interest rates. Yet empirical studies seem to suggest the contrary.

matter. Furthermore, they also argue that one can *explain* many aspects of institutions, for instance by looking at transactions-cost technology[4] or the imperfections and costs of information.[5] This book argues that financial institutions – banks – are critical in determining the behavior of the economy, and that the central features of banks and bank behavior can be understood in terms of (or derived from) an analysis of information imperfections.

The argument for looking at the banking system's institutional structure in detail as an intrinsic part of monetary economics has strong empirical support beyond that implicit in practical monetary policy discussions (which takes the importance of institutional factors as given). Over time, in closely observed systems like that in the United States, traditional monetary relationships have varied significantly, while in the same periods there have been equally important changes in the institutional structure of the banking system, or at least in the institutions within the banking system. Similarly, there are marked differences in the effectiveness of monetary policy in different countries, and similarly marked differences in their institutional structures. We argue that the changes in the monetary relations over time and differences across countries can be linked to institutional variations in the banking system. Frequently such changes become especially marked as the economy goes into a recession or faces a financial crisis. It is precisely when monetary policy becomes of crucial importance that the traditional models fail most dramatically. Later, we will argue that the failure to understand key aspects of financial institutions and their changes lies behind some of the recent failures in macro-economic policies, including the 1991 US recession and the severe recessions and depressions in East Asia that began in 1997.

An important reason for focusing on the impact of banking institutions is the rapid pace at which these institutions are changing. Existing theoretical models, largely institutionally independent, provide little or no guidance for assessing the effect of these changes on monetary policy. For example, transactions-

---

[4]  See Williamson (1979, 1985, 1999).
[5]  See, for example, Stiglitz (1974b, 1987b); Newberry and Stiglitz (1976); Braverman and Stiglitz (1982, 1986); and Braverman, Hoff and Stiglitz (1993).

based monetary theories that concentrate on money as a medium of exchange would tend to count money market accounts (which effectively monetize investments in short-term government securities) simply as an exogenous increase in the money supply and hence, of no particular significance for the incremental impact of central bank monetary expansions or contractions. Yet, in the context of an institutional banking system that competes with money market accounts for deposits, their long-run impact on the efficacy of monetary policy may be a far more difficult matter to assess. For policy purposes, it is important to understand the forces involved.

Still another reason for looking in detail at the structure of banking institutions arises from a series of questions concerning policies that directly or indirectly affect those institutions – and therefore the efficacy of monetary policy and the flow of funds towards investment in different kinds of enterprises. For instance, recent years have seen rapid globalization, and within Europe, monetary integration. With open capital markets, market rates of interest will equalize across countries in a monetary union. Similarly, as national economies become integrated, market rates will equalize across regions of a national economy. This means, for instance, that individual national monetary authorities or regional authorities (if they are small) cannot influence interest rates and hence, according to traditional monetary theory, cannot affect local economic activity (through monetary policy). Yet, such a conclusion may be unwarranted: local monetary authorities may be able to subsidize local banks (even though those banks face fixed interest rates) and in doing so, may stimulate local lending and local economic activity. The circumstances under which this may be the case require understanding the institutional structure of the banking system.

Similarly, many developing countries have been placed under strong pressures to open up their financial systems – a marked change in their institutional structure. Most of the arguments for this make standard appeals to an institution-free analysis – more competition increases economic efficiency. A closer look at the impact of such reforms on the domestic banking system, and on the flow of credit to small and medium-size enterprises (SMEs), suggests that there may be many circumstances in which these policy reforms have adverse consequences.

Part I of the book is divided into seven chapters. Chapter 1 sets out the problems with the current set of theories. Chapter 2 explains how financial markets (including the market for "loans") differ markedly from those for ordinary commodities. Chapter 3 develops the equity-based theory of banking, and uses it to derive the supply of loanable funds in an idealized competitive banking system toward which the world seems to be moving. Chapter 4 outlines the differences and similarities between the model banking system and the current system. Chapter 5 steps back and analyzes equilibrium in a simplified corn economy. Chapter 6 explains the important differences in the role of monetary policy in the corn economy and in a modern credit economy. Chapter 7 broadens the discussion towards a general equilibrium theory of credit. In part II of this book, the new paradigm is used to analyze a variety of aspects of monetary policy and to interpret several recent historical episodes.

# ONE

# Reflections on the current state of monetary economics

To theorists, monetary economics has long presented a challenge: finding the assumptions under which it does or does not matter. The challenge is all the greater because, while it is easy to construct models in which money matters, it is hard to believe that the quantitative effects in at least many of these are significant enough to account for observed behavior. For instance, macro-economists have often relied on the real balance effect, the fact that as prices fall, the real value of money increases, making individuals feel better off. However, for moderate rates of decline in prices, the magnitude of the real balance effect is too small to account, for instance, for an economic recovery.[1]

A second example concerns the refutation of the monetarist doctrine that prices move proportionally to increases in the money supply, for any monetary regime, so that there are no *real* effects of the increase in the money supply. Assume that were the case. Define a monetary regime as a rule of monetary expansion,

---

[1] Consider a dramatic fall in the price level by 50 percent. Assume that the ratio of money and dollar denominated government liabilities to GDP is 1, and that the coefficient on wealth in the consumption equation is 0.06. Then the increase in "autonomous" consumption from this fall in price – assuming that there is no Barro–Ricardo effect, so that consumers completely ignore the real value of their liabilities – would be 3 percent; even with a multiplier of 2, this would hardly offset a depression where GDP is down by 20 percent. To do that would require a fall in the price level three times greater.

depending on the state of nature, such that the expected rate of change of the money supply $E[d\ln M/dt]$ is a constant; the expected return to holding money is the same among monetary regimes given that prices move proportionally to $M$. However, if individuals are risk averse, then changes in the monetary regime will affect the probability distribution of returns, and hence, in general, the relative demand for money and capital, and therefore will have real effects, counter to the assumption. However, the issue is whether, given the degree of risk aversion in the market, the effects are significant for relevant changes in the monetary regime.

### Rigor, ad hocery, and relevance

Current dicta require that macroeconomics (treating here monetary economics as a branch of macroeconomics) be based on microeconomic principles. Some economists, who, in other respects, seem to insist that models should not be ad hoc, that they should be based on principles of maximization, took the low road around the difficulties posed by these strictures, putting money into the utility function or the production function – a trick, which repeated often enough, took on a semblance of respectability! Others took the high road, creating a demand for money by assuming that it is required for transactions, modeling it as an old fashioned cash in advance constraint – criticisms that it was an ad hoc assumption that was blatantly false being brushed aside with the remark that these were topics for future research.[2]

### The wavering case for the irrelevance of money

Research since 1970 has managed to both strengthen – and weaken – the argument that money does not matter. Extending

---

[2] On one occasion, when this objection was raised at a seminar at Princeton, a visiting professor from Chicago, while acknowledging that money was no longer required *in general*, pointed out that cash was still required for taxicabs. Surely, one does not want to construct a monetary theory on the basis that money is required for taxicabs and to purchase soft drinks in vending machines! Interestingly, when he submitted his bill for expenses, it showed that he had paid his taxicab fare on a credit card. And do we think that the new technologies which allow using cellular phones to purchase cokes in vending machines will lead to further changes in monetary theory?

the general equilibrium approach (Stiglitz 1969, 1974a) to show the irrelevance of corporate financial policy,[3] public financial policy was shown to have no effect.[4] Establishing a form of Say's law for government debt, Stiglitz (1988a) showed that if the government reduced taxes and increased its debt, the demand for government bonds increased by an amount exactly equal to the increase in supply. Furthermore, a change in the term structure of government debt has no effects. Of course, like any theorem, there were assumptions that went into the analysis. These seemed to be of two sorts: some, like the absence of distortionary tax effects, while they would alter the *qualitative* result that taxes had *no* effect, seemed an implausible basis for an argument about why monetary policy should be important: surely its effectiveness did not hinge on the real effects produced by the *difference* in the *change* in the dead weight losses arising from an increase in taxes in one year compensated by a decrease in taxes in some later years! Another assumption in the analysis was the absence of intergenerational redistributive effects. While one might agree or disagree with Barro (1974) that the economy is best modeled as a set of dynastic families, with no intergenerational effects, surely *short*-run monetary policy does not hinge on these intergenerational effects.

The other set of assumptions – concerning perfect capital markets (though the analysis does not require there be a complete set of risk and futures markets) – was no different from that assumed in conventional economic models. If that assumption were struck down, with it would fall much of the standard theory. Of course, practical people have long claimed that economists' models of capital markets are unrealistic, and a host of institutional economists (and theoretical economists, when they found it convenient) have made use of the imperfect capital markets assumption. However, higher-minded economists have looked derisively at those who made reference to imperfect capital markets, accusing them of, among other sins, ad hocery.

---

[3] A general equilibrium proof of Modigliani and Miller's classic (1958) analysis showing the irrelevance of debt–equity ratios.

[4] This result can also be viewed as a generalization of the Barro–Ricardo theorem (Barro 1974).

## The critical assumption: perfect capital markets

One of the most important developments in economic theory of the past fifteen years has been the exploration of the consequences of imperfect and costly information for the functioning of the capital market. It has been shown that models that assumed imperfect capital markets may have been much closer to the mark than those that assumed perfect capital markets.[5] These studies have shown that capital markets that are competitive – in the sense that that word is commonly used – may be characterized by credit and equity rationing. The models based on imperfect and costly information provide explanations of institutional details of the capital market, details which are either inconsistent with perfect capital market models or about which perfect capital market models have nothing to say; but they also provide a basis of explanation of the many aspects of macroeconomic (aggregate) behavior that seem inconsistent with the conventional neoclassical model.

In part I of the book, we argue that monetary institutions and policy do have important real effects, but for reasons quite different from those of the standard theory. Our objective is to explain both why it is that monetary policy is – sometimes – effective, and why the conventional explanation of the mechanism by which it works – particularly those versions based on the transactions demand for money – is inadequate.

We should say at the outset that we are not denying that there might be *some* grain of truth in these conventional explanations, only that they miss the *central* aspects of the mechanisms by which monetary policy works, and therefore are an unreliable basis for the analysis of monetary policy.

---

[5] Stigler (1967) tried to argue against capital market imperfections, suggesting that they were simply related to transactions costs, and that such costs were no less real than any other costs. But he failed to understand how imperfect information changed the nature of capital markets in far more fundamental ways, e.g. leading to credit rationing. For a more extensive critique of Stigler's position, see Stiglitz (2000c).

## A critique of the transactions-based theory of the demand for money

There are several reasons why one might be suspicious of traditional explanations. Keynes[6] was, perhaps, not as clear concerning the definition of money as he could have been. The absence of clarity may have been deliberate, enabling him to slip from one use to another, without the reader being aware. We focus our attention on demand deposits, because these are the part of money most directly under the control of monetary authorities, and then slightly more broadly, on M1, which includes currency.

Keynes spoke of three motives for holding money: the precautionary, the speculative, and the transactions motive. Given our definition, only the third is relevant. The other two motives are related to the use of money as a store of value; and as a store of value, money is dominated by T-bills and money market mutual funds, which yield higher rates of interest. Though some economists have suggested that Keynes' definition of money really did include these assets ("$L$" in the standard terminology), surely this broad aggregate is not under the control of monetary authorities. Even when monetary authorities set the money supply as a target, they never focus their attention on this broad measure. Empirical studies have concentrated their attention on narrower definitions, such as M1 (or, as M1 has done increasingly poorly, on M2).

Thus, an analysis of the demand for *money* (as opposed to dollar denominated government insured short-term assets) must focus on the transactions demand for money. (Of course, in a general equilibrium model, demands for all assets are interdependent. Still, it is useful to think of individuals as first deciding on how much they wish to hold in dollar denominated government insured short-term assets, and then to ask, of that total,

---

[6] We do not want to get into an exegesis of Keynes' work, to discuss the relationship between his *Theory of Employment* and his earlier *A Treatise on Money*, or between the true Keynes and Keynes as popularly interpreted, especially in the work of Hicks (1937). Our discussion is a critique of Keynes *as he has come to be understood*.

how much should be held in the form of money, for transaction purposes.[7])

The past fifteen years have witnessed remarkable changes in transactions technologies. Computers enable the velocity of circulation to become virtually infinite, for instance, in the use of money market accounts.[8] The relationship between conventionally measured money and income has not been stable in recent years. That it would change would be predicted by the theory, given the changes in transactions technology. But the fact that the relationship is not *stable*, that the changes in velocity do not seem to be *predictable*, not only undermines the usefulness of the theory for practical purposes. It also forces us to reconsider the foundations of the theory. Upon reflection, it becomes clear that the transaction-demand monetary theory was – and should have been recognized to be – badly flawed.

### Money is interest bearing, with a possibly low opportunity cost

A central quandary of modern economics in general, and monetary theory in particular, is this: today, in advanced industrial economies, most money – certainly money at the margin – is interest bearing, and the difference between the interest paid on money in, say, a cash management account[9] and a T-bill is determined not by monetary policy, but by transactions costs (see figure 1.1). In effect, with modern technology, individuals can use T-bills for transactions. There is no opportunity cost, at the margin, in holding "money." (To be sure, there is an opportunity cost in

---

[7] This approach would not even run into problems if the amount of money individuals wanted to hold for transactions purposes exceeded the amount of short-term government insured assets some people would wish to hold; in that case, they would simply sell short the T-bills.

[8] Funds are shifted out of a T-bill account into a checking account as a check is presented, so that balances in the checking account can be kept at zero.

[9] Cash management accounts (CMA accounts) are a registered trademark of Merrill Lynch, the first brokerage house to introduce these accounts which link money market funds and checking accounts in the way described in n. 8. For all intents and purposes, such accounts allow individuals to write checks against their T-bills, and T-bills are made infinitely divisible.

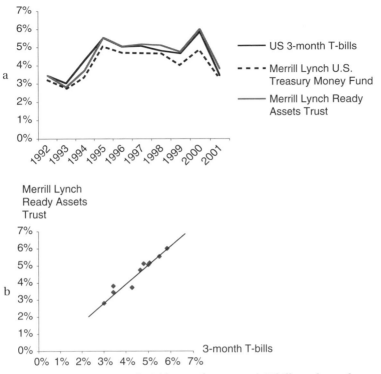

Figure 1.1 *Average annual yield rates for 3-month T-bills and a cash managment account, 1992–2001*

Deposits on a Cash Management Account® are implicitly invested in a money market fund of the account holder's choice, e.g. the Merrill Lynch U.S. Treasury Money Fund (holds only T-bills) or Merrill Lynch Ready Assets Trust (holds also commercial papers.)

a   Average annual yield rates, 1992–2001, in percentages
b   Relationship between yearly returns on T-bills and a CMA
*Sources*: 3-month T-bill rates: *Economic Report of the President*, 2001; CMA returns: Merrill Lynch U.S. Treasury Money Fund and Merrill Lynch Ready Assets Trust Fund Prospectus 2001; returns are net of operating expenses.

holding currency, but there are few economists who use currency in their regressions attempting to explain inflation or output.)

The monetary economics developed over the last twenty-five years is based on a money demand equation in which there is an opportunity cost for holding money. Standard monetary theories argue that monetary policy exerts its effects through changing the supply of money, which changes the interest rate; and changes in the (real) interest rate affect (real) economic behavior. Reducing the money supply increases the "price" of money – the interest rate – and that in turn reduces investment, reducing aggregate demand. In an open economy, there is one more channel through which monetary policy exercises its influence. The increase in the interest rate makes it more attractive for foreigners to put their money into the country (and less attractive for those within the country to invest their money abroad). The induced movement of capital into the country drives up the exchange rate, reducing demand for exports and increasing demand for imports.

The model was a useful one for policymakers, because at least some of the key relationships were stable. While the investment function was presumed unstable – shifting to the left in an economic slump – the money demand functions were presumed stable. Even with a variable level of investment, so long as the elasticity of response of investment to interest rate changes was stable, the government could easily predict the consequences of changes in policy. In many circumstances, the model did extremely well, but at other times – particularly in economic downturns associated with financial sector crises, such as that in the United States in 1991 and in East Asia in 1997–1998 – the model performed quite inadequately, and policies based on that model failed to deliver the right medicine in a timely way.

### Are most transactions income generating?

The fact that it did so well so often is perhaps the most remarkable aspect of the model. The problem noted above, that the interest rate is not the opportunity cost of an increasingly large fraction of the money supply, is but one of the problems facing the theory. The model assumes that the demand for money is a function of the value of national income, yet most transactions are not income generating, but rather are related

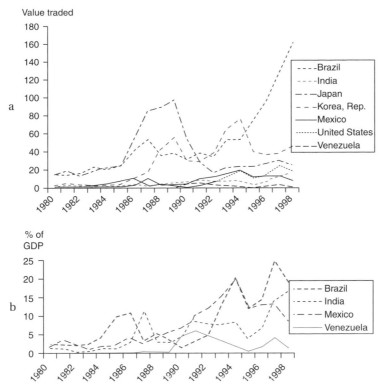

Figure 1.2  Stock value traded as a percentage of GDP various countries
The ratio of transactions to income is highly volatile.
a   Value traded
b   Percentage of GDP
Sources: GDP at market prices (current $US): Statistical Information
Management and Analysis; value traded, $US million: IFC Emerging
Markets Database, Emerging Stock Markets.

to the sales and purchases of assets, and these asset exchanges
bear no clear, stable relationship to the level of national income.
The annual variations in these transactions can be enormous
(see figure 1.2).[10]

---

[10]  The figure looks only at a subset of all transactions, but the results would surely
hold more broadly.

## And is money needed for transactions?

Moreover, most transactions do not require money, but can be mediated through credit; and this is increasingly the case. Indeed, the reason that credit could not previously be used as a basis of exchange was the informational problem of ascertaining whether or not a credit guarantor (a credit card company or a bank) had "certified" an individual as credit worthy. The decentralized nature of information in the market economy made the transfer of such information costly. Modern technology allows sellers to instantaneously communicate with the bank or credit card company to see whether or not the bank has "authorized" the issuance of credit in the given amount. Thus, the same technology changes that have enabled money to become fully interest bearing (or equivalently, T-bills to be used as money) have also enabled credit to be used as the basis of exchange.

## A first look at the data: movements in velocity

Monetarists were always skeptical about the interest rate mechanism so beloved both by neo-classical and traditional Keynesian economists. It was real interest rates that mattered, and real interest rates should be determined by real variables. Real business cycle theorists pushed this point perhaps even further than traditional monetarists. Money did not matter for anything real. Money affected only the price level. Increases in the money supply were translated into proportionate increases in the price level.[11]

Key in the monetarist formulation was the constancy of velocity. In fact, velocity has not been constant for many countries (see figure 1.3).[12] However, while standard transactions-based

---

[11] Earlier, we noted that if individuals are risk averse, the argument is incoherent, since different *ex ante* expectations concerning the rate of change of money supply then translate into different expectations about the probability distribution of price changes, affecting the attractiveness of holding money.

[12] Some monetarists claim that what is relevant for the *usefulness* of the theory is not the constancy, but the predictability of velocity, i.e. that it was changing

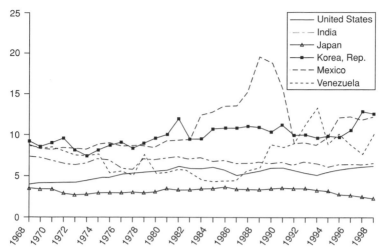

Figure 1.3 *Velocity*

For many countries, velocity has been far from constant.

*Sources:* Money (current LCU, million): *World Development Indicators.* Washington, DC: World Bank, 2000; GDP at market prices (current LCU, million): *World Development Indicators.* Washington DC: World Bank, 2000.

*Definition:* Money is the sum of currency outside banks and demand deposits other than those of the central government; this series, frequently referred to as M1, is a narrower definition of money than M2.

money demand stories postulate that velocity depends on the opportunity cost of holding money, the regression of velocity on the nominal interest rate shows that the interest rate changes explain only a relatively small fraction of the change in velocity

at a constant rate, or that the changes could be related to exogenous variables. Even if the expected value of the velocity next period is predictable (e.g. velocity is a random walk, with expected velocity next period being equal to that in this period), its usefulness is limited if there is a high level of variability around the expectation. But our objections go deeper. Even if velocity most of the time were relatively constant, if it changed dramatically in those few instances when the economy goes into a crisis, then its usefulness would be limited; the model would fail precisely when it is most needed for purposes of macro-economic stabilization. We should emphasize, however, that our dissatisfaction with the monetarist approach lies largely with its micro-foundations: the "stories" that have long been used to motivate it simply make little sense.

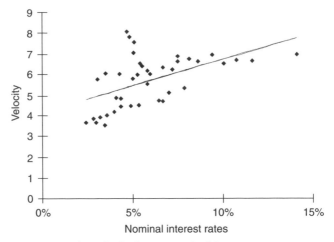

Figure 1.4 *Regression of velocity on nominal interest rates*
Variations in nominal interest rates explain only a small fraction of
the variability in velocity.
*Source*: *International Financial Statistics* (IFS). Washington,
DC: IMF, 2000.
*Data range*: US annual data, 1959–1999.
*Definitions*: Velocity is GDP divided by M1; nominal interest rates
are approximated by the T-bill rate, the discount on new issues of
3-month bills, and annual averages of these.

(see figure 1.4).[13] In light of the changing relationship between
money and income, there has been a search for alternative
definitions of money. However, this simply serves to show the
ad hoc nature of the enterprise. The failure of the money–
income relationship should spur a re-examination of the bases
of monetary theory, no less than the seeming failure of the inflation–unemployment trade-off in the later 1970s called for a
re-examination of other aspects of the postulates of traditional
Keynesian theory.

[13] Figure 1.4 provides the regression results of the US 1959–1999 annual data with
the velocity as the dependent variable and the nominal interest rate and a constant as the independent variables. The estimated coefficient on the nominal
interest rate is 0.2583 while the coefficient on the constant is 4.1719, with standard error 0.0655 and 0.4234, respectively. The $R^2$, in particular, is relatively
small, just 0.2852 when there are 41 observations. See Fair (1987), Mehra (1978),
and Fair and Dominguez (1991).

There are further objections to the transactions-based theory of money: When Ireland faced a strike that closed down the clearing mechanisms for checks, while the transactions-based theories might have suggested that the economy would have come to a screeching halt, alternative arrangements were easily worked out, and the effects were indeed limited. Italy has periodically gone through periods of small currency shortages, with little impediment to trade, the major effect perhaps being the increased number of cavities resulting from the slightly larger number of pieces of candy consumed, as candy became conventionally used for small change.

### Further problems

*What determines investment? Is it the short-term or long-term interest rates that matter? Interest rates or the price of equity? Nominal or real interest rates?*

However, the problems do not stop here. The demand for investment should, in principle, be related not to today's short-term nominal interest rate, but to the long-term real interest rate, or to the price of equity (Tobin's *q*). A number of empirical studies question this standard channel through which monetary policy is supposed to exert its effects.

If both nominal and real interest rates are included in a regression of investment, nominal interest rates typically appear to be more important.[14] While a persuasive case can be made that the price of equity is the most relevant of the various costs of capital measures, because it reflects market perceptions of the (average) risk associated with different investments, empirical studies have not lent strong support to the theory.[15] One explanation sometimes put forward is that in fact, relatively little

---

[14] Results appear to differ depending on the data sources and model specifications (e.g. lag structures). A typical straightforward regression of log (investment/GDP) on lagged nominal and real T-bill rates (deflated by CPI) and a constant yields a negative (and significant) coefficient on nominal interest rates and a *positive* (but insignificant) coefficient on real interest rates. Other data series seemed to generate a negative coefficient for real interest rates – but a coefficient that was smaller in absolute value than that for nominal interest rates.

[15] Abel and Blanchard (1989), Ferderer (1993).

new capital is raised through the equity market.[16] While true, this explanation is not completely convincing, since existing stockholders – in whose interests presumably investments are made – are concerned with the impact of the investment on the value of their equities, and this will depend on Tobin's $q$. One might argue that the problem is with the measure of the impact of the marginal investment on the value of equity;[17] with a constant (long-run) "equity" premium, a good surrogate measure is the interest rate. However, what should matter then is the long-term interest rate, not the short. And the question is, why should a change in the interest rate today affect beliefs about interest rates five, ten, or twenty years from now? In a market with risk neutrality, the long-term interest rate is the product of the (expected) short-term rates,[18] and for a change in today's short-term interest rate to have a significant effect on the long-term interest rate, it must presumably affect expectations of interest rates not just today, but for a long time in the future. However, why should that be so, when there is general agreement that monetary policy in the short run is related to short-run macro-conditions, while long-term interest rates should be linked to the long-term marginal productivity of capital?[19]

### Tobin's portfolio theory versus the Modigliani–Miller–Barro–Ricardo theory

Another theory that has enjoyed a great deal of popularity over the past twenty-five years is Tobin's portfolio theory. Tobin argued that the effects of monetary policy resulted from the monetary authorities changing the relative supplies, e.g. of money and bonds, or

---

[16]  See, for example, Mayer (1990).

[17]  That is, most empirical studies obtain a measure of *average q*, not *marginal q*.

[18]  That is, if $r_1$ is this year's short-term interest rate and $r_2$ is next year's, and $R$ is the long-term rate: $1 + R = (1 + r_1)(1 + r_2)$.

[19]  The same point holds if investors are risk averse, only now the long run can change not just with changes in mean expectations, but also with changes in risk aversion and risk perceptions, making the link between changes in short-term interest rates today and long-term interest rates even more tenuous.

short-term and long-term bonds (as in "Operation Twist"[20]).[21] In this theory, changes in long-term interest rates or the price of capital need not be simply related to changes in the short-term interest rates. In many ways, Tobin's theory is a marked advance over the earlier transactions-based theories. Note that this theory – like the transactions-based theories – is basically institution-free. What drove the economy was not the demand and supply of money alone, but the demand and supply of the entire portfolio of assets. The asset market adjustments engender changes in interest rates and returns on equity which, in turn, affect real economic activity.

However, as noted before, in a straightforward application of the Modigliani–Miller theorem to the public sector (or equivalently a generalization of the Barro–Ricardo theorem to cover a full range of public financial activities), public financial policy simply does not matter, under the standard perfect market assumptions. That is, a change in the ratio of long-term to short-term bonds would lead taxpayers (cognizant of the change in the implicit risks associated with tax liabilities that resulted) to adjust their bond holdings in such a way as to fully offset the effects.[22] Similarly, an open market operation is simply an exchange of T-bills for money, most of which is interest bearing, with an interest rate close to that of T-bills. Individuals' holdings of short-term dollar denominated government guaranteed assets would appear to be essentially un-changed. Why should this change have *significant* effects on the price of equity, as Tobin seems to claim?

If monetary policy is to be effective, it has to arise from some market imperfection or some distributive effect of the policy. However, one then needs to model that market imperfection or distributive effect directly, to ascertain the effects of monetary policy,

---

[20] In "Operation Twist" the Treasury retired long-term securities and issued short-term securities in order to improve the negative balance of payments while maintaining economic growth. This was based on the theory that it was the short-term rate that was relevant for international capital flows, while long-term rates were more relevant for the domestic economy, mainly because they affected the mortgage rate. See Holland (1969).

[21] Tobin (1969) argued that the effect of monetary policy on investment is mediated through the price of equity (Tobin's $q$). Earlier, we noted that empirical research had not provided strong support for that conclusion.

[22] See Stiglitz (1988a).

and it is not clear that there are persuasive effects.[23] For instance, while borrowing constraints mean that when the government substitutes taxes for debt, individuals may not be able to undo the effects, is it clear why if government substitutes long-term for short-term bonds, individuals cannot substitute one form of debt for the other? While the change in the debt structure may have implications for intergenerational risk bearing, do we really believe those effects are large enough to account for significant effects? If T-bills can be used for transactions purposes (as suggested above), at the margin, aren't money and T-bills close substitutes, especially in regimes in which the value of transactions services appears low; and why should the relative supply of these two securities have *significant* effects on the price of long-term bonds or equities, the variables that should be relevant for investment?

### Movements in interest rates

There is another anomaly, highlighted in figure 1.5. According to the theory, monetary policy exerts its effects through real interest rates. But figure 1.5 shows that for long periods of time, the real interest rate was a constant – there was no cyclical variability. It is possible, of course, that miraculously, monetary policy simply offset other changes in the economy – perhaps monetary authorities in these periods saw their job as keeping the real interest rate fixed. But even in that case, figure 1.5 makes clear that monetary policy did little more: it did not succeed in *lowering* real interest rates in response to a leftward shift in the investment schedule. And in this sense, monetary policy was perverse: As real incomes fell, as the economy went into a slowdown or recession, monetary policy was not even neutral. A neutral monetary policy would have kept the money supply fixed, thereby (in the traditional IS-LM framework) lowering the interest rate.[24]

But there is an alternative possibility, that underlies the analysis of this book, and that is that there are other channels than

---

[23]   See, for instance, Stiglitz (1983a).

[24]   The *nominal* interest rate would have been lowered. If the rate of inflation was reduced faster than the rate at which the nominal interest rate was lower, the real interest rate would have been increased. An *active* monetary policy would have sought to lower the real interest rate.

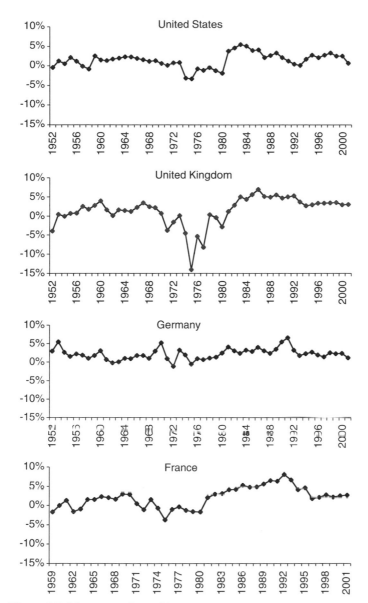

Figure 1.5 *Movements in real interest rates*

For long periods (with the exception of the time of the oil shocks in the 1970s), real interest rates have varied little in many countries, and it is hard to reconcile the relative stability of real interest rates with monetary theories which ascribe a central role to variations in the real interest rate.

Source: *International Financial Statistics (IFS)*, Washington, DC: IMF, 2002.

changes in real interest rates through which monetary policy exerts its effects. Monetary policy was operating, at least some times, in countercyclical ways, but not typically through interest rates.

## Interest rate spreads

Before leaving the discussion of these puzzles, let me say a word about the "spread" puzzle. Standard monetary theory focuses on the T-bill interest rate. However, economic activity depends on the interest rate that borrowers (investors) must pay. The presumption of the standard theory has been that the two closely track each other, adjusting for risk. The spread between the two often moves in strange ways. For instance, in the 1991 recession, the T-bill rate came down slowly, to between 3 and 4 percent, while credit card rates remained at 16–19 percent. It seems implausible that the "risk adjustment" just happened to change by the amount that the T-bill and deposit interest rates fell. Movements in other interest rates (e.g. prime rates) exhibit similarly anomalous behavior (though admittedly not as striking).

## Further dissatisfaction with the transactions-based theory of money

The transactions-based theory of money is not only unsatisfactory because its underlying premises are totally unpersuasive and because it leaves unresolved several key puzzles, but also because it provides little insight into explaining *changes* in the effectiveness of monetary policy, both secular and cyclical changes. In the standard model, increasing the money supply *may* be ineffective in a recession either because the interest elasticity of the investment schedule is very low or because of the "liquidity trap," namely increasing the money supply does not lead to significant decreases in the interest rate. The standard argument behind the liquidity trap, however, is no longer widely accepted. The standard argument is that investors, expecting that the low interest rate will not persist, become increasingly frightened of putting more and more of their money into long-term government bonds. Thus the long-term interest rate fails to fall – and so longer-term investments fail to increase. The reason that individuals become increasingly adverse to putting their money into long-term bonds is that they believe in mean reversion – that the low interest rates will not persist, so that the price of long-term bonds will fall. But not only is it the case that there is little evidence of mean reversion, but if there were, it would presumably already have been reflected in the price of long-term bonds, so that there would be no presumption of a large fall in price in long-term bonds.[25] The theory we develop below provides an alternative explanation for why monetary policy may be ineffective in bringing the economy out of a recession – it may be ineffective in inducing an increase in the supply of credit or in improving the terms at which credit is made available.[26]

Moreover, the standard theory does not provide a persuasive explanation or prediction of secular changes in the effectiveness of monetary policy (or, for that matter, in velocity itself). The only changes in technology that matter would be changes that affect the transactions demand for money; hence all the changes referred to earlier – the increased use of credit to mediate transactions – should have led to marked increases in the velocity of circulation (a reduced ratio of real money to income). If, as seems plausible, it is increasingly difficult to economize on the use of money for the remaining uses, then the elasticity of demand for money should become small, implying that given percentage changes in the supply of money should have increasingly large effects on interest rates; but given changes in T-bill rates, however accomplished, should have unchanged effects on investment and hence output. By contrast, the theories developed below suggest more profound secular changes in the efficacy of monetary policy.

---

[25] That is, the standard story is that the price of a long-term bond (perpetuity) is $1/r$, where $r$ is the short-term interest rate. That is, a bond that pays 1 dollar in perpetuity has a present discounted value of $1/(1 + r) + 1/(1 + r)^2 \cdots = 1/r$.

Hence, if $r$ is very low, with mean reversion, the expected price next period is less than the current price, and the expected return is not only less than $r$, but even negative. But the reason that the price is $1/r$ is that the interest rate is expected to be the same. If it were the case that the interest rate was expected to rise, then the price would be less than $1/r$.

[26] Either because the spread between T-bill rates and lending rates increases; or because the spread between T-bill rates and the longer-term rates which are relevant for firms' investment decisions increases.

# TWO

# How finance differs

This book focuses not on the role of money in facilitating transactions, but on the role of credit in facilitating economic activity more broadly. It is remarkably difficult to incorporate credit within the standard general equilibrium model. Credit can be created with almost no input of conventional factors, and can just as easily be destroyed. There is no easy way to represent the supply function for credit.

The reason for this is simple: credit is based on *information*. Ascertaining that an individual is credit worthy requires resources; and standing by that judgment, providing or guaranteeing credit entails risk bearing. There is no simple relationship between these economic costs and the amount of credit extended.

The physical capital with which we produce in our factories and fields may be slightly affected by outside disturbances – rain may lead to rust – but only major cataclysms, such as wars, can have a significant effect in the short run. However, informational capital can be far more easily lost or made obsolescent. Changes in relative prices, for instance, require a reevaluation of individuals and firms' credit worthiness.

### Interest rates are not like conventional prices and the capital market is not like an auction market

The standard general equilibrium model is not helpful in understanding credit markets, and may even be misleading. It is

misleading because we are apt to think of the price of credit –
the interest rate – being a price like any other price, adjusting to
clear the market.

The interest rate is not like a conventional price. It is a promise
to pay an amount in the future. Promises are often broken. If they
were not, there would be no issue in determining credit worthiness. As Stiglitz and Weiss (1981) have shown, raising the rate of
interest may not increase the expected return to a loan; at higher
interest rates one obtains a lower quality set of applicants (the adverse selection effect) and each applicant undertakes greater risks
(the moral-hazard, or adverse incentive, effect).[1] These effects are
so strong that expected net return may decrease as the bank increases the interest rate charged because the probability that borrowers don't pay back increases with higher interest rates. In figure 2.1a, the lender's expected return is maximized at $r^*$. Market
equilibrium may be characterized by credit rationing. That is, if the
demand and supply curves intersect at an interest rate above $r^*$,
$r^*$ is still the "equilibrium" interest rate and the demand for credit
(loans) exceeds the supply (see figure 2.1b). Lenders have no incentive to raise interest rate above $r^*$, because doing so will lower
their return.

That markets can be fundamentally different from conventional commodity markets should be familiar to us from another
context. None of the private universities in the United States – even
those, such as Harvard, Stanford, Yale, Princeton, and Northwest-
ern, where first-rate economists have served as Presidents,
provosts, and deans – has employed the price system to allocate
the scarce number of places for students. Let me remind you of
how we often talk about the auction for credit working: those who
have the best projects are willing to pay the highest interest rates,
and thus the auction market ensures that the best projects – and
only the best projects – get funded. Of course, we recognize the
possibility of human error. However, then we say, if the individual
makes a mistake in over-estimating the return, she bears the cost.
Similar language could apply to an auction for places in our universities. Those with the highest return to a Stanford degree would

---

[1] See also Keeton (1984).

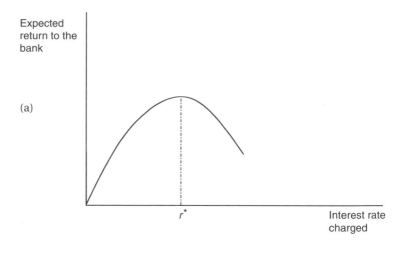

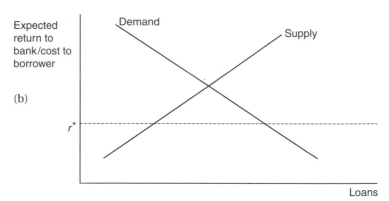

Figure 2.1 *The interest rate which maximizes expected return to the bank*
   a    There exists an interest rate which maximizes the expected
   return to the bank.
   b    At "equilibrium" interest rates, the demand for credit (loans)
   exceeds the supply

bid the highest, thus ensuring that the value added of scarce
university resources is maximized. If someone over-estimates the
value of a Stanford degree, she bears the costs. Lack of capital
should be no problem: the university would simply take an IOU.

   When it is put this way, we can immediately see the fallacies in
this reasoning. Students who bid too much will default on their
IOU – just as those who bid too high an interest rate on their loan

applications will default. Not only can we not rely on individuals' judgments, there may be reasons to believe that those who are willing to bid particularly high are more likely to default. The bank or the university bears at least some of the costs of these misjudgments. The scarce resources would not be used in a way that maximized value added. The auction system would result in the universities being flooded with over-confident and cocky students who are unpleasant to teach, combined with those natural charlatans and cheaters who feel no more moral compunction about defaulting on their student loans than they would on cheating on an exam.

So too in credit markets: in the face of uncertain prices, wages, and interest rates, the return to a project depends as much on expectations of those future prices as it does on the physical outputs. Those who are most willing to bid high for a loan are those who are most optimistic about future prices and are least risk averse, for whom the cost of default is lowest. However, there is no reason to believe that allocating credit to these individuals maximizes either the private return to the bank, or the social return to society.

Another anecdote illustrates the nature of what is at issue. A number of years ago, Stiglitz had a farm in New Jersey which he decided to rent out. It was not long after he had written the paper on credit rationing with Andy Weiss, but he failed to take to heart fully the message of that paper, with disastrous consequences. He held an informal auction for renting the farm, pleased that the winning bid was even more than he expected, but thought that perhaps the winner valued the aesthetics of the farm even more than he did, perhaps that he valued having a landlord that was honest and straightforward. What he hadn't fathomed was that the renter really understood the economics of the rental market better than Stiglitz did: if one doesn't plan to pay the rent, it doesn't matter much what rent one "promises" to pay. He knew how long it took, under New Jersey law, to evict someone. By promising to pay a high rent, he had succeeded in getting six months of free rent!

Just as universities spend resources screening applicants so too banks spend resources screening applicants.[2] The screening is far from perfect, yet some screening is preferable to none.

---

[2] The general theory of screening is set out in Stiglitz (1975a, 1975b).

There is another way to highlight the ways in which finance/ credit differs from ordinary goods and services. A central feature of the Arrow–Debreu model is the *anonymous* nature of markets. Nobody cares who supplies chairs or steel to a market, or who buys chairs or steel from the market. That is one of the wonderful things about competitive markets – they are entirely non-discriminatory.

However, credit is totally different. Supplying credit to John Rockefeller is different from supplying credit to Donald Trump or to anyone else. The terms on which credit will be supplied will depend on judgments about the likelihood that the loan will be repaid. That depends in turn on judgments about the financial position and incentive structures facing the individual or firm to whom credit is lent. Credit is thus highly individual, and the information relevant for providing the credit is highly specific. To be sure, there may be some information which is of generic value, e.g. information about the automobile market may be relevant for supplying credit to any car dealer or automobile manufacturer. By the same token, different potential lenders have different information bases. A lender who has dealt with a particular borrower over a long time has a much broader base to interpret data concerning the borrower's current economic circumstances. Moreover, expenditures to acquire this information are largely sunk costs, and indeed most of the information is not easily transferable or "marketable." It is hard to codify, often tacit in nature.[3] Inevitably, then, regardless of the number of potential suppliers of credit to any firm in the market, the number of firms actually providing credit, especially to a small or medium size firm, is likely to be relatively small.[4] Other lenders would have to expend considerable resources to obtain comparable levels of information. In short, regardless of the number of firms in the market, the market for credit is likely to be characterized by very

---

[3] There is a large literature on the difference between tacit and "codified" knowledge. See Stiglitz (2000a) and the references cited there.

[4] That is why governments need to be especially sensitive to the consequences of bank mergers. In assessing the impact of bank mergers, one needs to look at the impact on the market for the supply of loans to small and medium-sized enterprises (SMEs); competition in this market may be very limited, even if competition in, say, the market for depository services is highly competitive.

imperfect competition (better described by models of monopolistic competition than pure competition).[5]

## Credit and equity rationing

The informational problems just described imply that capital
markets behave markedly different from conventional markets.[6]
We have just noted that competition in such markets is likely to
be imperfect. There are more fundamental ways in which such
markets differ from classic markets. First, the information problems may easily give rise to credit rationing. Recall, again, the conventional stories: when there is an excess demand for credit, an
unsatisfied borrower offers the bank a higher interest rate. As interest rates rise, the demand for credit decreases, and the supply
increases, until equilibrium is attained. However, now, consider
what happens if, at the interest rate that maximizes the bank's expected return, there is an excess demand for credit. The bank
would refuse a customer who offers to pay a higher interest rate,
reasoning that he is a bad risk. The expected return for such a loan
would be lower than that for loans the bank is currently making.

  Banks will, of course, change the interest rate that they charge
as economic circumstances change. However, as we saw earlier,
there is no simple relationship between the interest rate
charged – or even the interest rate paid to depositors – and the

---

[5]  See, for instance, Jaffee and Stiglitz (1990) and Hoff and Stiglitz (1997). Stiglitz
    (1975b) describes the equilibrium in a model where, if two banks screen a bor-
    rower, they compete vigorously, so vigorously that the interest rate is competed
    down to the competitive level. There is a mixed strategy equilibrium, in which
    some individuals are screened only once – and the bank earns sufficient returns
    from the monopoly rents associated with this screening to compensate for the
    absence of returns on those that have been screened by two or more banks. In
    other models, those being screened bear the cost of screening. See also Stiglitz
    (1975a).
[6]  Thus, Stigler's argument against "imperfections of capital markets" (1967) is to-
    tally misplaced. He tried to argue that once one took account of real transac-
    tions costs, capital markets were little different from other markets. The fact is
    that even relatively small imperfections of information can lead to large conse-
    quences, e.g. credit and equity rationing, implying that capital markets behave
    in ways that are markedly different from how they would were information per-
    fect. See Stiglitz and Weiss (1981, 1983), Greenwald, Stiglitz, and Weiss (1984),
    Greenwald (1986), Hellmann and Stiglitz (2000), and Stiglitz (2000a).

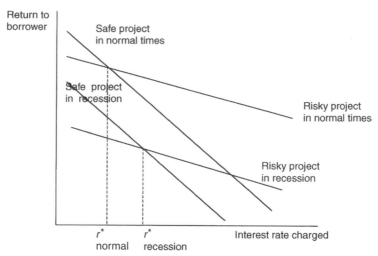

Figure 2.2  *Effect of recession on real lending interest rates*
While standard theories predict that real interest rates should fall in a
recession, credit rationing theories explain why the real lending interest
rate may well increase. $r^*$ is the highest rate the lender can charge without the borrower switching to the risky project. Lenders' expected
returns are higher with the safe project than with the risky one.

state of the economy. As the economy goes into a boom, the returns to all projects may increase, and one might be tempted
to argue that as a consequence the real rate of interest ought to
rise, presenting a quandary, since in *some* instances – such as
the Great Depression – the real interest rate moved counter-
cyclically rather than pro-cyclically (recall figure 1.5 and the
surrounding discussion)[7]. However, Stiglitz and Weiss (1981,
1991) have shown that there may be instances where the entrepreneurs' returns to, say, risky projects increase *relative* to
safe projects in booms, so the banks' optimal interest rate at
which their expected returns are maximized (and accordingly,
the market equilibrium interest rate charged to borrowers) actually falls (see figure 2.2).

---

[7]  Figure 1.5 shows that the real interest rate rose, for instance, in the 1979–1983
recessions, though it did not fall as the economy moved out of the recession. In
the Great Depression, real interest rates on commercial papers rose to 15.79 percent in 1932 from 6.19 percent in 1928. See Jones and Wilson (1987).

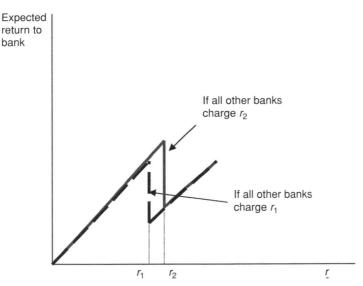

Figure 2.3 *The optimal interest rate charged by one bank may depend on that charged by others*

If all other banks are charging $r_1$, and one lender charges more than that, he gets only bad risks (those who have been rejected by others banks). If all others increase their interest rate to $r_2$, he can increase the interest rate he charges without an adverse selection effect.

Moreover, the optimal interest charged by one bank may depend on the interest rate charged by others. If all other banks are charging a low interest rate, then it may not pay one to increase the interest rate charged, since the only borrowers that one could attract are those that other lenders have rejected – which on average will be higher risk[8] (see figure 2.3). Even if there are not multiple (or a continuum of) Nash equilibria, the adjustment processes to a new equilibrium may be slow.

[8] Similar arguments have been put forward in the labor market, where adverse selection and incentive effects also play a role. The workers one attracts at any given wage depend on the wages others are paying. If one pays a lower wage than one's rivals, one attracts a lower quality labor force. See Rodriguez and Stiglitz (1991a, 1991b); Nalebuff, Rodriguez and Stiglitz (1993). In the labor market, norms may play a greater role: if one pays a wage lower than others, there may be adverse effects on effort arising from morale. See Stiglitz (1974c) or Akerlof and Yellen (1990).

### Equity rationing

Not only may informational problems give rise to credit rationing, they may also give rise to equity rationing: firms act as if they cannot raise additional equity capital. Empirically, there is considerable support for this conclusion; as we noted earlier, even in well-developed capital markets, a relatively small fraction of new capital is raised through new equity.

There are several reasons for this phenomenon which we refer to as "equity rationing." Though in many cases, firms might actually be able to raise new equity, they simply choose not to do so. They choose not to do so because issuing additional equity has a marked negative effect on firms' net worth,[9] net of the additional capital raised, so firms act *as if* they were equity rationed. These firms finance investment beyond retained earnings by borrowing.[10] When they are denied bank credit, they do not raise capital by issuing new equity, but rather constrain their capital expenditures to retained earnings.[11]

There are strong theoretical reasons why this should be so. The willingness of insiders to sell shares to outsiders conveys information; *on average* firms that are willing to do so are more likely to believe that the market has overpriced their shares. I illustrate this point to my students by holding an auction on the money in the wallet in my back pocket. The rules of the auction are simple. The winning bids are given 1 percent of the money in my wallet. I reserve, however, the right not to sell. I ask my students: What is the equilibrium bid? The brightest of my students immediately see the answer: zero. For they (perhaps mistakenly) believe that I know how much money is in my wallet, and know that I will only accept an offer if it represents *more* money than is in my wallet. That is, if there is $100 in my wallet, and a bid for 1 percent is less than a $1, I will reject it, and if it is more than $1

---

[9]  See e.g. Asquith and Mullins (1983).
[10] See Mayer (1990).
[11] See Hellmann and Stiglitz (2000) for a model combining equity and credit rationing. This behavior can also be explained, in some countries, by the structure of corporate and individual taxation (see Stiglitz 1973), but the behavior seems to occur even in contexts in which tax motivations are less compelling.

I will accept it. They are in a heads I win, tails they lose situation. This argument would suggest that there is never an equity market, but of course, in the real world, the original owners of a firm, while they may have more information than an outside investor, are still imperfectly informed, and are still risk averse; so they are willing to accept a bid at a price which is slightly lower than the actuarial value of their estimate of the value of the asset. Nonetheless, it is still the case that willingness to sell shares conveys a negative signal to the market and this negative signal is reflected in the price of shares. And accordingly, firms will be reluctant to sell shares, including selling shares to finance new investment.

Moreover, debt imposes discipline on managers, giving them less "free cash" with which to play. This is sometimes referred to as the "backs to the wall theory of corporate finance" – the necessity to meet high debt obligations gives them less "free cash" with which to play and therefore provides strong incentives for managers. The incentive effects of equity are mixed – to the extent that the owners are managers, the more equity the managers have the greater their incentives,[12] under modern managerial firms, where typically managers have negligible ownership shares, the effects of debt versus equity may be just the opposite.[13]

Other theories for the limited use of equity include those focusing on costly state verification.[14] The debt contract is a relatively straightforward one: to put it simply, creditors are paid a fixed amount, as long as debtors can; if they cannot, the debtors' assets are turned over to the creditors – providing a strong incentive for debtors to pay. The equity contract requires the firm to pay the shareholder a share of the profits. However, it is often hard to observe profits; they can be manipulated. At the extreme, if the owner of, say, a majority of the shares is also the manager, she can simply pay herself a salary equal to the residual income

---

[12] This was the point of the earliest papers on the principal–agent relationship. See e.g. Ross (1983) or Stiglitz (1974b).

[13] See e.g. Stiglitz (1982a), Greenwald, Stiglitz and Weiss (1984), and Myers and Majluf (1984) for a discussion of adverse selection model; or Stiglitz (1974b) or Jensen and Meckling (1976) for an analysis of incentive effects.

[14] See e.g. Harris and Townsend (1981).

of the firm – implying zero profits. More generally, entrepreneurs have found a variety of subtle (and in some cases, not so subtle) ways of diverting the returns of the enterprise toward themselves and away from minority shareholders. Indeed, it is only in a few countries with strong legal protections for minority shareholders that there exist many firms with diverse share ownership.[15]

## Risk aversion and equity rationing

Equity rationing is particularly important, because it means that firms cannot (or choose not to) fully diversify their risks; the original owners cannot fully share the risks throughout the economy, and consequently the firms do not act in a risk neutral manner. If firms have to rely on debt financing, there is a chance that they will not be able to meet their debt obligations, in which case they go bankrupt. There is a cost to bankruptcy not only for lenders.[16] Firms (and we need to think of banks as a special category of firm) maximize their expected profits, taking into account the effects of their decisions on their bankruptcy probability. Higher levels of production – for banks, as we shall see, this translates into higher levels of lending – imply higher probabilities of default.

If banks, and firms more generally, were not "equity-constrained," they would prefer to use more equity, as equity has a distinct risk diversification advantage over debt. In particular, the larger the

---

[15] See e.g. Dyck (1999). Strong accounting standards, accompanied by enforcement of fraud laws, also play an important role. For an early discussion, see Greenwald and Stiglitz (1992). Managers have also found a variety of ways by which they can divert a corporation's resources towards themselves and away from shareholders as a group – an art form which has been taken to new heights in the former Communist countries.

[16] See e.g. Greenwald and Stiglitz (1990a) for a discussion of the nature of these costs; these include both the direct costs of reorganization; the cost in terms of lost opportunities which arise as a result of the restrictions that are effectively imposed during the period of reorganization (e.g. the decreased willingness of others to engage in certain types of trades, including the lack of access to funds); and the costs to managers – not only the (often partial) loss of control, but also the consequences of the adverse signal concerning their competency which results from bankruptcy. We elaborate on the costs of bankruptcy in the context of banks in chapter 3.

fraction of outside finance that is raised through equity, the smaller the probability of bankruptcy.

### Risk averse firms

What is crucial for most of the analyses below is that the firms act in a risk averse manner. Besides equity rationing, there are other reasons to believe that firms are not risk neutral, or do not act as if they were. For example, in large corporations, decisions are made by managers whose compensation is almost always contingent on the performance of the firm. Such contingency pay is viewed to be necessary to provide the requisite managerial incentives.[17]

The two strands explaining risk averse behavior of the firm,[18] focusing respectively on bankruptcy and managerial incentives, are closely linked. One of the major concerns of management is avoiding bankruptcy. Not only does bankruptcy result in managers losing their current job, but also there is a stigma attached to having led a firm into bankruptcy that strongly adversely affects future job prospects.

In the case of regulated firms, the concern is not just bankruptcy, but also intervention by a regulator. For a regulated industry like banking, we should thus substitute the condition that firms are averse to going bankrupt with the condition that firms are averse to regulatory intervention, the strong form of which is a mandated change in management, as occurred in the case of Continental Illinois.

---

[17] In some cases, the possibility of bankruptcy may lead to behavior which appears to be risk loving; this will be true if firms are near bankruptcy. As we note further below, if there were no bankruptcy costs, then bankruptcy itself makes the firm's payoff function convex, inducing risk loving behavior. If bankruptcy costs are small enough, similar results hold. By the same token, poorly designed managerial compensation schemes can lead to risk loving behavior, as the firm absorbs the losses, and the manager is amply rewarded for the successes.

[18] There is ample evidence that firms behave in a risk averse manner. Even if markets fully diversified risk, the remaining aspect of risk with which firms would still be concerned is correlation with the market. In fact, firms care about the own risk of a project, not just its correlation with the market. Other examples are discussed in Stiglitz (1989b).

*With credit rationing, monetary policy exerts its effects not only through interest rates, but also through credit availability*

Credit and equity rationing – or, more broadly, the informational problems associated with the capital market – provide insights into three of the puzzles we have noted above. *If* credit rationing is important, it could explain *both* why corporate financial policy is not irrelevant and why public financial policy is not irrelevant. Public financial policy matters because individuals cannot fully offset reduced borrowing and increased taxes by the government by increased borrowing on their own account, if they are credit constrained. While the magnitude of their credit constraints may be altered as a result, they will not in general be altered in a fully offsetting way. Corporate financial policy matters not only because individuals may not be able to borrow in a way to fully offset reduced borrowing on the part of a firm in which they own shares, but increased corporate indebtedness, beyond a point, leads to an increased probability of default, and so long as there are real bankruptcy costs, this has real consequences.

It could also explain our findings concerning the seeming unimportance of real interest rates (both absolutely and relative to nominal interest rates) in explaining variation in economic activity at certain times. When the economy is credit rationed, it is the *quantity* of loans, not just the interest rates charged, that is critical. With nominal debt contracts, it is not just the *ex ante* expected real interest that matters. A higher than expected rate of inflation redistributes income from creditors to debtors and conversely for a lower than expected rate of inflation; and these redistributions have real effects. With high inflation and high nominal rates, cash flow constraints are more likely to be binding. For instance, with a real interest rate of 5 percent and an inflation rate of 50 percent, so that nominal interest rates are 55 percent, if the firm borrows $1,000 to buy an asset worth say $2,000, yielding a 10 percent return, then even though the asset is worth $3,000 at the end of the year, its cash flow is only $200, not enough to pay the $550 owed. To be sure, the lender should be willing to lend the difference – after all the dollar value of the asset has increased by $1000. But as long as the lender is not *committed* to making the loan, the borrower bears a risk that the lender will not provide the additional capital; and when there are several lenders, each lender may worry that other lenders will not provide the requisite capital, or only at highly unfavorable terms, forcing the firm into bankruptcy, and hence each lender himself may tighten credit standards, e.g. insist on more collateral. These problems are particularly severe if there is the possibility of future credit rationing: the borrower may simply not be able to obtain the credit required to repay. Hence, borrowing *even at the same level of real interest rates* will be less attractive: nominal interest rates matter. Even if the variability of future real interest rates remains unchanged, higher levels of nominal interest rates imply changes in risks borne by both the lender and the borrower.[19]

## Equity rationing and risk divestiture

However, even when the economy is not credit rationed, equity rationed firms (or more generally, risk averse firms) may not be willing to borrow much more, even as interest rates are lowered, given that they cannot divest themselves of the risk associated with production and investment (in the absence of perfect futures markets). So long as a firm's sales are not assured, there is a risk with all production (let alone all investment). There is always a chance that the production will simply have to be held in inventory, or that the firm can sell it only at a price considerably

---

[19] The previous discussion makes clear the difference between the impacts of higher *levels* of nominal interest rates and *changes* in the nominal interest rate (in both cases associated with corresponding changes in the inflation rate). Unexpected increases in inflation lead to redistributions which typically are beneficial to debtors and, if they do not disrupt the financial system too much, may actually stimulate investment, while higher levels of inflation with concomitant increases in interest rates involve more risk bearing by borrowers, and therefore hurt investment. Note that these points are quite different from the argument often put forward that, as a matter of experience, higher inflation rates are associated with higher variability in inflation and in real interest rates. While that in fact may be the case, one has to be careful about the causal links: higher inflation is often the result of large unanticipated supply or demand shocks, and it is the uncertain adjustment to these shocks which is the source of variability, not the inflation itself.

lower than the price, say, today. As the economy enters a recession, this risk is increased. Moreover, if the firm has not fully anticipated the recession – as is typically the case – as it enters the recession, it also finds its net worth depleted, as it fails to sell all that it had anticipated selling, or sells it only at a lower price.[20] This means that at the same time that the magnitude of the risk has increased, the firm's ability and willingness to bear the risk has decreased.

This has effects on each of the decisions of the firm: pricing, hiring, wage setting, layoffs, inventory management, production, investment, and in a series of papers we have explored these various decisions.[21]

For now, we note that as the economy enters a recession, not only is the aggregate demand curve shifted to the left, a point emphasized in standard macroeconomics, but so too is the aggregate supply curve, reinforcing the downward movement in the economy (see figure 2.4). At any price level, the firm is willing to produce less. Our analysis suggests that often aggregate supply is as important as demand – in some cases, as in a small open economy facing a fairly elastic demand curve for its products, more important; and that the two are intricately intertwined. But equally important, the elasticity of demand for investment too may fall; small changes in the nominal (or even real) interest rates charged will not induce much additional investment. One way of thinking about this heuristically is to note that as an economy goes into a recession, the combined effect of increased risk perception and reduced willingness and ability to bear risks is to increase the risk-adjusted cost of capital enormously. Hence, a given change in borrowing rate represents a smaller percentage change in the "cost of capital" than during a boom time.

Moreover, as we shall see later, banks themselves become more risk averse, so that the spread between the T-bill rate and

---

[20] These problems are exacerbated in firms with large debts, especially when the interest rate is not variable: as the economy goes into a recession, prices are likely to be lower than anticipated, so that the real payments to creditors increase, making it more likely that it will go bankrupt.

[21] See Greenwald and Stiglitz (1987a, 1988b, 1989b, 1990a, 1990b, 1993a, 1995).

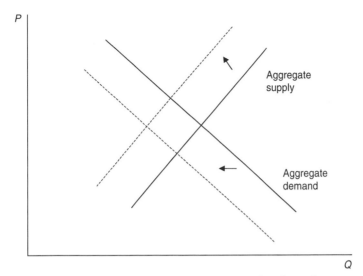

Figure 2.4 *Effect of recession on aggregate demand and supply curves*
As the economy enters a recession, both the aggregate demand
curve and the aggregate supply curve are shifted to the left.

the interest rate they charge borrowers increases (see figure 2.5);
hence a given change in the T-bill rate may translate into a
smaller percentage change in the lending rate.[22] All of these are
part of the explanation for the traditional characterization of
monetary policy at such times as ineffective as pushing against
a string.[23]

These are the themes that we will elaborate upon in following chapters. For now, we simply note that credit and equity

[22] There is a further effect, which may be important in practice: the lowering of
interest rates may adversely affect expectations. Investors may reason that if
the central bank is lowering interest rates, it must be because matters are worse
than had previously been expected. These expectation effects become particularly important in the short run; the Fed, for instance, hesitates to make a large
change in interest rates, even when the economic data might warrant such a
change, because of worries about "scaring" the market.

[23] Borrowers, moreover, when they think about making an investment worry not
just about the interest rate this period, but the interest rate over the life of the
investment. Long-term interest rates may not move in tandem with short-term
interest rates; in some cases, they may even move in opposite directions. Again,
the Fed, in focusing on the short-term T- bill interest rate, may not be focusing
on the variable which matters most. (Expectations, including of inflation, play
an important role in these movements of the term structure.)

Figure 2.5 *Junk Treasury spread, 1988–2000*
There are large movements in the spread between the T-bill rate and
the lending rate. What matters for the level of economic activity is
the lending rate, while the Fed, and economic analysis, has
traditionally focused more on the T-bill rate. Changes in the T-bill
rate may not be translated into corresponding changes in the
lending rate.

rationing are pervasive in the economy, that credit and equity
rationing – for both firms and banks – will be important in the
sequel,[24] and that firms (and banks) act in a risk averse manner. Most importantly, one should not think of equilibrium in
the market for loans as similar to the market equilibrium for
aluminum or other commodities. The supply of loans involves
information processing and risk bearing by banks. Their ability and willingness to bear these risks – to make loans – is a
central determinant of the level of economic activity. In chapter 3, we shall show how shocks to the economy and policy
affect banks' lending behavior.

---

[24] As we shall see, most of our analysis does not require the presence of both credit
and equity rationing, only one or the other.

# THREE

# The ideal banking system

To understand how our current banking system works, we need to think through how an idealized banking system might work – a banking system not too different from what may emerge in the fairly near future in the USA. The central features of this banking system are (a) government-insured deposits; (b) government-imposed reserve requirements, with reserves held at the central bank in interest-free accounts; and (c) no transactions costs. The banking system must compete against money market mutual funds, which invest in government T-bills, and which provide checking services comparable to those provided by banks. They have no reserve requirements, and they pay an interest rate equal to the T-bill rate. (This follows from assumptions concerning competition in the industry and no transactions costs.) Here, we want to highlight certain fairly obvious implications of the model.

The fact that deposits are government-insured means that depositors should be indifferent between holding their funds in the money market accounts and in banks. This means that the interest rate paid by banks to their depositors must equal that on government T-bills. Each bank thus views itself as facing a horizontal supply curve for funds. If it pays epsilon more than its competitors, it can get as much funds as it wants.

The key to understanding the supply of loanable funds (credit availability) is to understand the behavior of banks. We will argue that banks behave in a risk averse manner. We will justify this assumption on the basis that banks – like the firms discussed in chapter 2 – face limits on their ability to diversify and divest risks; e.g. they are equity constrained. To expand, they need to accrue debt that increases the probability of bankruptcy, and the costs associated with bankruptcy lead to risk averse behavior.

### Implications of risk averse behavior

Banks' risk averse behavior has some immediate and important implications. For instance, it means that banks' level of net worth affects their behavior. This is an important departure from the standard neo-classical paradigm with perfect risk sharing.[1] In a complete market with perfect information and without a solvency constraint, risks are effectively spread throughout the economy, and banks (at least with respect to risks that are uncorrelated with the business cycle) act in a risk neutral manner.[2] Since (under those assumptions) banks can easily raise capital, the amount of a bank's net worth is of no relevance: if there are good lending opportunities, the bank can instantaneously raise the funds with which to make the loans and raise the funds in a way that imposes no additional risk of bankruptcy.[3]

---

[1] Some research, such as Kehoe and Levine (1993), Kocherlakota (1996), and Alvarez and Jermann (2000), derives imperfect risk-sharing in complete-market settings by introducing some forms of borrowing constraints. However, these general equilibrium models do not explain why there are such borrowing constraints. Our analysis derives these constraints on the basis of asymmetries of information.

[2] In fact, since many of the important risks upon which we shall focus are business cycle risks, some of our results would obtain even if banks were not equity constrained.

[3] When a bank's net worth is too low, in the formulation in which banks maximize expected terminal wealth *minus* expected bankruptcy costs, they will actually act as risk preferers: bankruptcy itself, as is well known, introduces a non-concavity into the payoff function, which at low levels of net worth, more than offsets the concavity introduced by the expected bankruptcy costs. This non-concavity is important in understanding the risk taking behavior of the S & Ls in the United States during the 1980s – leading to the eventual demise of so many of them. See Kane (1987) and Stiglitz (1992a). In the discussion below, we shall assume throughout that the bank's net worth remains at a sufficiently high level that it acts in a risk averse manner. One of the purposes of bank regulation is to ensure that bank capital remains at a high enough level that it indeed does act in a risk averse manner. (See chapter 9, p. 206.)

In the analysis below, we shall see how the hypothesis that banks are risk averse (a) explains how changes in economic circumstances affect the supply of loanable funds in the market – and thus the level of economic activity; and (b) explains how monetary policy can alter the supply of loanable funds, with larger impacts under some circumstances than others.

### The loanable funds theory

The theory that we develop can be thought of as a generalization of the loanable funds theory. In the 1930s, there was a strong competing theory to that of Keynes, the loanable funds theory, advocated, for example, by Robertson.[4] In that model, the interest rate is determined as the intersection of a downward sloping demand and an upward sloping supply curve of funds (see figure 3.1). In accordance with standard economic precepts, both depended on real interest rates: there is no money illusion. As the economy moves into a recession, the demand curve (derived from the demand for investment goods) shifts markedly to the left, while the supply of funds (from savings) also shifts to the left, as savings fall in response to decreasing income. In this simple rendition, there is an automatic stabilizing force: the shift in the demand

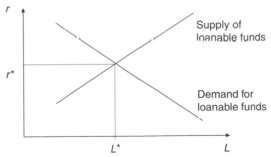

Figure 3.1  *Loanable funds model, no credit rationing*

---

[4]  See Robertson (1922). The hostility between these alternative schools was so strong that when Stiglitz studied and taught in Cambridge, in the mid- and late 1960s, Keynes' disciples' "secret seminar" was still an ongoing institution – a seminar from which Robertson and his followers were deliberately excluded.

for funds typically is greater than the shift in the supply, so real interest rates fall, and this leads to more investment, helping restore the economy towards full employment.

We argue that what matters is not just a supply of savings, funds that are not spent on consumption goods, but a supply of *credit*, credit that can finance investment of firms or consumption of households; that financial institutions play a pivotal role in determining the supply of credit; that there may be large changes in the supply of credit over the business cycle – the decrease in the supply in a recession may well outpace the decrease in the demand for funds, so that even if interest rates were determined by the intersection of the supply and demand for funds, the real interest rate facing borrowers could rise, thereby exacerbating the downturn. To be sure, if funds are not flowing to households and firms inside the country, they must be flowing somewhere else – to the government, or in an open economy, abroad. The government may find itself paying lower and lower interest rates. This may be all to the good for the government's cash flow, but there is no Ricardian equivalence: the improvement in the government's position does not translate directly into an improvement in the position of firms and households, at least not in a way which can lead to their spending more.

Credit rationing complicates matters further: with credit rationing, interest rates may not be determined by the intersection of the demand and supply of loanable funds, so that the decrease in the supply of loans translates directly into a reduction in economic activity (e.g. as a result of less investment which firms can finance), not mediated at all by a change in the real interest rate (see figure 3.2).

Indeed, the real interest rate charged may increase or decrease with changing economic circumstances. The possibility of this should have been clear from our earlier discussion of credit rationing, where we showed that a risk neutral lender would never lend at a rate that exceeded the rate at which the expected return was maximized (see figure 2.1). But the expected return/interest rate charged-curve may well shift with changing economic conditions. Figure 3.3a shows a case where the interest rate increases, while figure 3.3b shows a case where it decreases. Consider, for instance, the simplest adverse selection model of credit rationing, where there are two groups of borrowers. The "safer" borrowers

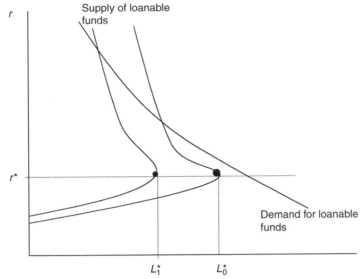

Figure 3.2 *Loanable funds model with credit rationing*
   With credit rationing, the equilibrium interest rate (the rate which
   maximizes expected returns for the lender) is below the level at
   which the demand for loanable funds equals the supply. A leftward
   shift in the supply curve for loanable funds leads to less lending but
   no change in the interest rate: the extent of credit rationing is
   increased. (Because expected returns actually decrease when the
   interest rate exceeds $r^*$, the supply of loanable funds decreases.)

drop out at the interest rate $r^*$, so that if the lender charges more
than $r^*$, he gets only the riskier, lower expected return borrowers.
Hence, $r^*$ is the interest rate charged by the lender. If worsening
economic conditions imply that the safe borrower actually drops
out of the market at a lower real interest rate than before, then
lenders might lower the real interest rate charged (figure 3.3c). On
the other hand, consider the simplest adverse incentive model, in
which the riskier project becomes more attractive at higher interest rates. (Higher interest rates reduce the expected return to the
investor on a riskier project by less simply because there is a lower
probability that she will actually pay the higher interest rate, that
is, there is a higher probability that she will default.) If an economic
downturn lowers the expected return to the riskier project more

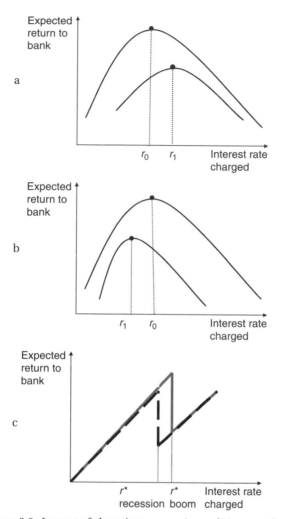

Figure 3.3 *Impact of changing economic conditions on the equilibrium interest rate with credit rationing*

The equilibrium interest rate with credit rationing is the interest rate that maximizes expected returns.

a   Interest rate is increased

b   Interest rate is decreased

c   The case of an adverse selection model where, as a result of a recession, the low-risk borrowers drop out of the market at a lower interest rate.

than the safe project, then the critical interest rate at which borrowers switch is increased; and hence lenders may increase the interest rate charged without worrying of a switch to greater risk taking (recall figure 2.2). The point is that in different circumstances,
different effects may predominate; with credit rationing there is no
clear relationship between the real interest charged and the economic cycle. Later, in our discussion of *risk averse* lenders, we shall
show that there is, in fact, a systematic force leading to an increase
in real interest rates charged as the economy goes into a recession.

The cornerstone of our analysis is thus the behavior of banks,
to which we now turn.

### The bank's portfolio problem

Given its equity, the bank must decide how much to lend, how
thoroughly to screen loan applicants, how much to retain in government T-bills, how many funds to acquire through deposits,
what interest rate to charge on loans, and what interest to pay on
deposits. There are other decisions: how much to spend on monitoring loans, how much of the portfolio to devote to real estate,
and within real estate, to, say, commercial properties. For each
borrower, the bank must decide on the size of the loan that it is
willing to provide, the non-price terms (such as collateral), and
what restrictions to impose on other borrowing by the firms to
which it lends. In this chapter, where we are focusing on competitive banks, we assume that the bank faces a given deposit
rate, $\rho$, at which it can acquire as many funds as it wants. We can
write the bank's gross returns from its loan portfolio as

$$Y = Y(N, r, e, \Theta) \qquad (3.1)$$

where

$N$ = total number of dollars lent
$r$ = interest rate charged on loans
$e$ = expenditures on screening and monitoring
$\Theta$ = state of the business cycle, representing the
undiversifiable risk of the bank's portfolio.

Without loss of generality, we assume that a large value of $\Theta$ represents a good state of the business cycle, i.e. $Y_\Theta > 0$.

In this simple model, we focus on three decisions of the bank – how much to lend, what interest rate to charge, and how much to spend on screening and monitoring. $e$ can in fact be thought of as a vector representing all other decisions (other than the amount of lending and interest rate charged), including, for instance, whether the bank makes a few large loans or many small loans.[5]

From (3.1), given the state of business cycle, the three variables $\{N, r, e\}$ will determine the probability distribution of the bank's gross returns. We will elaborate on them a bit further before setting up the model.

(i) *The total number of dollars lent* We assume that the returns to the different loans (the bankruptcy probabilities) are not independent. There is a strong cyclical component to bankruptcy. Normally, banks have specialized information about firms with whom they have regular relationships; they have less information about others. As they grant more loans, their ability to screen accurately is reduced, because they "go down the list" of borrowing prospects. At the same time, lending more to the same borrowers increases the risk of default of each. For these reasons, the more the bank lends, the greater the risk of bankruptcy,[6] and more broadly, the lower the mean return and the higher the standard deviation.

(ii) *The interest rate charged* Normally, we would have expected an increase in the interest rate charged to increase the bank's

---

[5] Standard diversification theory would suggest that the bank make many small loans. However, there are important fixed costs, e.g. associated with screening and monitoring, and these costs lead banks to limit the number of those to whom they lend money.

[6] Even with loans with independently distributed returns, additional loans increase the variance of the return, even if the variance per dollar lent decreases. Bankruptcy is more closely related to the former than to the latter.

expected return. Because of adverse selection and incentive effects, the expected return may actually be lowered as the interest rate charged increases, as we noted at the beginning of chapter 2 (see figure 2.1a).

These interest rate effects arise because the bank has only imperfect information, both concerning the nature of the loan applicants and the actions that loan applicants undertake. Of course, the bank has *some* information, and it has *some* control over what borrowers do with its funds. However, as long as its information is imperfect, and its control is limited, the effects that we have just described may occur, and they may be important.

(iii) *The bank's expenditure on screening loan applicants and monitoring the uses of its funds* The screening costs, in particular, represent up-front expenditures, the return to which accrues only subsequently, when the loans are repaid. They are sunk costs. They are, in these senses, risky investments. Moreover, screening expenditures borne by the bank are long-term investments, likely to bear their full fruit only over a long period of time. In an economic recession, where the bank's horizon may be shortened – or it believes that the life prospects of the firms to which it is lending are shortened – the returns on these investments are reduced. Hence, just as firms do not undertake the fixed costs of hiring workers in a downturn, banks do not undertake the fixed costs of screening new firms in a downturn. Just as the former implies that workers who are laid off, e.g. by firms going out of business or contracting their size, will find it difficult getting rehired, so too here, firms that have their supply of funds cut off, e.g. by banks going bankrupt or contracting their lending portfolio, will find it difficult getting taken on by an alternative bank.

There are other determinants of the probability distribution (mean and standard deviation) of returns of the bank's loan portfolio, e.g. its collateral requirements. For simplicity, we shall ignore these other determinants.

## THE BASIC MODEL

To simplify matters, we formulate the bank's problem in a two-period model[7]. The bank has an initial net worth, $a_t$. It can invest an amount $N$ in loans yielding gross return $Y$ and an amount $M$ in T-bills with interest rate $\rho$.[8] This is also the rate which it must pay depositors.

As deposits are subject to reserve requirements, the bank cannot use all its borrowed funds to invest, but must set aside a proportion of them. Thus, if $k$ is the reserve requirement, and if a bank wishes to make $B$ of investments financed by borrowing, it must borrow $D$, where

$$D(1 - k) = B \tag{3.2}$$

These reserve requirements can also be viewed as a "tax" $\rho$ on the interest payments on deposits, defined by

$$1 + \tau = 1/(1 - k) \tag{3.3}$$

The cost of the borrowed funds, i.e. the total repayment to depositors is consequently

$$D\rho = B\rho(1 + \tau) \tag{3.4}$$

Therefore the end-of-the-period net worth of the bank, taking account of the possibility of bankruptcy, is:

$$a_{t+1} = \max \{ Y + M(1 + \rho) - B(1 + \rho(1 + \tau)),\ 0 \}$$

| | | | |
|---|---|---|---|
| gross returns from loans | gross returns from T-bills | payments to depositors | (3.5) |

---

[7] A more comprehensive approach would entail using dynamic programming; the bank chooses a sequence of portfolios for each time, assuming for instance that the state of the economy follows some Markov process. For tractability and the purpose of illustrating the main points of this book, we just set up a two-period model here. All the choice variables are determined in the first period $t$. The bank's initial wealth $a_t$ is given; it corresponds to the state variable in a dynamic programming setting. The bank's terminal wealth $a_{t+1}$ is determined by its portfolio choice. The two-period setting can also be conveniently converted into a mean-variance framework. In the following notation, we drop the time subscript of the bank's choice variables. For example $N$ just means $N_t$.

[8] Since in this simple model we assume that the inflation rate is fixed, changes in the nominal deposit interest rate translate directly into changes in the real interest rate.

where by assumption $B \geq 0$. To balance the bank's budget,[9] it must hold that $B$ equals total expenditures (ignoring taxes, which are paid at the end of the period) minus initial wealth

$$B = \underset{\text{loans}}{N} + \underset{\text{T-bills}}{M} + \underset{\substack{\text{expenditures} \\ \text{on screening}}}{e} - \underset{\substack{\text{initial} \\ \text{wealth}}}{a_t}$$

There are effectively two regimes – one in which the bank borrows ($B > 0$, it is a depository institution), and the other in which the bank only invests its own assets ($B = 0$, it is an investment bank). If the bank is an investment bank, it simply invests what it does not lend into T-bills.[10] Using the budget constraint, we can rewrite the maximization problem (3.5) for a depository institution as:

$$a_{t+1} = \max \{Y(N, r, e, \Theta) + M(1 + \rho) \qquad (3.5')$$
$$- [N + M + e - a_t](1 + \rho(1 + \tau)), 0\}$$

and for an investment bank as:

$$a_{t+1} = \max \{Y(N, r, e, \Theta) + [a_t - N - e](1 + \rho), 0\} \quad (3.5'')$$

The bank goes bankrupt if $a_{t+1} < 0$. Recall $Y_\Theta > 0$ by assumption. Accordingly, there exists a critical value $\hat{\Theta}$ such that the bank goes bankrupt if $\Theta \leq \hat{\Theta}$, and not otherwise. Let $F(\hat{\Theta})$ be the probability that $\Theta \leq \hat{\Theta}$; then this is the probability that the bank goes bankrupt. We will let $c$ represent the cost of bankruptcy.

### Avoiding bankruptcy

There are two alternative ways of modeling bank behavior. They both yield similar results, namely, that the bank acts in a risk averse manner. The first is based on the assumption that the bank is risk neutral, provided it does not go bankrupt, but there is a

---

[9] Throughout, we assume the only way the bank can amplify its resource basis is by accepting deposits. We ignore the possibility of new equity or bond issues.
[10] Later, we shall expand the set of portfolio allocations to allow banks also to invest in, say, long-term government bonds.

high cost to bankruptcy, so it naturally wishes to avoid bank-ruptcy.[11] Formally, we assume the bank[12]

$$\max_{\{N,\ M,\ r,\ e\}} E(a_{t+1}) - cF(\hat{\Theta})  \qquad (3.6)$$

s.t.

$$N \le N^d(r,\ e)  \qquad (3.7)$$

where $N^d$ is the demand for loans at the interest rate $r$, and where $c$ is the cost of bankruptcy. There are several alternative inter-pretations to this cost. Most obviously, it includes the actual transactions costs associated with bankruptcy, which can be sub-stantial. Typically, in the process of bankruptcy, there is signifi-cant loss of informational and organizational capital; some of the bank's best workers look elsewhere for employment, given the uncertainty of the bank's future prospects; units of the bank may be disbanded. Since many of the bank assets are loans, and there may be large asymmetries of information concerning the true value of these assets, they often sell at a substantial discount.[13] Typically, too, in the process of bankruptcy, bank activities are limited, if not suspended, and there is often a high cost associ-ated with this disruption. In addition, there are personal costs that accrue to the managers of bankrupt organizations, the stigma that they may well bear in the future. From the point of view of decision making, what matters are the costs borne by the decision maker, and these costs can be real and large.

[11]  See the discussion above and Greenwald and Stiglitz (1988a, 1990a) for alter-native interpretations of this assumption – e.g. it may represent the conse-quences of managerial behavior.

[12]  As noted in n.7 a more rigorous way to set up the bank's problem is to use dy-namic programming, where the objective of the firm is to maximize the present discounted value of dividend streams *plus* terminal wealth.

[13]  While from a social view, these losses may be viewed as purely distributive – the losses from the perspective of the seller being gains from the perspective of the buyer – from the perspective of the decision making bank, they are a real cost; also, there is a real social cost associated with the increased uncertainty associated with the transfer of assets. Moreover, the recognition of these costs affects lending behavior, and thus has real consequences. The fact that "used" loans (loans previously made) can be resold only at a discount is called the "lemons discount factor" (Akerlof, 1970) and plays a role in the later analysis of the consequences of changes, e.g. in reserve requirements or interest rates.

Finally, there are the costs associated with the loss of *franchise* value, the expected present discounted value of the future profits that the bank would receive were it to remain viable. In a sense, there is an option value of survival; and bankruptcy destroys that option value.

The bankruptcy cost $c$ thus depends on a number of factors, and some of these costs may change with changes in economic conditions. In a recession, for instance, especially one which is expected to be long in duration, the franchise value may decrease markedly. The "managerial" stigma value may either decrease or increase; the fact that labor mobility is more difficult in a recession means that the cost of the stigma may be larger; on the other hand, if many firms are failing, the magnitude of the stigma may be smaller; there is a greater chance that an inference will be made that the manager himself is less to blame – the bankruptcy was due to circumstances beyond his control.

The bankruptcy costs are also likely to increase with the scale of the firm, though not necessarily proportionately.

In short, $c$ can be viewed as a measure of the aversion to bankruptcy. For the most part, with one important exception,[14] in the subsequent analysis, we will focus more on the determinants of the changes in the marginal probability of bankruptcy, rather than on changes in the costs of bankruptcy. But it is easy to adapt the analytic framework to explore the consequences of changes in $c$ itself.

This formulation recognizes that banks might want to choose an interest rate below that at which demand equals supply; but that they cannot "force" borrowers to borrow. When the constraint (3.7) is not binding, it means that there is credit rationing; the amount that people are willing to borrow at the interest rate offered by the bank exceeds the loans that the bank is willing to grant. We shall concentrate our attention on that regime, because it is both simpler and more interesting; it represents the most marked deviation from the standard regime, for interest rates are then *set* by the bank, not by standard market forces of demand and supply. When the constraint (3.7) is binding, banks' loan interest rates are determined

---

[14] Namely, in the discussion of regulation below, we shall analyze how regulatory changes affect the franchise value of the bank.

by market forces, by the demand and supply of loans, not by banks themselves. However, most of our results remain valid even in the absence of credit rationing, as we shall see.

Problem (3.6) says that the bank chooses its loan portfolio, its loan policy (here reflected in the interest rate charged and management cost $e$) and its investments in government bonds to maximize the expected value of its terminal wealth $a_{t+1}$, *minus* the expected value of the bankruptcy penalty.

The solution to this problem is easy to describe. We focus our attention first on the amount of lending. Banks pursue lending to the point where the expected *marginal* gross return of loans equals the costs of the funds, including the increased expected bankruptcy costs[15]:

$$EY_N = (1 + \rho) + \phi \quad \text{if the bank is not borrowing} \qquad (3.8)$$
$$EY_N = (1 + \rho(1 + \tau)) + \phi \quad \text{if the bank is borrowing}$$

where $\phi$ is the marginal bankruptcy cost (MBC)[16]

$$\phi = \partial cF/\partial N > 0 \qquad (3.9)$$

Figure 3.4 shows marginal bankruptcy costs rising as the bank lends (and borrows) more. In the absence of bankruptcy costs, we obtain the standard neo-classical result – the marginal return on a loan is equal to the cost of capital (figure 3.5). In the absence of bankruptcy risk, the marginal return on a loan is just the interest rate charged. But with bankruptcy there may be a marked discrepancy between the interest rate charged and the expected marginal return to lending, and between the expected marginal return to lending and the cost of capital; the latter difference is the marginal bankruptcy cost, $\phi$.

To foreshadow what will follow, standard analysis has focused on how changed economic circumstances (e.g. an economic downturn) shift down the expected return, thus lowering lending

---

[15] In (3.8), $Y_N$ depends on $r$. $r$ is either the optimally chosen interest rate (in the event of credit rationing) or the market interest rate (when there is no credit rationing).

[16] In the following, the term *marginal bankruptcy cost* (*MBC*) shall refer to the marginal change in expected bankruptcy costs due to a change in the amount of lending $N$.

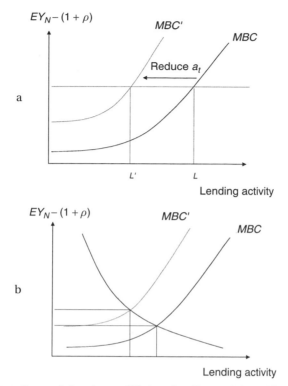

Figure 3.4  Determining the equilibrium lending activity with
bankruptcy

The equilibrium lending activity is that where the difference
between the expected marginal return and the cost of capital
$EY_n - (1 + \rho)$ is equal to the marginal bankruptcy cost. Shifts in the
marginal bankruptcy curve (here, as a result of a decrease in the
bank's net worth $a_t$) lead to changes in the level of lending.
a    The case where the expected marginal return to lending is
constant
b    The case where the expected marginal return to lending
decreases as the amount lent increases.

(figure 3.5a); and how government policy shifts down, say, the cost
of capital, thus increasing lending (figure 3.5b). By contrast, our
analysis, while not denying the importance of the role of these shifts,
also emphasizes the role of shifts in the marginal bankruptcy curve
(the dotted line in figure 3.4) as a result of a decrease in the bank's

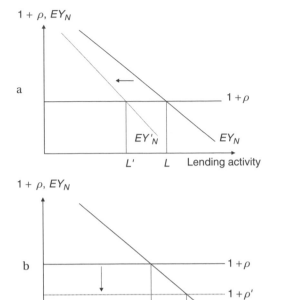

Figure 3.5 *Traditional model with no bankruptcy*
The equilibrium level of lending is that where the expected marginal return equals the cost of capital $\rho$.
a   A decrease in the expected marginal return leads to a reduction in lending activity
b   A decrease in the cost of capital leads to an increase in lending activity

net worth $a_t$. (Panel a illustrates the case where $EY_N$ is a constant, panel b where there are diminishing returns.)

The bank's decision on $e$ and $r$ can be analyzed in a similar way.

$$EY_e = (1 + \rho(1 + \tau)) + \partial cF/\partial e \quad \text{if the bank is borrowing}$$
$$(3.10)$$
$$EY_e = (1 + \rho) + \partial cF/\partial e \quad \text{if the bank is not borrowing}$$

Note that since expenditures on screening are likely to reduce the risk of bankruptcy by reducing the probability of default on

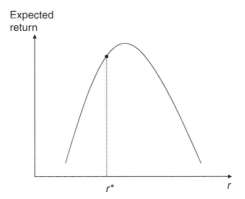

Figure 3.6 *Interest rate determination with credit rationing and bankruptcy*

The bank chooses an interest rate which is below that which maximizes the expected return, because further increases in the interest rate would increase the probability of bankruptcy.

loans, they are likely to be pushed further than they would if the bank were risk neutral, that is, if there were no costs of bankruptcy.

Finally, when there is credit rationing, so the bank can choose the interest rate charged, $r$ is chosen so that[17]

$$\overline{EY}_r = \partial c\overline{r}/\partial\overline{r} \tag{3.11}$$

That is, the bank does not choose the interest rate which maximizes the expected return (that is, for which $EY_r = 0$) because it realizes that it increases the risk of bankruptcy in doing so (see figure 3.6).

---

[17] When there is no credit rationing and the bank expands its loan portfolio by increasing the amount lent to any particular borrower, the bank can normally increase the interest rate charged to reflect the increased riskiness of the loan, but the amount by which the interest rate increases is determined competitively, that is, there is a critical threshold interest rate above which the bank will not be able to lend to that borrower, and others similar to him. In a sense, we can think of the market determining the interest rate for every "risk category"; a larger loan moves a borrower from one risk category into another. If the market were risk neutral, it would set the interest rate on a safe loan, and the interest rate charged on all other loans is then determined as the interest rate which yields the same expected return, taking into account bankruptcy. But the essential point of the analysis here is that markets are not risk neutral. Unfortunately, there is no simple way of calculating the certainty equivalent return.

The first-order conditions (3.8), (3.10), (3.11) can be solved simultaneously in the case of credit rationing for the level of lending, screening, and the interest rate charged, as functions of the bank's wealth, the market rate of interest, and other parameters (to be discussed below):

$$r^* = \Phi^r(a, \rho, \tau, c; \dots)$$ (3.12)
$$e^* = \Phi^e(a, \rho, \tau, c; \dots)$$
$$N^* = \Phi^N(a, \rho, \tau, c; \dots)$$
$$M^* = \Phi^M(a, \rho, \tau, c; \dots)$$

When there is no credit rationing, and the bank must take the interest rate charged (on a group of seemingly homogeneous borrowers, even though, after private information is acquired, they are heterogeneous[18]) as given, we similarly obtain

$$e^* = \Phi^e(a, \rho, \tau, r, c; \dots)$$ (3.13)
$$N^* = \Phi^N(a, \rho, \tau, r, c; \dots)$$
$$M^* = \Phi^M(a, \rho, \tau, r, c; \dots)$$

Solving for the impact of changes in any of the parameters $\{a, \rho, \tau\}$ is typically a complicated matter of differentiating the sets of equations simultaneously, with results depending on the nature of cross-derivatives. Since our point in this book is to provide a general framework rather than detailed and definitive results, we will normally slide by these niceties, focusing (using diagrammatic) techniques, on what we see as the "normal" case.

### Mean–variance analysis

The alternative formulation is simply to assume that banks act in a risk averse manner; that is, they maximize the expected utility of the wealth at the end of the period, $EU(a_{t+1})$. We assume utility is a continuous and strictly concave function of wealth,

---

[18]  We have clearly overly simplified. In the case where there is only an adverse incentive problem, then it makes sense for all banks to charge the same interest rate, but when there is also an adverse selection problem, the interest rate charged is likely to differ depending on the number of banks who have ascertained that the borrower is "good" and are therefore competing to lend to him. See Stiglitz (1975b).

i.e. $U'' < 0$. A special case of this, which will be particularly useful for diagrammatic analysis, is that in which[19] the bank can be viewed to maximize a utility function represented as a function only of the mean and standard deviation of end-of-period wealth.[20] For the representative bank, we can write the mean and variance of its terminal wealth as functions of $N$, $M$, $r$, $\rho$, $\tau$ and $e$:

$$\mu(a_{t+1}) = \mu(a_t\, N,\, M,\, r,\, \rho,\, \tau,\, e) \tag{3.14}$$

$$\sigma(a_{t+1}) = \sigma(a_t\, N,\, M,\, r,\, \rho,\, \tau,\, e) \tag{3.15}$$

Then, the bank maximizes:

$$U = U(\mu(a_{t+1}),\, \sigma(a_{t+1})) \tag{3.16}$$

Or more precisely, the bank's problem is

$$\max_{\{N,\, M,\, r,\, e\}} U(\mu(a_{t+1}),\, \sigma(a_{t+1}))$$

s.t.

$$N \le N^d(r,\, e)$$

where the constraint is not binding if there is credit rationing, and is if there is not.

For simplicity, in the analysis below, we will focus on the mean and standard deviation of *income* rather than *terminal wealth*, but it is easy to translate results from one frame to the other.[21]

---

[19] We assume that the pattern of returns and the utility functions satisfy one of the conditions under which mean–variance analysis is valid. See Cass and Stiglitz (1972), Stiglitz (1972a). Alternatively, we can think of mean–variance analysis as a simple heuristic, that enables us to obtain insights of more general validity.

[20] For simplicity, when we use the mean–standard deviation model, we shall ignore the implications of bankruptcy for the mean and standard deviation of return. The mean–standard deviation diagram is presented as only a heuristic for understanding what is going on, and the corrections required to incorporate bankruptcy are sufficiently complicated that they blur the essential points that we wish to emphasize.

[21] The only difference is that if the true utility function is defined over $a_{t+1}$, then shifts in $a_t$ that leave income unchanged in each state of nature may change choices (in effect, they shift the indifference curves in the space of mean and standard deviation defined over *income*). It should be emphasized that we are using mean-variance analysis as a simplifying heuristic. There are some restrictive utility functions for which mean-variance analysis is valid, but we do not want to limit our analysis to these highly restrictive cases.

For most of the analysis, we will also assume constant returns to scale in risky investment (loans), so that the mean and standard deviation of the net return of the bank's loans are:

$$\mu_Y = N\mu^*(M, r, \rho, e) \tag{3.17}$$

$$\sigma_Y = N\sigma^*(M, r, \rho, e) \tag{3.18}$$

where $\mu^*(M, r, \rho, e)$ represents the mean net return for one unit of loans and $\sigma^*(M, r, \rho, e)$ represents the standard deviation of the net return for one unit of loans. Then the mean and standard deviation of the bank's net income at the end of the period is:

$$\mu = N\mu^* + M\rho - \rho(1 + \tau)(N + M + e - a_t) \tag{3.19}$$
$$\text{for } N + M + e - a_t \geq 0$$

$$= N\mu^* + M\rho \quad \text{for } N + M + e - a_t < 0 \tag{3.20}$$

$$\sigma = N\sigma^* \tag{3.21}$$

where (3.20) just describes the case when there is no borrowing from depositors, so the bank does not need to pay any interest on deposits.

### The diagrammatic analysis of the mean–variance model

One of the reasons that the mean–variance framework is so attractive is that there is a simple diagrammatic exposition. Assume the bank took all of its net worth and spent it on loans and related screening and monitoring expenditures. By choosing its policies efficiently, it can generate a mean–standard deviation frontier, illustrated in figure 3.7, denoted by *RR*, which is also called the *loan opportunity set*. The bank can obtain higher returns by undertaking greater risk – e.g. by charging higher interest rates (*the interest rate effect*), changing the composition of their portfolio, for instance towards riskier loans (*the loan-composition effect*) and, say, monitoring less intensely. Thus, at every point on the *RR* curve, there is a set {*e, r*} that represents the "efficient" set of policies for maximizing

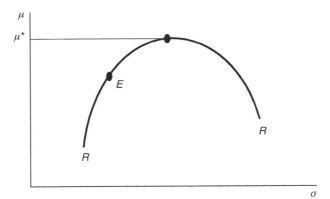

Figure 3.7 *Loan opportunity set (mean–standard deviation frontier)*
In the mean–variance model, *RR* is the loan opportunity locus, the
mean and standard deviation that could be obtained if the bank spent
all of its money on lending activities. $\mu^*$ is the point where expected
return is maximized. *E* is the point the risk averse bank chooses.

the mean at the given variance.[22] As the bank moves to the right
along the *RR* curve, the interest rate charged increases and the
expenditure on screening presumably decreases.

It is useful for later analysis to consider two special cases. The first
is where the *only* decision of the bank is the interest rate charged.
Earlier, it has been shown that the mean return increases, and then
decreases, as *r* increases. However, as *r* increases, typically the variance increases too. Hence, the mean–variance frontier appears as
in figure 3.7, as an inverted *U*-shape. Risk neutral lenders always operate at the peak – an implicit assumption in Stiglitz and Weiss (1981)
and the subsequent literature. Risk averse banks, however, always
operate to the left of the peak – at an interest rate lower than that
maximizing the expected returns. Therefore, in the subsequent discussions we shall often only show the left-hand side of the curve.

The second case is that in which the bank faces a given interest
rate because in a competitive market, it cannot attract borrowers

---

[22] Thus, the efficient frontier represents the solution to the following problem: If
$N = a_t - e$, i.e. the bank spends all of its wealth on lending activities
$$\max_{\{e, r\}} \mu_Y \quad \text{subject to} \quad \sigma_Y = \sigma_Y^*$$

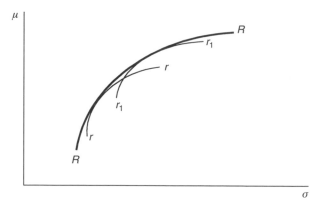

Figure 3.8 *Mean–variance model with interest rate fixed and variable*
With the interest rate fixed, the mean–variance frontier is *rr*; if the
interest rate can be varied, the bank can obtain the outer envelope
of the *rr* curves, the *RR* curve, which is flatter.

unless it charges an interest rate less than or equal to what is determined by the market for loans, say, $r^*$. Then there is still a
mean–variance frontier, so long as the bank has other instruments
under its control. If we label the mean–variance frontier with $r^*$
fixed as $rr$, then the *RR* curve depicted earlier, in which *e* and *r*
are both controllable, can be viewed as the outer envelope of the
set of *rr* curves corresponding to different loan rates (see figure
3.8). The loan opportunity set with fixed interest rate is thus more
"curved" than the opportunity locus with variable interest rates.[23]

Besides making risky loans, the bank can also lend at the safe
rate of interest (i.e. buy T-bills).[24] Point *S* along the vertical axis
in figure 3.9 represents the outcome if it were to take all of its
portfolio and put it into short-term government bonds. By
allocating different proportions of its wealth between T-bills and
loans, the bank can also obtain any point on the straight line
through *S* which is tangent to the loan opportunity set, *RR*, at *P*.[25]

---

[23] Some actions (like increased screening) require increased expenditures, leaving
fewer funds left over for lending. The mean–variance frontier takes this into account.

[24] Actually, in terms of real consumption, government bonds are not safe. Mean–
variance analysis can be extended in a straightforward way to situations in
which the "safe" asset is still risky, as long as it represents the minimum variance asset. See Cass and Stiglitz (1970).

[25] This is the standard portfolio separation theorem of mean variance analysis.
See Tobin (1958).

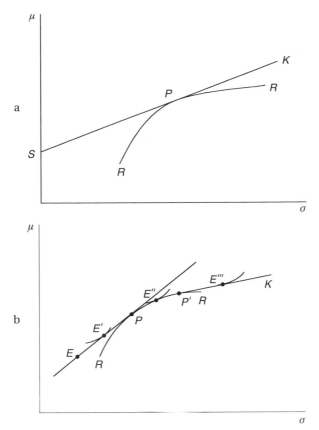

Figure 3.9 *Mean–variance model, credit rationing, with and without reserve requirement*

a   Without reserve requirement

*S* is the mean and standard deviation if the bank puts all its net worth in T-bills, *RR* if it puts it all into loans. The full opportunity locus is the line *SPK*: to the left of *P*, the bank accepts no deposits, but holds T-bills; to the right of *P*, the bank accepts deposits and lends more than its net worth.

b   With reserve requirement: bank's full opportunity locus

If the bank puts all of its money into loans, its opportunity locus is *RR*; *S* is the return if the bank puts its entire worth in T-bills (the safe asset); it can obtain any point on the locus *SP* (the tangent line to *RR* through *S*) by changing the proportion of assets invested in T-bills; by borrowing and lending it can obtain any point on the locus *P'K*. Where the bank chooses to operate depends on its risk aversion: if it is very risk averse, it chooses *E*, near *S*, putting most of its existing net worth into T-bills; if it is not very risk averse, it accepts large amounts of deposits, and chooses point *E'''*. At *E'* it invests mainly in loans, at *E''*, it holds neither deposits (borrows) nor T-bills.

If there were no reserve requirements, the bank could also borrow at the same cost that it could lend to the government,[26] so that its whole opportunity set is the extension of the straight line through $S$ that is tangent to $RR$ (see figure 3.9a). However, as long as there are reserve requirements and reserves pay a lower interest rate than government T-bills, the bank must borrow at a higher cost than the T-bill rate. As a result, the bank's total opportunity set looks as illustrated in figure 3.9b. It can borrow (accept deposits) at a net cost of $\rho(1 + \tau)$ per dollar borrowed (taking into account the reserve requirement) and lend out the proceeds. The mean–standard deviation is given by the line $P'K$, where the slope of the line $P'K$, (which is tangent to $RR$ at $P'$) is determined by the net cost of funds.[27]

The bank can operate at four different points along the opportunity locus. In the first three cases, the bank accepts no deposits, i.e. it is acting as a closed investment bank. First, it could simply buy government bonds (point $S$): the bank is, in those circumstances, hardly operating as a bank. Second, it can take some of its funds and invest them in T-bills, and it can lend the remainder out. These are the points along the locus $SP$. Third, it can take all of its net worth to make loans, neither investing in T-bills, nor accepting deposits. These are the points along the loan opportunity locus between $P$ and $P'$.

In the fourth case, where it accepts deposits and lends the proceeds (beyond what it has to keep in reserves), the bank is acting as a conventional (depository) bank. Then it chooses one of the points along the line $P'K$.

The bank's choice depends on its attitudes towards risk, as well as on the trade-offs it perceives. Figure 3.9 illustrates the four possibilities. If it expects the return on T-bills is close to the maximum it can obtain on its loan portfolio, the portfolio choice is more likely to be close to the corner solution $S$.[28] Similarly, if the bank is so

[26] Assuming that deposits are viewed as riskless, or close to being so, as they would be with government deposit insurance.

[27] More precisely, the slope of the line $SP$ is $(\mu_Y - \rho)/\sigma_Y$ and the slope of the line $P'K$ is $(\mu'_Y - \rho(1 + \tau))/\sigma'_Y$ where $\{\mu_Y, \sigma_Y\}$ and $\{\mu'_Y, \sigma'_Y\}$ are the mean and variance at $P$ and $P'$ respectively.

[28] If T-bills were perfectly safe, a bank would not be at the corner solution unless T-bills yielded the same expected return as the loan portfolio. However, because of uncertainties associated with inflation, T-bills are, in real terms, risky, and so it is conceivable that there be a corner solution, even when T-bills yield a lower expected return.

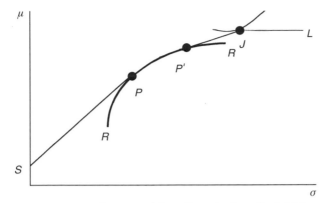

Figure 3.10 *Mean–variance model, credit rationing, diminishing returns to lending*
   If there is a limited supply of good lending opportunities, the
   opportunity locus eventually bends down. Here, we depict the
   situation where there are a fixed number of good lending
   opportunities and an unlimited number of lending opportunities at
   somewhat lower expected returns. There is a kink at the point where
   the good lending opportunities run out, point *J*.

risk averse that it requires a large increase in mean return to compensate for additional risk, the solution is also likely to be near *S*.
On the contrary, if the bank perceives the expected return to loans
as much higher than what it must pay to obtain funds and it is not
very risk averse, then it will borrow a great deal (accept many deposits), and lend a great deal. It will choose a point such as *E'''*, at
which an indifference curve is tangent to *P'K* far to the right of *P'*.

   So far we have implicitly assumed that the mean and standard
deviation of returns per dollar lent is independent of the scale of
lending. If, however, there are diminishing returns, then the bank's
opportunity set appears as in figure 3.10, where we assume that
there is a fixed supply of good loan opportunities (greater than the
amount that it has in its own net worth), and a perfectly elastic supply of second-rate lending opportunities. Under these assumptions, there is a kink in the total opportunity set facing the bank.[29]

---

[29] Note that these opportunity sets are defined *relative to the information of the
   bank*; that is, additional loans may be perceived to be riskier, simply because
   the bank has little information on these new borrowers, and is unable to screen
   them perfectly.

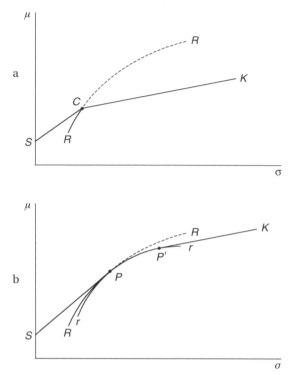

Figure 3.11 *Mean–variance model, no credit rationing*
   a   Interest rate competitively determined, no other control
   instrument. If the interest rate that banks can charge is limited
   (to *C*) because of competition, and banks have no other control
   instrument, then the opportunity locus (with reserve requirements)
   is the line *SCK.*
   b   There are other control instruments
   If there are other control instruments, then the bank's opportunity
   locus is the tangency between a line through *S* and the curve *rr* –
   representing the opportunity locus when all variables other than the
   interest rate are chosen efficiently.


   The bank's total opportunity set illustrated in figure 3.9 pre-
sumes the bank can get as many loan applicants as it wishes at
any interest rate it charges, i.e. there is credit rationing. Figure
3.11a illustrates what happens in the absence of credit rationing
if the only control instrument of the bank is the interest rate and

under competition, the bank can only charge an interest rate, say $r^*$ or lower, and can get any positive amount of deposits. Then, the (relevant) loan opportunity set, represented in terms of mean and standard deviation, is a single point $C$. Assume all loan applicants are identical; then the bank can get as many borrowers as it wishes if it offers the competitive terms of contract. In the case without credit rationing, the bank's opportunity locus is thus the kinked line $SCK$. More generally, if there are other control variables, the opportunity set is similar to figure 3.9b with one difference: the interest rate, $r$, is no longer chosen by the bank (see figure 3.11b), so that the loan opportunity locus is the curve $rr$ rather than $RR$.

### Basic propositions

We summarize the implications of this model for bank behavior in seven propositions:

PROPOSITION 1    *The bank never borrows to buy government bonds.*

That is, if $(1)\,\tau > 0$, i.e., there is a strictly positive reserve requirement and (2)

$$B = N + M + e - a = \text{bank deposits} > 0 \qquad (3.22)$$

then $M = 0$.

This follows from the fact that there is a tax on deposits and the bank must pay (before tax) an interest rate equal to the interest rate received on government bonds. Thus, in every state of nature, $a_{t+1}$ is lower if the bank borrows to buy government bonds. Hence $Ea_{t+1}$ is lower and the probability of bankruptcy is higher. (Moreover, if the cost of bankruptcy increases with the size of the bank's assets or liabilities, the cost of borrowing also increases.)

The implications of this theorem are striking. It means that, were we in a competitive banking regime, we should never see a bank with deposits holding government T-bills.

There are, to be sure, dynamics that are more complicated than those captured in our simplified model. Banks may hold T-bills or any other liquid asset for "liquidity" purposes, because they may expect to invest them next period and it can be costly to ramp deposits up or down quickly, to liquidate loans or other assets, or otherwise to obtain funds needed. Thus, there is a shadow value associated with some level of deposits not already committed to loans, and this shadow price may more than offset the tax.

Formally, the maximization problem (3.6) is modified to read

$$\max EV(a_{t+1}, M_t) - cF$$
$$\{N, M, r, e\}$$

s.t.

$$N \le N^d(r, e)$$

where $V$ is the terminal valuation function, which takes into account that the value of the firm depends not just on its total end-of-period wealth, but on its "liquidity" at that time. Alternatively, we can say the bank

$$\max Ea_{t+1} - cF + \lambda_{t+1} M_t$$

where $\lambda_{t+1}$ is the shadow price of liquidity at time $t+1$. For the bank to be willing to borrow to invest in T-bills, $\lambda \ge \rho\tau$, the "extra" value of liquidity must be greater or equal to the tax.[30]

(In this highly simplified model of perfectly competitive banking, where banks can get an infinite supply of deposits, the shadow price would presumably be zero. In fact, there are a variety of reasons, outside this simplified formulation, why there might be a positive shadow price. Without deposit insurance, depositors would worry about the risk of being repaid; some banks may not be able to get funds. Later, we shall show that if there is limited competition or if banks cannot be sure of facing a perfectly horizontal supply curve of funds, there are circumstances in which banks hold T-bills in

---

[30] Note that even though the maximand appears linear in $M_t$, in fact since the bank has to pay more in interest than it gets back in returns (net of "tax"), as $M$ increases, the probability of default increases. More generally, the value of liquidity will depend on the level of liquidity, i.e. $\lambda_{t+1} = \lambda(M_t)$.

their portfolio.[31] Nevertheless, the basic insight – that with competitive banking, one should not expect to see banks holding significant amounts of T-bills in their portfolios – remains valid.)[32]

Now we can use our analytic framework to establish our remaining propositions. Propositions 2 and 3 focus on how changes in the economic circumstances of the bank – its net worth or the perceived risk of its lending portfolio – affect bank behavior. Propositions 4 and 5 focus on how monetary policy – changes in the T-bill rate or the reserve requirement – alter its behavior. Proposition 6 and 7 focus on how regulatory policy – changes in capital adequacy requirements or risk adjustments within the capital adequacy requirements – alter bank behavior.

## The impact of changes in bank net worth

### Impacts on lending

PROPOSITION 2 *A decrease in bank's net worth leads to a decrease in bank lending.*[33]

As we noted, banks pursue lending to the point where the expected marginal gross return of loans equals the costs of the funds, including the increased marginal expected bankruptcy costs:

$$EY_N = (1 + \rho(1 + \tau)) + \phi \qquad (3.23)$$

---

[31] Even when the shadow price of liquidity exceeds the tax, there will be limited holdings of T-bills. Capital adequacy requirements imply that the capital leverage ratio $a_t/(M + N)$ may be required by regulation to be greater than some lower bound $\alpha^*$, and this requirement will restrain the bank from holding too much in the form of T-bills. For a more complete discussion, see below.

[32] Besides T-bills, as we have already noted, the bank can also hold long-term government bonds. However, if capital markets – and risk regulation – worked "perfectly," the higher interest rate on long-term bonds would simply compensate for the higher risk associated with such bonds. In practice, particularly given the absence of appropriate risk adjustments in both capital adequacy requirements and deposit insurance premia, there can be strong incentives to holding long term-bonds. See the discussion on pp. 86–88 below.

[33] Assuming that after the decrease, $a_t$ is still greater than the critical value we identified earlier as the point where the bank becomes a risk lover.

where $\phi$ is the marginal bankruptcy cost

$$\phi = \partial cF/\partial N > 0 \tag{3.24}$$

Under mild restrictions, it can be shown that

$$\phi_a < 0 \tag{3.25}$$

that is, if the bank initially has less net worth, it must borrow more to maintain a given level of loans, but the return on the loans is risky. With the higher amount "borrowed" by the bank, there is a higher probability that

$$Y < D(1 + \rho) \tag{3.26}$$

i.e. the bank will not be able to pay back its depositors. Thus, reducing $a_t$ at a fixed $N$ increases the default probability, $F$. Under suitable and plausible restrictions, this also increases the marginal bankruptcy cost. Thus with a fixed cost of funds, $\rho$, the effect of a reduced $a_t$ is to increase, at any level of lending activity, the marginal bankruptcy cost ($MBC$), as illustrated in figure 3.4, leading to a lower level of lending.

## Portfolio composition effects and red-lining

When there are several distinguishable categories of loans and there is credit rationing, the earlier literature (Stiglitz and Weiss, 1981) pointed out that there may be red-lining; certain categories of loans will simply be denied credit. Figure 3.12a illustrates the case where the cost of capital is $\rho$, lenders are (in effect) risk neutral, and lend to all of those categories for which they can obtain a return in excess of $\rho$, but deny credit to groups (here, to group $B$) for which a loan, at every interest rate charged, yields an expected return less than $\rho$. They noted too that changes in market conditions (here, an increase in $\rho$) may result in some groups that formerly received credit being denied credit, while other groups will face higher interest rates. Thus, monetary policy exercises its influence both through the *availability* channel and the normal interest rate channels. When banks are risk averse, similar issues are at play. Now, a group with a lower maximum expected return than

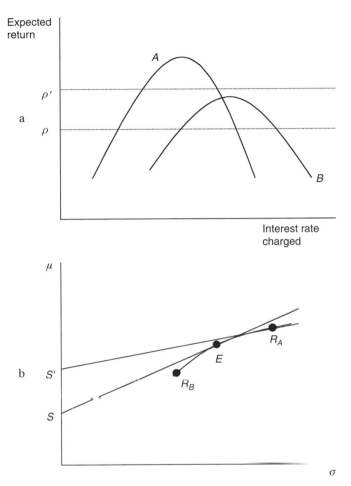

Figure 3.12 *Effects of change in cost of capital when there are two or more groups in the population*
When there are two or more groups in the population, changes in the cost of capital $\rho$ can result in some groups being excluded from credit. Each group has its own mean–standard deviation locus.
a    Risk neutral lender
As $\rho$ increases, group $B$, whose maximum return lies below $\rho'$, is excluded from credit
b    Risk averse lender
Similar results hold when the returns to the two are highly correlated. Here, with the increase in interest rates, the bank goes to the "corner" solution of lending only to group $A$.

$\rho$ will clearly be excluded from the market, as before. But so too may a group where the maximized expected return exceeds $\rho$, but which has high risk and is highly correlated with other loans with a lower variance. In figure 3.12b, the loan opportunity locus goes from $R_A$ where the entire portfolio is lent to type $A$ to $R_B$ where it is all lent to type $B$. If the safe interest rate is very high, the bank might have wanted to go "beyond" $R_A$, that is to lend to type $B$ short; but clearly, this is not feasible.

### Impacts on interest rates charged

While the bank contracts its lending, it will also normally adjust the interest rate charged (when there is credit rationing). The lower wealth means that there is a higher probability of bankruptcy at the old level of lending, and this will normally be the case even after it contracts its lending. With normally shaped distributions, not only will the average probability of bankruptcy be higher, but so will the marginal probability of bankruptcy $\partial F/\partial r$, so that the bank will actually reduce the interest rate charged. However, note that in this seemingly anomalous case, the extent of credit rationing may be increased markedly, as the demand for funds increases and the supply of loans decreases. Seemingly tighter monetary conditions are not associated with higher interest rates – a marked departure from the standard paradigm (figure 3.13).

### Impacts on lending and interest rates charged in mean variance model

Figure 3.14 illustrates the same results in a mean–variance diagram. The reduced bank net worth shifts the loan opportunity locus $RR$ and the point $S$ (investing the entire bank net worth in T-bills) down proportionately, to $R_1R_1$ and $S_1$, respectively. The tangency points $P$ and $P'$ shift down to point $P_1$ and $P'_1$, respectively. Thus the new opportunity locus looks just like the old, but "shrunk" to the origin.

Again we need to distinguish among the different regimes.

The most interesting is that where the bank is neither borrowing nor buying T-bills. The bank has chosen a point on the locus

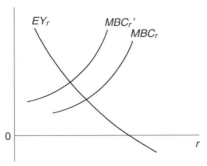

Figure 3.13 *Impact of lower bank wealth on interest rate charged,*
*bankruptcy model*
Lower bank wealth shifts the marginal bankruptcy curve with respect to r up, and leads the bank to charge lower interest rates.

$R_1 R_1$ (see figure 3.14a).[34] Let $E_0$ be the initial equilibrium, at the
tangency between the indifference curve and the opportunity
locus along $RR$. If the bank undertakes the same actions –
charging the same amount for loans, engaging in the same
amount of screening activity per loans – but reduces the number
of loans proportionally to the size of its diminished portfolio, then
mean and standard deviation are reduced proportionally. The
point $X$ on the new mean–standard deviation opportunity locus
corresponds to the original equilibrium, $E_0$. Now, as the bank is
"poorer," it acts in a more risk averse manner and chooses a point
to the left of $X$ – the point marked $E_1$. This point represents a
lower interest rate, as we suggested would normally be the case
in the "bankruptcy" model.

The more general case is where the bank either holds T-bills
or borrows. In either case, the bank's opportunity set shrinks in
proportionately, as before (see figure 3.14b). Because of the "proportionate reduction" effect, the points $P_1$ corresponding to $P$
and $P_1'$ corresponding to $P'$ have the bank taking precisely the
same actions with respect to its risky loan portfolio – that is the

[34] If the bank is not borrowing, less risk may also (through the portfolio-
composition effect) entail a more diverse loan portfolio and/or it may entail
charging a lower interest rate, when there is credit rationing. (Recall from Stiglitz
and Weiss (1981) that lower interest rates are associated with banks obtaining
a less risky pool of borrowers, and borrowers undertaking less risky actions.)

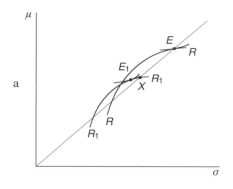

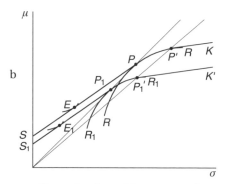

Figure 3.14 *Impact of lower bank wealth, mean–variance model*
The opportunity cost shrinks in towards the origin.
   a   The bank lends out all its wealth, neither borrowing (taking
   deposits) nor holding T-bills. At lower wealth, the bank is less willing
   to accept risk, and hence charges a lower interest rate.
   b   The bank holds T-bills
   The optimal lending portfolio is exactly the same as before (scaled
   down), and hence there is no change in the interest rate charged.
   The bank shrinks the amount of lending more than proportionally.

bank charges the same interest rate and engages in the same
amount of screening. If banks exhibit absolute decreasing risk
aversion, the absolute amount of risk that they are willing to undertake at the lower level of wealth is lower, and hence the
amount of lending is reduced.

   Note that in both of these cases, tighter credit conditions are
associated with *no* change in the interest rate charged (though

to be sure, this is an extreme result derived from the particular properties of the mean–variance model).

## General equilibrium effects

When there is not credit rationing, banks cannot choose freely the interest rate they charge. Now, we note one further effect: there is a general equilibrium effect. When all banks face a contraction in their net worth, there will be a decreased level of lending; in the absence of credit rationing, this will normally result in an increase in the interest rate on loans (for any risk category).[35] The effects of an increase in interest rates are described in proposition 5.

## Impact of an increase in risk on lending

PROPOSITION 3 A *mean-preserving increase in risk reduces lending activity and leads to a lowering of the certainty equivalent interest rate for a risk-neutral lender, though the actual interest rate charged is likely to increase.*

A mean-preserving increase in risk means that any given loan to a firm has a higher probability of default. If the bank were to keep the interest rate it charged fixed, this would mean, in effect, a lowering of the risk-adjusted rate to the borrower (who, were she risk neutral, would clearly find the loan more attractive).

   This makes an important point: *When there is an increase in the interest rate charged as a result of an increase in risk, it does not mean that credit conditions are really tighter.* Nor will the higher interest rates in such a case necessarily discourage investment. What matters is whether the increase in the interest rate charged is greater than necessary to offset the higher probability of default. We focus on the expected return and call this the certanty equivalent interest rate for a risk-neutral lender. We ask, in other words, what happens to the risk neutral risk-adjusted interest rate.

---

[35] Because banks are risk averse, under credit rationing, they may exclude certain categories of borrowers. What happens to the average lending rate is therefore more ambiguous.

This is a knotty issue, simply because the probability of default is subjective, and may differ markedly between the borrower and the lender. The borrower may believe that the interest being charged more than offsets the probability of default (and especially at the margin, if the lender charges higher and higher interest rates the more the borrower borrows), while the lender believes that he is not even charging a risk premium. See Stiglitz (1972c).

If the safe interest rate was $\rho$ and banks were risk neutral, then the risk-adjusted interest rate $r_a$ is found by solving the following system of two equations:

$$\rho = r_a(1 - P_b) \quad + \quad \int_{\Theta_f}^{\infty} \left( \frac{Y_f - c_f}{B} - 1 \right) dF(\Theta) \quad (3.27)$$

receipts in the event     +     receipts in the event
of no bankruptcy                of bankruptcy

Here B is the amount the bank lends to the firm, $c_f$ is the firm's bankruptcy cost, and $Y_f(\cdot, \Theta)$ the return on the firm's implemented project, which depends on the state of the business cycle $\Theta$, where $\hat{\Theta}_f$ is the value above which the firm goes bankrupt (compare to the analysis of the bank on p. 49). $P_b$ is the bankruptcy probability of the firm:

$$P_b = \text{Prob}\{Y_f(\cdot, \Theta) \leq (1 + r_a)B\} \quad (3.28)$$

The risk premium charged by a risk-averse bank (or the market) is then the excess of the interest rate charged $r$ over $r_a$. Note that for the firm the interest rate charged looks higher than that received by the bank, as it loses all its output $Y_f$ in the event of bankruptcy, while the bank can extract only the amount $(Y_f - c_f)$ from the bankruptcy assets. To illustrate this, let's assume that the bank charges exactly the certainty-equivalent interest rate for a risk-neutral lender, $r_a$ (as defined above). Then the subjective interest rate for the firm (expected net cost of the loan for the firm), $r_f$, is clearly greater than $r_a$ (expected net return to the bank):

$$r_f = r_a(1 - P_b) + \int_{\Theta_f}^{\infty} \left( \frac{Y_f}{B} - 1 \right) dF(\Theta) \quad (3.29)$$

For a bank with a widely diversified portfolio, what matters, of course, is not the probability of default of a particular loan, but whether there are so many defaults that its own probability of

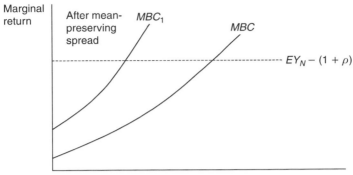

Figure 3.15 *Impact of mean-preserving spread (increase in risk) of the borrower's return on lending, bankruptcy*
   A mean-preserving increase in risk shifts the marginal bankruptcy curve up, leading to less lending activity. Here we assume a constant marginal return to lending

default increases. Clearly, if the bank were to charge only the interest rate that would offset the increased risk, then its mean return would remain unchanged, but the variability of its return would increase – there is a larger chance, for instance, that a large fraction of its loans will default.

To see this most simply, consider the case where the bank has made two loans, each loan has three outcomes – a very low return, a medium return, and a high return. Assume the bank goes bankrupt if both firms go bankrupt, i.e. both firms have the very low return. This occurs with probability $(p_L)^2$ where $p_L$ is the probability of the low return occurring, and for simplicity we assume the outcomes of the two loans are independent. A mean-preserving spread then increases $p_L$ and therefore the probability of the bank going bankrupt.

It thus seems plausible that an increase in risk increases the probability of default – at the certainty equivalent interest rate for a risk-neutral lender – at any given level of loan activity. Under plausible restrictions this also means that the *marginal* probability of the bank going into bankruptcy, at any given level of lending activity, is increased, as illustrated in figure 3.15. Lending activity is accordingly reduced.

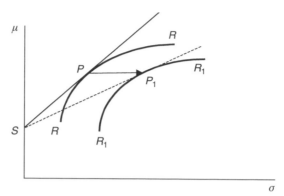

Figure 3.16 *Effect of mean-preserving increase in risk*
The loan portfolio curve shifts to the right and also down, because
the maximum amount that the lender can extract from the borrower
is reduced (e.g. there will be more screening). The optimal loan
portfolio entails higher risk.

Figure 3.16 shows the same result in terms of a mean–standard
deviation diagram. The loan opportunity locus shifts to the right,
and this has both a wealth effect and a substitution effect, both
of which serve to reduce lending activity.[36]

### Impacts on lending rates

By the same token, a mean-preserving increase in the risk of
loans leads to an increase in the probability of default and, presumably, in the marginal bankruptcy cost of the bank (unless the
bank is, as noted earlier, so close to bankruptcy that it becomes
risk-loving). As in the discussion on p. 74, there is hence a presumption that the bank will reduce the spread it charges over the
certainty-equivalent interest rate for a risk-neutral lender. However, the average interest rate charged may actually increase
because of a higher certainty-equivalent interest rate.[37]

---

[36] Not only is the level of risk assumed in equilibrium reduced as a result, the level
of lending activity required to attain that level of risk is reduced.

[37] This result is harder to see using the mean–variance diagram. The mean-
preserving increase in risk shifts the loan opportunity locus to the right, as we
have already noted. It also shifts the locus down; the maximum amount that

If firms were risk neutral, the reduction in supply would increase the gap between the demand and supply for funds; but with risk averse firms, the greater risk which they face reduces also the demand for funds. Hence it is ambiguous whether the gap between the demand and supply of funds increases or decreases.

Similarly, in the absence of credit rationing, at the old certainty equivalent interest rate for risk-neutral lenders, both the demand and supply of funds will have decreased, and *a priori*, it cannot be determined which has decreased more. Hence, a mean-preserving increase in riskiness may lead to an increase or decrease in the equilibrium certainty equivalent interest rate.

We can now see why as the economy enters a recession, there is no clear presumption concerning movements in interest rates, even if there are clear presumptions concerning the level of lending activity.

### Impact of increases in reserve requirements

PROPOSITION 4 *For a depositary institution an increase in reserve requirements leads to reduced lending and to charging higher interest rates, under normal conditions.*

An increase in reserve requirements, at a fixed set of policies by the bank (including a given interest rate charged to borrowers), increases the cost of funds to the bank (remember the characterization of reserve requirements as a tax on borrowing by the bank). This increases the bankruptcy probability at any level of borrowing, and under normal conditions, this increases the marginal bankruptcy cost. The increase in the marginal cost at each level of lending implies that the amount of lending will be reduced, because the bank lends up to the point where the net marginal (expected) return per dollar lent, $EY_N - (1 + \rho(1 + \tau))$, equals the marginal bankruptcy cost, $\phi$ (see figure 3.17).

the lender can extract from the borrower is likely reduced. If, at the old risk neutral risk-adjusted interest rate, the extra return that can be extracted from charging a higher interest rate increases less than the extra risk that it generates (measured in terms of standard deviation), it means that at the old risk neutral risk-adjusted interest rate, the loan opportunity locus is flatter. Since the marginal return relative to the marginal risk is lower, the bank lowers its risk neutral risk-adjusted interest rate.

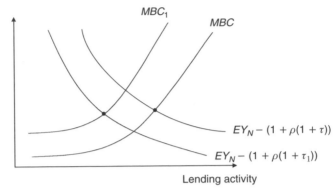

Figure 3.17 *Impact of increase in reserve requirements, bankruptcy model*

An increase in reserve requirements shifts the marginal net return curve down and the marginal bankruptcy curve up, leading to less lending.

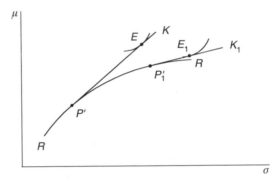

Figure 3.18 *Impact of increase in reserve requirements, mean–variance model*

Here we focus on a bank which accepts deposits. The increased reserve requirements shift the opportunity locus from $RP'K$ to $RP'_1K_1$, implying a higher interest rate but much less lending. ($E_1$ is much closer to $P'_1$ than $E_0$ is to $P'$.)

Again, under "normal" conditions, the adjustment of the various terms of the loan contract will not alter this basic conclusion.

Figure 3.18 illustrates the same results in a mean–standard deviation diagram for a bank that accepts deposits. The higher reserve requirement has both a wealth effect (the bank is worse off) and a substitution effect (the net cost of funds are higher) and both of these lead to less lending. The bank moves from $P'$ to $P'_1$ on its loan opportunity locus, i.e. it charges a higher interest rate, leading to higher mean returns and higher risk. Thus, to get the same amount of risk in its total portfolio, it needs to lend less. Note that in figure 3.18 $E_1$ could be close to $P'_1$, in which case the bank would be making almost no loans other than out of its own portfolio (i.e. it would accept no deposits). The reduction in the amount of lending may be far larger than the traditional money multipliers would have led one to believe. The traditional literature emphasized the *ability* of banks to lend, assuming that the amount that they wanted to lend was constrained only by this. Here, we assume that each individual bank is able to obtain the level of deposits it wants. The reduction in the amount of lending is determined solely by the bank's *willingness* to lend.

When interest rates are determined by the market (no credit rationing), an increase in reserve requirements would flatten the $P'K$ curve for any given interest rate. As before, income and substitution effects would lead to less risk taking, and hence less lending. The supply curve of loanable funds would shift to the left and the equilibrium interest rate charged would have to increase. The new market equilibrium (discussed at greater length in chapter 5) will therefore entail less lending and a higher interest rate.

### Impacts of an increase in the T-bill rate

PROPOSITION 5 *Under normal conditions, an increase in the rate of interest on T-bills leads to less lending for banks that accept deposits and to higher lending rates.*

For such banks, the analysis is exactly the same as for an increase in the reserve requirement. Note that for banks that do not accept deposits but invest in T-bills, an increase in the interest rate paid on T-bills has a positive wealth effect and a negative substitution effect, so the net effect on lending activity is ambiguous (figure 3.19).

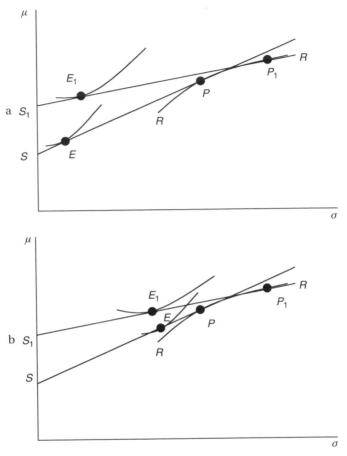

Figure 3.19 *Impact of increase in interest rates*
   An increase in the interest rate paid on T-bills for a bank who holds
   T-bills in its portfolio has a wealth and a substitution effect which
   work in opposite directions.
   a   A case where lending is increased (wealth effect prevails)
   b   A case where lending is decreased (substitution effect prevails)

### *Impact of an increase in capital adequacy requirements*

Regulators impose not only reserve requirements, but also capital
requirements. Under the BIS standards, these capital requirements are risk-related. We simplify by assuming that the bank's
net worth, *a*, must satisfy the constraint given by

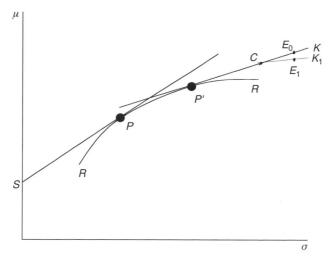

Figure 3.20 *Impact of increase in capital adequacy requirements*
Capital adequacy requirements impose a limit on the amount of
lending that a bank with a fixed asset base can engage in. Given the
additional restriction, the bank undertakes more risk within its
portfolio, monitoring less and charging a higher interest rate. The
opportunity locus moves from $SPP'K$ to $SPP'CK_1$.

$$a \geq N^*Z_L + M^*Z_T \tag{3.30}$$

where $Z_L$ is the net worth requirement per unit of outstanding
loans, and $Z_T$ is the net worth requirement per unit of T-bills held
in the bank's portfolio.[38]

Now when the bank maximizes (3.6) or (3.16), i.e. the expected
terminal wealth *minus* the bankruptcy costs or the expected
utility in the mean–variance framework, it does so with one
additional constraint, (3.30).

In the case where there are only two assets, T-bills and loans, the
opportunity set of the bank with restricted lending appears as in
figure 3.20: for low levels of risk, it is the same opportunity set as
before, but it is truncated at the point $C$. In figure 3.20, the constraint is binding. The bank would like to lend more but cannot.

Increasing the capital requirements leads to a reduction in the
amount of outstanding loans. It is clear that when these regulatory

---

[38] Regulators could impose further requirements related to the liability structure,
e.g. if a bank had an uninsured tranche of long-term debt, $b$, outstanding, then
they could impose a constraint of the form $a + \xi b \geq N^*Z_L + M^*Z_T$.

constraints are binding, they can have every bit as large an effect on lending (and therefore on macro-economic activity) as can standard macro-economic control mechanisms – regardless of their intention. Later, in chapter 9, we shall discuss the justification for, and risks associated with excess reliance on capital adequacy requirements.

The effects of capital adequacy requirements are, however, not limited to the level of lending. Given that the bank would like to engage in more risk taking, it does so now in an "inefficient" manner, raising interest rates, moving to a riskier loan portfolio, and investing less in screening and monitoring. The modified opportunity locus is depicted as $SPP'CK_1$.[39] The bank does not move from $E_0$ to $C$, but rather from $E_0$ to $E_1$.

More interesting is the situation where there are two types of government bonds, T-bills and long-term bonds. Long-term bonds are risky from our two-period perspective[40] since there is a chance of a change in the capital value. We simplify the analysis by assuming that there is a single type of loan, but that banks can allocate their risky portfolio between loans and long-term government bonds. In figure 3.21, $R_L$ is the mean–standard deviation of an all-loan portfolio, $R_G$ is the mean–standard deviation of an all-bond portfolio, and the curved line between them represents various combinations. We have drawn the opportunity locus $SPK$, as before, which maximizes mean return for any given standard deviation. We have assumed for simplicity no reserve requirement. Now, consider what happens when capital adequacy standards are imposed. Assume that the net worth requirement for holding bonds is set equal to zero, so that the government regulator focuses only on default risk, not the true measure of risk facing financial institutions. The constraint is not binding to the left of $C$, but to the right, any additional risky funds must be allocated solely to the long-term government bond. We thus obtain the locus $SPCK_1$. Now, the capital adequacy constraint results in the bank holding more long-term bonds, rather than lending. In the example illustrated, there is little change in the total riskiness

[39] That is, the modified opportunity set is given by the solution to max $\mu$ s.t. $\sigma \leq \sigma^*$ and $a \geq N^*Z_L + M^*Z_T$.

[40] For a discussion of the meaning of risk in this context, see Stiglitz (1970).

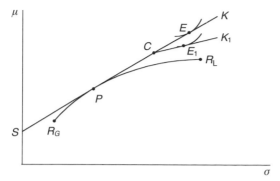

Figure 3.21 *Impact of capital adequacy requirements*
   When banks can either invest in long-term bonds or loans, an
   increase in the capital adequacy requirement may lead to little
   reduction in risk, but a large reduction in lending.

of the bank's portfolio, though there can be large changes in the
amount of lending.

### Impact of a change in risk adjustment

As we shall note in chapter 14, this is precisely what happened
in the 1980s. The problem was exacerbated by the substantially
higher returns earned on long-term government bonds – returns
which, in a perfect capital market, would simply reflect the risk
associated with these assets. In a sense, one might have argued
that one should not have treated these extra revenues as "income" but rather set them aside as a contingency fund, in the
event that long-term interest rates rise (the value of these long-
term assets falls). In any case, neither the standard accounting
nor regulatory frameworks forced banks to take adequate account
of the risks associated with long-term bonds.

   Had they done so, banks might have been encouraged to engage in more lending – and less holding of long-term government
bonds. To see this, consider the effect of an increase in $Z_T$ in the
capital adequacy constraint

$$a \geq N^*Z_L + G^*Z_G + M^*Z_T \tag{3.31}$$

where $G$ is the holdings of long-term bonds and $(Z_G - Z_T)$ is the
capital adequacy risk premium on these long-term bonds. Then

an increase in the risk adjustment associated with long-term bonds offset by a reduction in the risk adjustment associated with loans may actually lead to more lending. In effect, there is an increase in the "net" return to lending relative to the "net" return to holding long-term bonds.

### Capital adequacy requirements and risk taking

There is one other important consequence of an increase in capital adequacy requirements. The restriction reduces the franchise value of the bank (clearly, forcing the bank to do something that it does not want to do reduces the expected present discounted value of future profits), and the reduced franchise value of the bank induces the bank to undertake more risk. Hellmann, Murdoch and Stiglitz (2000) show that this effect is so large that an increase in capital adequacy requirements may actually lead to more risk taking. In our model, this can be interpreted either as a reduction in the cost of bankruptcy $c$ or a change in the indifference curves between mean and standard deviation, making them flatter.

### Extensions of the basic model

#### Limited number of good lending opportunities

Earlier, we saw that when there are a limited number of good loan opportunities, but an unlimited number of second-rate lending opportunities, there is a kink in the bank's overall opportunity locus (figure 3.10). It is easy to see the consequences for policy: if the bank is lending to all good loan opportunities and only to good loan opportunities, changes in reserve requirements or interest rates (or even bank net worth) may have no effect on lending. The bank operates at the kink, both before and after the change. Of course, large enough changes in interest rates, reserve requirements, or bank net worth move the bank away from the kink.

More generally, the elasticity of response will be low if there are rapidly diminishing returns, i.e. the mean return on marginal loans is substantially lower than that on existing loans, and risks are substantially higher.

## Inflation risk

What happens when there is uncertainty about the rate of inflation, so that there is risk (in real terms) even associated with T-bills? Now, the point $S$ is no longer associated with zero standard deviation. There is a general theorem, called the two-fund theorem,[41] which maintains that under mean–variance analysis, the optimal portfolio can be described as consisting of a linear combination of the minimum variance portfolio (here still assumed to be just T-bills) and one other portfolio. However, now, the locus between these two points, in the mean–standard deviation space, is no longer a straight line.

The one important difference is that at zero risk, individuals act in a risk neutral manner, i.e. indifference curves are normally drawn as having a zero slope as they approach the vertical axis. This precludes the possibility of a "liquidity trap," where the bank would want to hold all of its assets in T-bills.[42] However, with inflation risk, the slope of the indifference curve through $S$ will not be flat, and a liquidity trap is clearly possible.[43]

### European banking

If the central bank pays interest equal to the T-bill rate on reserves, as is the case in the euro area, then reserve requirements have, in our model, no effect. As long as there is a perfect financial market for deposits, the analysis of figure 3.9a applies. Otherwise there is a small tax on deposits given by the difference between the brokers' and the reserve rate.

---

[41] See Cass and Stiglitz (1970).

[42] It is not in general possible to go short on loan portfolios, so points to the left of $S$, where banks hold more than 100 percent of their portfolio in T-bills, are really not feasible.

[43] We shall obtain similar results later, in chapter 4, where we analyze the impact of changes in interest rates when individuals cannot costlessly dispose of existing risky loans: then all marginal investments are put into the safe asset.

# FOUR

# Restricted banking (or, the banking system of today)

The model of the banking system that we have described in chapter 3 has some similarities with common views of our current banking system, but there are also some important differences. Most importantly, in our model, the interest rate paid on deposits is identical to the interest rate on T-bills. The reason for this assumption is that with modern transactions technologies, money market funds and investing in T-bills can provide essentially the same transaction services provided by banks. With government provided insurance, banks have the same safety,[1] the same liquidity, and provide the same transactions services as money market funds, and thus must pay the same interest rate.

In fact, banks usually pay a lower interest rate. We need to ask why. That question has two components: demand and supply. Why do banks pay lower interest rates? And why do individuals deposit their funds in accounts paying less than they could receive elsewhere? The answer, historically, to the first question is that banks were regulated in the interest rate that they could pay.[2]

---

[1] Note that without government insurance, banks that invested part of their portfolio in loans would be riskier than money market funds, and thus could attract funds only if they paid a *higher* interest rate. See Greenwald and Stiglitz (1991a, 1993a) for an analysis of interest rate determination without government insurance.

[2] However, see p. 92 below for a discussion of why that constraint may not have been binding.

One answer to the second question – the one to which we are most attracted – is that there are lags in the market adjusting to the new economic environment. People have always used banks for writing checks. They think that there is something that they are getting in return for the lower interest rates paid. Eventually, it will dawn upon them that there is not. (At one time, they used to get pleasure from dealing with a person, a bank teller, as this seemed superior to having to deal through the mail with an anonymous money market fund. However, with the spread of ATMs, banks have joined the ranks of the anonymous institution.[3]) Banks have come to rely on these lags – lags that are sufficiently long to approach "irrationalities." Thus, some years ago when there was a debate over whether banks should be allowed to pay interest rates to depositors, a key element in that debate was the effect of competition on the viability of the banks. On the one hand, if banks were restricted not to pay interest, the flow of funds out of the banks into the money market funds would eventually drain the banks of most of their funds. On the other hand, if interest rates were bid up to the money market levels, banks, which had counted on obtaining cheap funds in making their loans, would be in a precarious position. What saved the banks is that there are a large number of small, financially unsophisticated depositors who seemed content to leave their funds in low interest rate time deposits. These deposits were completely dominated by money market funds, which had greater liquidity and were equally safe. The banking authorities are willing to let the financially unsophisticated be exploited to maintain the viability of the banking system.[4]

---

[3] Furthermore, for those who still like the personal touch, they can go down to their local brokerage house, both to cash checks and make deposits in the money market fund. Admittedly, these have fewer branch offices. People may be willing to pay a little more for these branch offices. However, presumably, with competition, differences in interest paid on deposits in such branch offices should closely reflect the added costs of running the branch offices. With a slight modification, the model of chapter 3 should apply directly.

[4] Along the same lines, one of the authors, Stiglitz, recalls an experience when he was in Princeton; a bank official asked him whether he wanted to transfer funds from a "type 1" account to a "type 2" account, which was identical to type 1 account except that the type 2 account paid a quarter of a percent higher interest rate, and was "newer." The bank realized that there were some people

There are other possibilities. One may be that the lower interest rate is offset by other services provided by the bank to those who have funds deposited in the bank. This may be true, and to the extent that it is, it suggests that the model of chapter 3 may in fact have considerable applicability, even under a regime of regulated interest rates. That is, even in the presence of regulated deposit rates, the "effective" interest rate paid on deposits was set competitively. Banks provided other services, e.g. extending a credit line at below "the fair market value" of such a credit line or lending funds at a lower interest rate. In a competitive market, one would expect banks to compete in the provision of these auxiliary services when they cannot compete directly in terms of interest rates paid. In this view, the regulations may have had only a limited effect, and the model presented previously, where there was no regulation, may accordingly provide a good approximation.

## Policy under restrictive banking vs. competitive banking

Here, we want to formulate a slightly different model, one that captures the notion that competition among banks may be limited and that, accordingly, there may be rents within the banking sector. The assumption seems particularly plausible in those European countries, like Britain, where relatively few banks dominate the industry. The existence of limited competition *within the banking sector* alone does not resolve our quandary about the

---

who were interest sensitive, and it was willing to accommodate them by paying higher interest rates. However, it was perfectly willing to pay others a lower interest rate.

It is fruitless to try to reconcile such behavior with "rational, informed" consumers. One can, tautologically, claim that the extra costs of filling out the form to transfer the funds from a type 1 to a type 2 account obviously exceeded the differences in expected returns. The value of the time to sign the form, for virtually all customers, obviously was less than the value of the expected increment in earnings. Thus, one can only account for the failure to transfer funds to the higher paying accounts by "psychological costs." What those costs might be, or how they could possibly be so large, remains a mystery. Though saying that there are "consumer irrationalities" may not enhance our understanding of the underlying behavior any further, it at least alerts us to the fact that consumer behavior cannot easily be described as a weighing of costs and benefits.

persistence of profits. So long as there are money market funds providing transactions services, banks – no matter how few they are in number – should be forced to pay the T-bill rate. Thus, we shall have to assume that such money market funds do not exist – an assumption that was realistic prior to 1970 in the United States and remains realistic today in some countries.

There are, of course, good reasons that competition in the lending business may be limited.[5] There may even be good reasons for government to restrict competition.[6] Individuals entrust their funds to a bank, and in the absence of deposit insurance, they have to be confident that this trust will not be abused. While high moral character may have sufficed in the early, ethnically related banking communities, more narrowly defined economic incentives are required in larger communities. Reputation is a most effective incentive mechanism, but banks have to have an incentive to maintain their reputation: the stream of future profits that they can earn, their franchise value, provides that incentive. Excessive or, indeed, "normal" competition – driving profits to zero – attenuates those incentives.[7] And establishing a reputation acts as a barrier to entry.[8]

---

[5] That is, expenditures on screening are up-front expenditures, fixed costs; in the extreme case where two or more banks ascertain that a given potential borrower is a "good" borrower, intense (Bertrand) competition between them will ensure that the borrower will obtain the loan at an interest rate which is commensurate with his actual risk, and accordingly, the lender who has invested in screening will not obtain any return on his investment. For the general theory, see Stiglitz (1975a, 1975b). The evidence is that there is, in fact, limited competition in the market for small business loans. That is, even though there may be many suppliers of such loans, any given borrower will face one, two, or at most a very limited number of suppliers. See Jaffee and Stiglitz (1990) and the references cited there.

[6] See Hellmann, Murdoch and Stiglitz (2000).

[7] This has obvious and important implications for policy discussions, focusing on enhancing competition within the banking sector. In some countries, the absence of *sufficient* competition can have very adverse effects. But so too can excessive competition, particularly if there is a margin of "overly enthusiastic" firms that incorrectly anticipate the potential for profits within the industry, enter, and drive down the profits of the more established firms. Traditional discussions have focused on the fact that because of deposit insurance, such banks impose a burden on the public, and if only deposit insurance were eliminated, the only consequence of their over-enthusiastic lending activities would be on the equity owners of the bank. But there is an externality on other banks; and their adverse effect on franchise value on these banks leads to more risk taking by these banks; if these banks have deposit insurance, there is an externality on the public via this channel.

The existence of profits (rents, or franchise value[9]) implies that government regulatory or monetary policy will have impacts on the bank's net worth, and therefore on its willingness and ability to bear risk – and hence to make loans. Both the amount of lending and the riskiness of lending may be affected. This, of course, was also true in chapter 3, but there is one difference. Now the deposit rate is fixed at zero, so that an increase in the T-bill rate increases the profitability of a bank which holds T-bills, even if nothing else changed. This *seigniorage* effect (a particular form of a *wealth effect*) on lending is the first important way in which the restricted banking model differs from the competitive model of chapter 3.[10] Traditional monetary policy may, indeed, have had its most significant effect on the level of economic activity through this channel.

There is a second way in which *restricted banking* – when deposit interest rates are fixed – differs from *competitive banking* and that is that while in the competitive banking model, in the case of depository institutions, banks *choose* their level of deposits (how much they borrow), in the case of restricted banking, banks take the level of deposits as fixed. In competitive banking, banks that are borrowing normally hold no (or minimal) amounts of T-bills (proposition 1); under restrictive banking, the allocation of their fixed wealth- plus-deposits between T-bills and loans becomes the central decision, for it is that decision which determines the supply of loans.

Because under competitive banking, the level of borrowing (deposits) is the decision variable of central concern, the implicit

[8] This holds particularly if capital markets are imperfect, as we have argued they are. Many of the expenditures on establishing a reputation are up-front expenditures, e.g. on impressive bank headquarters, that are sunk costs. For a discussion of the role of sunk costs as entry barriers see, e.g., Stiglitz (1988c) or Farrell (1986). For a discussion of reputation and competition, see Stiglitz (1989c).

[9] For much of the following analysis, which focuses on short-run equilibrium, it does not matter whether there are profits in the long run or not; all that matters is the existence of profits in the short run, which can be increased or decreased, without being quickly offset by entry or exit, so that the franchise value is affected. It is also important for the purposes of this chapter that competition be sufficiently limited that deposit rates are not driven up to a level which eliminates profits or rents at the margin (as was the case in chapter 3). For simplicity, as we have noted, we assume in this chapter that deposit rates are fixed at zero.

[10] As we shall see below, the magnitude (and even the sign) of the seigniorage effect is more complicated than this discussion might suggest, because changes in T-bill rates also affect the magnitude of deposits.

tax rate on deposits (the reserve requirement) becomes of first-order importance. It has a *substitution* effect, discouraging lending. Under restricted banking, unless holdings of T-bills are included in reserves, changing the tax rate on deposits has a wealth effect, but no substitution effect (simply because deposits are *exogenously* determined).[11]

Thus, without credit rationing, under competitive banking, substitution effects are greater than the wealth effect. To be sure, there is still a wealth effect in competitive banking, but especially in the absence of credit rationing, the magnitude of this wealth effect is limited, since changes in the lending rate will largely offset changes in the deposit rate. (This is a general equilibrium effect, which will not be fully analyzed until later chapters.) The wealth effect arises only as a result of a change in the spread induced by the change in monetary policy: once again, we see the central role played by the spread between lending and deposit rates. The magnitude of the substitution effect may be far less than the magnitude of the wealth effects through which monetary policy has traditionally exercised its impact, and this is one of the reasons why monetary policy may be less effective in the future.[12]

On the other hand, when there is credit rationing, the effectiveness of monetary policy (e.g. an increase in reserve requirements) may be less attenuated, as competition in the banking sector increases. Then there is a wealth effect – possibly smaller than before, but nonetheless present – as the banks' effective cost of funds is increased without an offsetting increase in the lending rate.[13]

---

[11] There is a substitution effect in the general equilibrium analysis, to which we turn in a later chapter: as banks change their portfolios, the demand for T-bills and hence the equilibrium T-bill interest rate changes. As we shall see, there will then be second-round effects on the level of deposits.

[12] There exist models which lie between the extremes of "restricted" banking and competitive banking, as modeled here. One variant is monopolistically competitive banks, where firms compete for depositors and borrowers, but do not face perfectly elastic supplies of either. Monetary and regulatory policies will then affect the deposit rate (which will typically differ from the T-bill rate) as well as the lending rate, even though profits are competed away in the long run. See Hoff and Stiglitz (1997) and Hellmann (2000).

[13] More precisely, as we have seen, there will be an increase in the lending rate, but because of the envelope theorem, this has a second-order impact on the bank's expected utility.

## The basic model

We now provide a simple model illustrating these points. For simplicity, let us assume that the government fixes the interest rate on deposits at zero, that banks have a monopoly on "*liquidity services*," that those liquidity services are valued by consumers, and that accordingly, they are willing to deposit funds in banks even though they yield a zero return. Now, the banks take as exogenous their deposits; they are simply equal to[14]

$$D = D(\rho, y) \tag{4.1}$$

a function of interest rates (on T-bills) and income, $y$.[15] Beyond this, we shall assume that banks can obtain brokered funds at the T-bill rate. We also assume that the same reserves are required on the brokered accounts as on deposits.

The expression for the expected value of the bank's terminal wealth is the same as before, except that now there is no interest paid on deposits:

$$Ea_{t+1} = E[\max\{Y(N, r, e, \Theta) + (1 + \rho)M - D, 0\}] \tag{4.2}$$

where

$$D = (1 + \tau) B = (1 + \tau)(N + M + e - a_t)$$

and by assumption $(N + M + e - a_t) \geq 0$ $\tag{4.3}$

Note that if the bank is an investment bank, $D = B = 0$, so that there is no difference from the ideal banking system described in chapter 3.

---

[14] While the supply of deposits to the banking system as a whole is exogenous, the supply of deposits to any particular bank may not be. Banks may engage in non-price competition to garner more deposits for themselves. Such non-price competition may, of course, even affect the aggregate supply of deposits. For simplicity, we ignore this competition, assuming, for instance, that the banking system acts collusively enough so as to preclude these forms of competition. The model of this chapter is meant to be a polar model: the more effective the competition, the closer the resulting equilibrium is to the competitive model that we focused on in chapter 3.

[15] Ignoring, for the moment, the important observation made earlier that the demand for money is related to the volume of transactions, which is not necessarily directly related to the level of income.

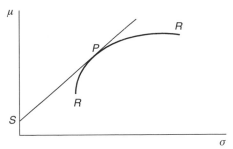

Figure 4.1 *Opportunity locus, mean–variance model, restricted banking*
If the bank takes all of its deposits and net worth and lends it out, its
opportunity locus is *RR*, if it puts the funds into T-bills it is at point
*S*. It can obtain any point on the locus *SPR*.

Again, we can use mean–variance analysis to depict the
bank's opportunity set. There is only one modification to the
previous analysis. Now, since the magnitude of deposits is outside the bank's control, it makes sense to add these to its initial
wealth. Thus, the locus *RR* now represents the mean and standard deviation, assuming the bank lends out all of its own
wealth plus all of its (exogenously given) deposits (less, of
course, those funds required to be on deposit at the central bank
as non-interest bearing reserves). Similarly, if the bank takes all
of its available funds and invests them in T-bills, then it obtains
the point *S*. (See figure 4.1.) Under the assumptions given above,
the bank can obtain any linear combination between *S* and a
loan portfolio on *RR*. The best set of such combinations is given
by the line *SP.*

(The bank could, of course, go beyond (to the right) of *P*, by
borrowing funds under brokered accounts. However, we will
focus on the case of the "representative" bank where the bank
holds some T-bills, and thus is located somewhere along the
locus *SP*.)[16]

---

[16] For the banking system as a whole, the level of deposits is given. Additional
funds can be obtained only by paying returns commensurate with T-bill rates,
risk-adjusted. If the banking system as a whole is in this situation, the analysis
of chapter 3 largely applies.

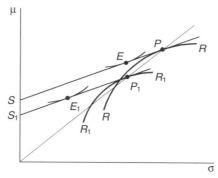

Figure 4.2 *Impact of reduced bank wealth, restricted banking*
Reduced bank wealth shrinks the opportunity locus towards the
origin and leads to less lending.

The analysis of the restricted banking model (with credit
rationing) is essentially identical to that of the competitive
banking model, with one important difference. Now, policies
which affect the supply of deposits affect the curve $RR$, and thus
the opportunity set $SP$.

The analysis of a reduction in bank net worth is thus similar to
the earlier analysis. The loan locus $RR$ and the whole opportunity
locus shrink towards the origin (with mean and standard deviation reduced proportionately). The higher leverage induces the
bank to act in a more risk-averse manner: interest rates charged
remain unchanged[17] but the amount lent decreases (figure 4.2).

### Impact of higher interest rates

The impact of higher interest rates is, however, somewhat more
complicated. Before, higher interest rates on T-bills exercised their
impact on banks that take deposits through the impact on the cost
of funds, in a similar way to what we discussed in figure 3.18. Banks
would be induced to have a riskier portfolio (possibly charging
higher interest rates), but (normally) also engage in less lending.

Now, another mechanism is at work: The higher T-bill rate leads
to smaller deposits and shifts the entire $RR$ locus down and to
the left (mean and standard deviation are reduced). The point $S$

[17] If we perform this analysis using the concept of marginal bankruptcy costs (see
p. 59), interest rates charged would actually decrease.

may shift up or down depending on the elasticity of supply of deposits, as the bank earns higher returns on a smaller deposit base. To see this, note that $S$ is the return of the all T-bill portfolio, $\rho D(\rho)$, and its change is given by

$$\frac{dD(\rho)\rho}{d\rho} = \frac{\partial D(\rho)}{\partial \rho}\rho + D(\rho) = D(\rho)(\varepsilon_{D,\rho} + 1) \qquad (4.4)$$

where $\varepsilon_{D,\rho}$ is the elasticity of supply of deposits with respect to the T-bill interest rate. The return on the all T-bill portfolio will increase if the absolute value of $\varepsilon_{D,\rho}$ is smaller than unity, and in this case the increase in T-bill rates will cause a positive wealth effect.[18] If $\varepsilon_{D,\rho}$ is less than unity in absolute terms, the wealth effect will be negative. Note that the change in T-bill rates affects only the supply, not the cost of funds under restricted banking.

Under competitive banking and credit rationing, there is also a wealth effect due to increased costs of funds to the bank, equal to $-D$, the value of deposits. Since the interest rate is chosen optimally, the change in profits due to the adjustment of lending rates in reaction to the change in the cost of funds can be ignored.[19] Thus, in this case, what matters is the initial level of deposits, rather than changes in the spread or changes in deposits, both of which are endogenous.

These potentially large negative wealth effects which are likely to arise under both regimes lead to less risk-taking.[20] In addition, there is also a substitution effect towards the higher-yielding T-bills. Both of these effects therefore lead to less lending.

Figure 4.3 illustrates alternative possibilities for the case of restricted banking. In panel (a) the elasticity of supply of deposits

[18] In mid-2001, the Thai government raised the interest rate, arguing that doing so would lead to increased lending activity, using arguments that were only partially related to those put forth here.

[19] Consider the terminal valuation function $V^* \equiv \max_{r,N,e} Ea_{t+1}$ given $\{a_t, \rho, \tau\}$, where $M$, the holdings of T-bills, is defined by the budget constraint. Applying the envelope theorem, $dV^*/d\rho = \partial V^*/\partial\rho$, which yields the described result.

[20] If the interest rate change is believed to be permanent (e.g. if interest rates follow a random walk), there will be a decrease in the franchise value of the bank. Since the bank loses its franchise value when it goes bankrupt, a decrease in franchise value can be thought of as decreasing the cost of bankruptcy, and hence as inducing more risky behavior, i.e. more lending. It is unlikely, though, that this indirect effect will dominate the direct negative wealth effect.

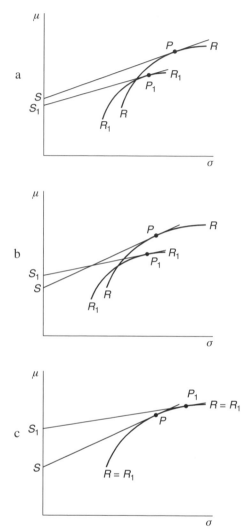

Figure 4.3 *Impact of increased interest rates, restricted banking*
Increased T-bill rates can lead to smaller deposits, shrinking *RR* towards the origin.
a   High elasticity of the supply of deposits: *S* shifts down, the *RR*
locus shrinks towards the origin
b   low elasticity of deposits: *S* may shift up
c   zero elasticity of deposit: *S* shifts up strongly, the *RR* locus remains
unchanged

is high in absolute value: an increase in T-bill rates leads to a strong decline in deposits and hence a negative wealth effect for the bank. The point $S$ shifts down and the $RR$ locus shifts inwards. Both substitution and wealth effects lead to a decline in lending. Panel (b) illustrates a case where the elasticity of supply of deposits is low. Depositors withdraw only a small fraction of their savings from the bank in reaction to the increase in interest rates. The higher interest outweighs the lower deposit base and leads to a positive wealth effect for the bank. In panel (c) we depict the limiting case when the supply of deposits has zero elasticity with respect to the T-bill rate: the amount of deposits does not react to the increase in interest rates, so that the RR locus remains unchanged. At the same time the higher interest rate shifts $S$ outwards. In this extreme case we would have a strongly positive wealth effect, but still a negative substitution effect.

Without credit rationing, the bank cannot freely choose the interest rate it charges. This may seem a curious assumption in the restricted banking model: competition is sufficiently limited that there are profits, but sufficiently keen that banks are price-takers in lending. The net effect on lending behavior then can be ascertained only in a general equilibrium model in which the interest rate on loans is determined simultaneously with the amount of lending.

Alternatively, we could assume that each bank faces a demand curve for loans (of a given quality, i.e. risk) which is a function of the interest rate it charges, $r$, and the interest rate charged by other lenders, $r'$. Then $N$, the amount of lending, is a function of $r$ and $r'$. The mean-standard deviation frontier now has a bow-shaped curve, and $S$ is still the all-T-bill portfolio. Each bank takes $\rho$ and $r'$ as given. An increase in $\rho$ shifts $S$ up or down depending on the elasticity of supply of deposits. The change in the mean and variance of the pure loan portfolio is somewhat more complicated. If the spread is unchanged (i.e. $r$ increases by the same amount that $\rho$ does) and the coefficient of variation $\sigma / \mu$ is unaffected by the scale of lending, the $RR$ locus shrinks towards the origin. There is no substitution effect. It is possible, of course, that the increase in $r$ associated with the increase in $\rho$ leads to riskier behavior by borrowers, in which case the reduction in

standard deviation is less than that in mean. Then, there is a substitution effect away from (risky) lending.


### Impact of a change in reserve requirements

As another application of these basic ideas, consider the impact
of a change in reserve requirements. Under restricted banking,
this leads to a wealth effect. The bank takes its deposits as given.[21]
The increased reserve requirement reduces the amount of funds
(its own net worth combined with the deposits, net of those that
have to be held in reserve) that can either be loaned out or invested in T-bills. The opportunity locus thus moves from $SP$ to
$S_1P_1$ (see figure 4.4). Now there is no substitution effect. With normal utility functions (i.e. with decreasing absolute risk aversion
with respect to wealth) the bank invests absolutely less in the
risky asset, i.e. it makes fewer loans.[22]

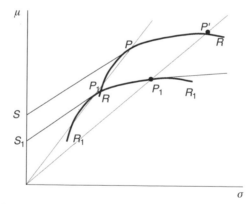

Figure 4.4 *Impact of increased reserve requirements*
Increased reserve requirements have the same effect as a reduction
in bank net worth for banks that hold T-bills in their portfolio,
leading to less lending. There is no substitution effect.

---

[21] We focus on a *partial equilibrium* analysis in which the T-bill rate, $\rho$, is taken
as given.
[22] The change in mean at $S$ is now unambiguously negative (whereas before it
depended on the elasticity of the supply of deposits).

By contrast, an increase in reserve requirements in the competitive bank model acts just like an increase in the interest rate on deposits – it increases the cost of capital to the bank. For borrowing banks, there is effectively no difference between an increase in the deposit rate and an equivalent increase in reserve requirements.

Contrasting the impact under the two regimes, we note that the wealth effect in both is proportional to the size of the deposits;[23] while there is no substitution effect under restricted banking,[24] there is under competitive banking (see figure 3.18). As a result, we expect increases in reserve requirements to have a stronger effect on lending activity under competitive banking. This is reinforced, in the case of competitive banking, by the portfolio-composition effect, which leads to higher interest rates and a more risky loan portfolio. The bank gets more of its desired risk profile through these means than by lending, which, in effect, is being taxed.[25]

---

[23] That is, an increase in the reserve requirements is equivalent to an increase in the tax on deposits.

[24] That is, the amount that the bank has to invest either in loans or T-bills depends only on the T-bill rate and the reserve requirement, and $SP$ is thus parallel to $S'P'$. This is not the case if the bank bought additional funds at the T-bill rate, but we assume it does not.

[25] Thus, any horizontal distance, say, from $P$ to $P'$ in figure 3.9b, represents a smaller increment in lending.

# FIVE

# Market equilibrium

In previous chapters, we have constructed the basic building blocks of our alternative theory of monetary economics, which argues that the focus of monetary policy should shift from the role of money in transactions to the role of monetary policy in affecting the supply of *credit*. We have shown how imperfect and costly information both leads to imperfections of capital markets and creates an important function for banks – screening among potential borrowers, monitoring borrowing activity, and enforcing debt contracts. We have then shown how the extent to which banks are willing to lend (and the terms at which they are willing to lend) are affected by changes in the external conditions facing banks and by monetary and regulatory policy, and how the impacts of monetary and regulatory policy in turn depend on the nature of competition in the banking sector.

We have developed the basic insights in terms of partial equilibrium models, focusing on the behavior of a representative bank. But assessing the full impact of monetary policy requires embedding the representative bank into a general equilibrium model. This is the topic of this chapter and chapters 6–7. Our focus, however, is on the linkages *within* the financial system, not the linkages among factors of production and outputs, which is the subject of standard general equilibrium analysis.

In this chapter and chapter 6, we center our attention on the links between deposit rates and lending rates in simple general equilibrium models. In chapter 7, we investigate the links between trade credit and bank credit.

But before analyzing the relationship between money and credit, it is useful to consider banking in a non-monetary economy. At first blush, this might seem strange: can there be banks without money? A look at a simple, primitive corn economy – and contrasting that economy with a monetary economy – will help clarify the distinctive role played by *money*.

## The corn economy

We begin our analysis with a simple model of a corn economy, a particular case of an economy without money. At the end of each harvest, farmers must decide how much seed they want to plant next year, and how much seed they want to consume today. Some farmers will want to save (not consume) more than they want to plant. Thus is created a capital market – a market where those with excess demand for seed are brought together with those with an excess supply. However, in this seed market corn today is traded for a promise of more corn tomorrow. The problem is that those promises are often broken, for a variety of reasons. the borrower may never have intended to repay because he wants the corn for his current consumption; the borrower may have had the best of intentions, but bad weather may have destroyed his crop. Lending is a risky business, and not surprisingly, specialized institutions develop to handle the risk. Those with excess corn seed bring their excess seed down to such a specialized institution, the bank, which promises a particular rate of return. The bank in turn lends to many different borrowers. It screens borrowers, ascertaining who has the highest likelihood of repaying; it visits farms to ensure that the seed is used in the way promised; it helps collect payment, should any borrower waver in his resolve to repay; and it provides a guarantee, promising to pay back a fixed amount, regardless of the amount of collections. Among all these services, perhaps the most important is the certification, ascertaining who is in fact credit worthy.

We assume that there are a limited number of institutions with the skills to perform these services. The representative bank has capital $K$. For simplicity, we assume there are two groups of farmers in the economy, type 1, the savers, and type 2, the borrowers. There are a very large supply of deadbeat farmers willing to borrow from the bank, but who will not repay. The bank sorts through the loan applications to find the good borrowers. For notational convenience, we assume the number of good borrowers is equal to the number of savers, and that there are $n_0$ farmers of each of these two types per bank. We assume that bank bankruptcy costs are sufficiently high so that if the bank goes bankrupt, its depositors receive nothing back. Similarly, if a farm to which the bank has lent money cannot repay the promised amount, the bank recovers nothing. There are two interest rates, $\rho$, the interest received by savers, and $r$, the interest paid by borrowers. Savers care about $\rho$ and $p$, the probability that a bank will repay the promised amount.[1] This determines their supply of savings:

$$S(\rho, p) \tag{5.1}$$

The analysis is simplest in the case where, because of transactions costs, each farmer deposits his corn in only one bank, the "representative bank."[2] In this case, a perfectly competitive bank takes the utility of depositors (type 1 farmers), $v$, as given, which is expressed as a function of the interest rate paid and the probability of default of the bank:

$$v = U(S, \rho, p) = V(\rho, p) \tag{5.2}$$

This gives us a representation of $\rho$ as a function of $p$ and $v$:

$$\rho = V^{-1}(p, v) \tag{5.3}$$

---

[1] Thus, in our primitive corn economy, the government has not provided full deposit insurance. One of the important points thus raised in this chapter is that many of the results of chapters 3 and 4 do not in fact depend on the assumption of full deposit insurance – though to be sure, the interest rate paid by banks to depositors will have to differ from $\rho$ if there is not full deposit insurance. The result that depositors care only about the probability of default follows from the assumption that in the event of default, they receive nothing. Clearly, if there is residual wealth to be divided among depositors, the magnitude of these amounts will be of relevance. Incorporating these complicates the calculations greatly, but adds no new insights.

[2] In the more general case, farmers will spread their savings among the banks, so savings will depend on the entire vector $\{\rho, p\}$.

Equations (5.1) and (5.3) imply:

$$S = S(V^{-1}(p, v), p) \equiv \Xi(v, p) \tag{5.4}$$

All good borrowers are assumed identical. The probability that they repay a loan of size $s$ and interest rate $r$ is $P(s, r, z)$, where $z$ is a vector of environmental variables, i.e., weather conditions.[3]

There are two versions of the model that can be explored at this point, with and without credit rationing. The information theoretic problems that give rise to credit rationing and that were described in earlier chapters apply as well to the corn economy. Farmers' behavior, for instance, may be affected by the interest rate that they have to pay.

### The corn economy with credit rationing

The simplest case is that where there is credit rationing, so that, at the interest rate which maximizes the bank's expected return, the demand for funds is greater than the supply. The magnitude of the loan demanded by the representative borrower is given by

$$d \equiv d(r) \tag{5.5}$$

The expected utility of profits of the bank, $\Pi$,[4] and its probability of default, $p$, depend on the interest rate it pays, the interest rate it receives, the size, $s$, and number, $n$, of its loans, the size of its deposits, $D$, and its initial capital, $K$, the corn endowment it carriers over from previous period:[5]

$$\Pi = f(\rho, r, s, n, D, K, z) \tag{5.6}$$
$$p = g(\rho, r, s, n, D, K, z) \tag{5.7}$$

---

[3] One of the advantages of the simple corn model is that bankruptcy probabilities depend only on the individual's own efforts and an externally given environmental variable, $z$, not on macroconditions, which are affected by the level and terms of lending of the representative bank.

[4] Again, we can model this either as a risk averse bank or a risk neutral bank facing a cost of bankruptcy. Since our interest here is only in exposing the structure of the argument, the results do not depend on the formulation chosen.

[5] We assume that there may be a fixed cost associated with managing the account of any particular borrower, so that risk is not necessarily reduced by increased diversification, i.e. by making more, smaller loans. This would also be the case if there is an underlying variable, e.g. rainfall, causing all loans to default simultaneously.

Substituting (5.3) into (5.6) and (5.7), and simplifying, we obtain:

$$\Pi = \pi(r,\, s,\, n,\, D;\, v,\, K,\, z) \tag{5.8}$$

$$p = \rho(r,\, s,\, n,\, D;\, v,\, K,\, z) \tag{5.9}$$

The bank chooses $r$, $s$, $n$, and $D$, given $v$, $K$, and $z$, to maximize the expected utility of its profits, subject to the constraint $s \leq d(r)$, yielding $r^*$, $s^*$, $n^*$, and $D^*$. In short, as in our earlier analysis, we assume competition in the deposit market is keen; but what depositors care about, in the absence of deposit insurance, is not just the promised return, but also the probability of default. (There are constraints on these choices that we ignore for the moment; that is, we are assuming that we are in the credit rationing regime, where the demand for funds (corn), by those wishing to plant more seed than they have exceeds the supply.) We denote the solution by $\{r^*[v,\, K,\, z],\, s^*[v,\, K,\, z],\, n^*[v,\, K,\, z],\, D^*[v,\, K,\, z]\}$, and the associated values of $p$ and $\Pi$ by the corresponding notation.

## Market equilibrium with credit rationing

An equilibrium is defined as a value of $\{v\}$ such that

$$n^* \leq n_0 \tag{5.10}$$

and

$$D^*[v,\, K,\, z] = S(\rho,\, p) = \tilde{S}[v,\, K,\, z] \tag{5.11}$$

the desired loans made by banks equal the supply of seeds provided by depositors. If banks wanted to lend more seeds than they had seeds deposited, they could improve the terms they pay to depositors, i.e. increase $v$.

The underlying hypothesis to these calculations is simple: lending is risky (even with good screening). If banks are risk averse, the amount of lending that they will be willing to engage in depends on the state of nature, their initial wealth $K$, and the cost of funds, which is effectively summarized by "$v$." In equilibrium, banks' demand for deposits must equal the supply of deposits by (risk averse) farmers.

Not surprisingly, if the representative bank has more capital, it will be willing to engage in more lending activities and more risk taking (which, in this case, *may* be reflected in lending at a higher interest rate and/or making bigger loans to fewer borrowers). Moreover, savers will be willing to supply more funds to it at a lower interest rate (because of the higher level of safety). The increase demand for funds (corn) will result in the banks bidding up the interest rates they are willing to pay depositors.[6]

Thus, an increase in $K$ will result in a lower cost of intermediation, i.e. smaller spread between the interest rate paid to depositors and the interest rate paid by borrowers. The spread is the effective compensation that the banks require to compensate them for the risk which they bear and the expected losses from bankruptcies of their borrowers. In equilibrium, a decline in this cost entails more financial intermediation – the higher interest rate paid to depositors will result in more seeds being saved and planted. The corn economy does not have any "equilibrium" problems: the demand and supply of seed are always in equilibrium; and savings equal investment. If a bank has seeds, it will lend them – especially if they rot when not planted. The prices in the market (e.g. utilities of lenders) adjust to equilibrate the market. Presumably, there is no reason that they could not equilibrate rather quickly. The bank would quickly see that it has some seed on hand that it is not lending, and would adjust the terms of loans or the terms of deposits until the two are matched.

### Market equilibrium with all borrowers receiving credit

Little is changed if all potential borrowers get credit, except now each bank has to compete for customers; it takes the expected utility of its customers, $u$ for borrowers, $v$ for depositors, as given. The utility depends on the size of the loan and the interest rate charged, $u = u(s, r)$.[7] Thus, it chooses among a set of loan packages $\{r, s\}$,

---

[6] Formally in the credit rationing regime, the bank chooses $s^*$ as well as $n^*$.

[7] In this model, all potential borrowers have access to credit, but banks still limit the size of their loans, reflecting the increase in the probability of default. Alternatively, banks could confront borrowers with an interest rate schedule $r = r(s)$.

which generate that level of expected utility, the one which maximizes its expected utility of profits. We denote the solution by $\{r^*[v, u, K, z], s^*[v, u, K, z], n^*[v, u, K, z], D^*[v, u, K, z]\}$, and the associated values of $p$ and $\Pi$ by the corresponding notation. An equilibrium is defined as a value of $\{u, v\}$ such that

$$n^* = n_0 \qquad (5.10a)$$

the demand for loan contracts must be equal to the supply, and

$$D^*[v, u, K, z] = S(v, u, K, z) \qquad (5.11a)$$

again, the deposits desired by banks equal the supply of seeds provided by depositors. An increase in $K$ will normally make banks more willing to lend, increasing their demand for loan contracts and deposits. In the process, both $u$ and $v$, the utility level of borrowers and depositors, will be bid up. As part of that process, normally the supply of seeds, $S$, will increase, the average size of loans, $s^*$, will increase, the equilibrium interest rate on loans, $r^*$, will decrease, and the equilibrium interest rate paid on deposits, $\rho$, will increase, so that the spread between borrowing and lending rates will decrease.

### Comparing "nominal" and risk-adjusted changes in spreads

These formulations correspond closely to the traditional formulations, in which interest rates are determined to equate the demand and supply of loans, except that the interest rate itself does not seem to appear explicitly. The reason is clear: loan contracts are far too complicated to be described by a single variable, the interest rate. Also relevant is the size of the loan and the probability of default. The formulation presented here shows how all of these can be solved for simultaneously, and how the market equilibrium will be altered, say, by a change in the net worth of banks, $K$. We argue, in effect, that $u$ and $v$ represent simple summary statistics of the market, the benefits of lending to the depositors and of borrowing to the borrower.

Hidden beneath the changes in interest rates charged and paid are changes in the probabilities of default, which are themselves *endogenous*. The *apparent* changes in interest rates charged borrowers and paid depositors may be larger or smaller than the "nominal" changes. Making the interpretation of these changes all the more difficult is the fact that often, a change in the external environment, $z$, will subsequently lead to a change in the value of bank net worth $K$.

Thus, as $K$ increases, the associated decrease in $r$ reduces the probability of default by the borrower, while the increase in $s$ increases it. If the net effect is an increase in default probability, then the fall in risk adjusted real interest rates charged borrowers is *greater* than the apparent fall. On the other hand, the higher probability of default by borrowers leads to a higher probability of default by banks, so that the true increase in the interest rate paid deposits $\rho$ is actually smaller than the apparent increase. But because of the diversified nature of the bank portfolio, the latter effect is likely to be small. On net, then, the true reduction in spread is greater than the apparent reduction.

### An alternative formulation

The use of $u$ and $v$, the utility levels of depositors and borrowers, as surrogates for the interest rate paid and charged (but embracing other relevant attributes of the deposit and loan contracts) has one major disadvantage: $u$ and $v$ are not directly observable. There is a slight modification of the above analysis which allows us a reformulation closer to the traditional loanable-funds model. Here, we assume a continuum of farmers, with say different risk preferences denoted by a parameter $\alpha$, where higher $\alpha$ represents higher risk aversion. At any interest rate charged for borrowing seeds or paid depositors for putting seed in the bank (with an associated probability of the bank defaulting), each farmer decides whether to borrow or lend. For simplicity, we assume that farmers have available to themselves only two technologies, a seed-intensive technology, and a "normal" technology, and that if a farmer chooses the seed-intensive technology, he must borrow a fixed number of seeds, $n^d$ (demand for loans), while if he chooses the normal technology, he has available a surplus of seeds, $d^s$ (supply of deposits). We now let $x$ be the fraction of the farmers who choose the seed-intensive technology, so that the demand for seed from banks (the demand for funds) is just

$$xn^d$$

and the supply of seeds from depositors to banks is

$$(1 - x)md^s$$

The expected utility of a farmer of type $\alpha$ who chooses the seed-intensive technology is denoted by $u$ and is a function of the interest rate charged (now all loans are identical in size)

$$u = u\,(r,\,\alpha)$$

The expected utility $v$ of the farmer who uses the normal technology is a function of both the interest paid depositors, $\rho$, and the probability of the bank's defaulting, $p$. But $p$ itself is a function of the interest rate charged to borrowers and the set of borrowers. We have parameterized the model such that those with low $\alpha$ choose the seed-intensive technology. We can thus characterize the set of borrowers by $\alpha^*$, the farmer who is indifferent between using the seed-intensive technology and the normal technology (with all farmers with $\alpha \leq \alpha^*$ choosing the seed-intensive technology). Thus,

$$p = p(r,\,\alpha^*;\,K,\,z)$$

$$v = V(\rho,\,p,\,\alpha)$$

$\alpha^*$ is defined by

$$V(\rho,\,p(r,\,\alpha^*;\,K,\,z),\,\alpha^*) = u(r,\,\alpha^*) \tag{5.12}$$

Assuming that we can solve for $\alpha^*$ as a function of the interest paid and charged[8]:

$$\alpha^* = \psi(\rho,\,r,\,K,\,z) \tag{5.13}$$

---

[8] In adverse selection models, there are often multiple equilibria. Here, we ignore that possibility.

If $F(\alpha^*)$ is the fraction of the population with $\alpha \leq \alpha^*$, then

$$x = F(\psi(\rho,\, r,\, K,\, z)) = x^*(\rho,\, r,\, K,\, z) \tag{5.14}$$

We can then solve for the demand for seed (loans):

$$N^d = x^* n^d = N^d(\rho,\, r,\, K,\, z) \tag{5.15}$$

We can also solve for the supply of seeds (deposits) to the banking system $D^s$

$$D^s = (1 - x^*) d^s = D^s(\rho,\, r,\, K,\, z) \tag{5.16}$$

Competition among banking is sufficiently high that each bank takes the interest rates it must pay depositors and it can charge customers as fixed. For simplicity, we assume it cannot distinguish among borrowers, and in particular, cannot observe any particular farmer's $\alpha$, though it knows (or can infer from the level of market activity) the value of $\alpha^*$ and hence the probability of default on its average loan. Thus, the expected utility of profit of the bank is given by

$$\Pi = \Pi(\rho,\, r,\, N^s,\, \alpha^*;\, K,\, z) \tag{5.17}$$

where $N^s$ is the supply of loans by the bank. The bank recognizes that the default probability on an additional loan is

$$p = p(\rho,\, r,\, \alpha^*;\, K,\, z) \tag{5.18}$$

The representative bank thus chooses the number of loans to make (the supply of funds) and its corresponding demand for deposits, $d^d$, to maximize its expected utility[9]:

$$n^s = n^s(\rho,\, r,\, \alpha^*;\, K,\, z) \tag{5.19}$$

$$d^d + K = n^s \tag{5.20}$$

---

[9] In this formulation, we assume that the bank lends out all of its seed, e.g. because seeds that are not replanted will not last until the next season. The bank may have available alternative seed storage activities, e.g. which entail some deterioration in the supply of seeds (in effect, the expected return is negative), but in which there is low variance. Then the risk averse bank may decide not to lend out all of its capital base ($K$). The bank then has to decide how much to store, $M$, how much to lend, and how much to borrow, with $M + n^s = K + d^d$.

If there are $\zeta$ banks, the aggregate supply of funds is just

$$N^s \equiv \zeta n^s(\,\cdot\,) = N^s(\rho, r, \alpha^*; K, z) \tag{5.21}$$
$$= N^s(\rho, r, \psi(\rho, r; K, z); K, z)$$
$$= N^s(\rho, r; K, z)$$

The aggregate demand for deposits by all the banks, $D^d$, can similarly be solved for, which in reduced form, we express as

$$D^d = \zeta d^d(\,\cdot\,) = D^d(\rho, r; K, z), \tag{5.22}$$

Market equilibrium requires the demand for funds (corn) by those using the seed intensive technology to equal the supply of funds by banks,

$$N^d(\rho, r, K, z) = N^s(\rho, r, k, z) \tag{5.23}$$

and the demand for deposits by banks to equal the supply of funds (corn) by farmers who save:

$$D^d(\rho, r; K, z) = D^s(\rho, r; K, z) \tag{5.24}$$

We thus have two equations and two unknowns, the rate of interest charged borrowers and paid lenders. We can solve the two equations simultaneously, and describe how changes in the parameters of the problem, e.g. bank capital, $K$, or the environment, $z$, affect the two interest rates.

It may be useful to go one step further – to try to draw a standard loanable-funds diagram, showing the interest rate as determined by the demand and supply of loanable funds. The trick here is that demand and supply depend on different variables, the interest rate paid and the interest rate charged, and the spread between the two is endogenous. Equation (5.24) provides a heuristic way out. We solve (5.24) for the spread

$$\xi \equiv r - \rho = \xi(r; K, z) \tag{5.25}$$

and substitute back into (5.23):

$$N^d(r - \xi(\,\cdot\,), r; K, z) = N^s(r - \xi(\,\cdot\,), r, K, z) \tag{5.26}$$

Figure 5.1 shows the equilibrium interest rate as the intersection of the demand and supply of loanable funds (corn). The analysis would be essentially identical to the standard analysis *if*

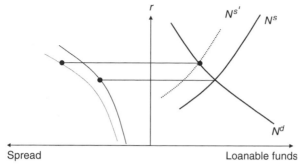

Figure 5.1 *Equilibrium interest rate in the corn economy*
The equilibrium interest rate is the intersection of the demand and
supply curves for "seed." A decrease in the amount of "capital" of
corn banks leads to a decrease in the supply of loanable corn, an
increase in the lending rate but, because the spread has increased,
not a commensurate increase in the deposit rate.

the spread were constant and if the probability of default were
constant (or ignored). For then, the supply of funds would just
depend on the interest paid, $r - \xi$, and the demand for funds
would depend just on $r$. Our analysis reflects a whole series of
more complicated interactions resulting from the probability of
default: (a) default affects the likelihood that a borrower will
repay, and hence both the "true" cost to the borrower and the
return to the bank; (b) default on the part of the bank affects the
relative attractiveness of a farmer depositing his money in the
bank; (c) the interest rate charged may affect the actions of borrowers, and therefore the probability of default; (d) the interest
rates charged and paid affects the mix of borrowers, and hence
the probability of default; (e) economic circumstances and the
net wealth of banks affects their willingness to bear risk, to accept deposits and lend, and the equilibrium spread.

For instance, an increase in the net worth of banks will normally be expected to reduce the spread, while an increase in the
interest rate charged might normally be expected to increase the
overall riskiness of borrowers. Hence, we assume

$$\xi_K(r; K, z) < 0$$

$$\xi_r(r; K, z) > 0$$

Thus, in figure 5.1, a reduction in $K$ will *shift* the supply curve of funds to the left. There may be a slight effect on the demand for funds – the lower interest rate paid on deposits might, at any given lending rate, induce some farmers to become borrowers rather than lenders – but this is likely to be second-order. Hence, there will be an increase in interest rates charged, as depicted. The reduction in $K$ also increases the spread at any given interest rate charged. And as the interest rate charged increases, the spread increases further, so that only a fraction of the higher lending rate is "passed on" to depositors. But this second increase does not really represent a higher cost of intermediation – it represents the fact that at the higher interest rate, the probability of default is higher.

### Employment and credit creation

We can modify the model so that productive employment depends on, say, $z$ and $K$, e.g. if the amount of seed planted determines the demand for agricultural workers. Then we can even generate "cyclical" unemployment, if workers do not move easily between planting activities and other activities. However, the more serious macro-economic problems arise when we move from this simple corn economy into a monetary economy, to which we now turn.

# SIX

# From the corn economy to the monetary economy

The essential difference between a corn economy and a monetary economy is that in a monetary economy, banks do not actually have to give out seed to borrowers. They lend, creating a "deposit" which the borrower can use to obtain seed on the market. The deposit is, in effect, a "certification of credit worthiness." The bank bears the risk of the borrower not repaying. Anyone who supplies seeds to farmers will be more willing to accept these certifications than to provide credit directly to the farmer himself. It is this certification which facilitates the transaction between the borrowing farmer and the seed supplier.

There are three problems posed by moving from the simple corn economy to the monetary economy with certifications. First, what ensures that the supply of these "certifications" will be equal to the supply of seeds on the market? Indeed, the fundamental macro-economic problem arises from the fact that it can be either greater or less than that number. Second, why is the process of screening linked to the process of banking? In principle, the bank's information services/activities could be separated from its lending activities. Why is that not more prevalent? And third, what is the role of public regulatory policy? While a fuller analysis of regulatory policy is postponed to part II, it is worthwhile at this juncture explaining the *rationale* for such policies.

### Certification

Clearly, if these certifications are to have value, they must be accepted by others. While in principle, each seller of seed could engage in his own inspection of the certifiers, this would be extremely costly and inefficient – almost, but not quite, as inefficient as having to obtain information about each borrower directly.

Information about the certifier – like many other forms of information – is a public good (because the marginal cost of an individual enjoying the benefit of that knowledge is zero[1] and because it is hard to exclude others from enjoying the benefits of the information[2]). It is thus natural that the information is publicly provided and this is also a key rationale for public prudential regulation of banks.[3] Concern about systematic risk also naturally leads government to regulate banks' certification activities. Systematic risk, and the possibility of runs, has led most governments in advanced industrial economies to provide deposit insurance, which provides another rationale for regulation – to avoid the moral hazard associated with the insurance. As fire insurance companies require commercial buildings to install sprinklers, providers of deposit insurance require banks to hold a certain level of capital.

Without such regulation, and with imperfect information in the market, the temptation for fraud might be enormous. In fact, one can certify for oneself, or one's friends, with no intention to repay. In the absence of government regulation, if sellers' costs of discriminating between fraudulent certifiers and good certifiers are high enough, the market for certification services will dry up (this is an extreme version of the adverse selection

---

[1] Though, to be sure, the marginal cost of transmitting the information may be positive.

[2] That is, while a private agency could sell the information, if the behavior of those to whom the information is sold is observable, outsiders can make inferences about the information from looking at the behavior. For instance, if all depositors who subscribed to the information service suddenly pulled out their money from a bank, others would infer that the depositors have received adverse information concerning the bank's balance sheet.

[3] See Stiglitz (1993a).

problem.[4] The market will revert to the "corn" economy of chapter 5).[5]

Similar considerations affect the analysis of why it is that screening and monitoring services are linked to lending services. Statements about the credit worthiness of a particular borrower are more meaningful when those making the statements are willing to put their money where their mouth is, to put at risk at least some of their own capital. Having money at risk also enhances incentives to do a better job of screening and monitoring. That is why certifications of a bank that has no capital have little credibility. The information about the net worth of "certifiers" is again a public good, and there is a role for public regulation to gather, analyze, disseminate, and possibly act upon this information. In chapter 7, we shall look at other dimensions of the linkage between credit and information.

However, even with appropriate regulations, there is no need for a bank to restrict its lending (its certification services) to its capital base, or even to the capital base *plus* deposits. Even if the supply of "certifications" (loans) is a multiple of deposits, the probability of the bank not being able to repay depositors as promised may be limited. The problem of the bank is parallel to that in the corn economy, but now the bank is not limited in its lending activities to lend an amount equal to its deposits. Of course, if bankruptcy is costly, the bank will want to keep a certain amount of money (corn) on hand, in case depositors want their deposits back, or to balance off the risks associated with lending. That is, given the return on lending, there is an optimal portfolio allocation that will entail a certain amount of reserves (money held in T-bills, corn held in storage). If the government provides (implicitly or explicitly) deposit insurance, this optimal amount of reserves will be less than what is socially optimal, or optimal from the perspective of the best insurance contract, in which case the government (the insurer) will impose reserve requirements.[6]

---

[4]  See Akerlof (1970).

[5]  Another way of putting the matter is that there is an externality exerted by bad certifiers on good certifiers. See Greenwald and Stiglitz (1986a). See also Stiglitz (1975a, 1975b).

[6]  In the case of an optimal insurance contract, the insurer would provide a set of contracts, offering different premia at different levels of reserve. Each of these contracts would be break even (if the insurer were risk neutral) or would yield

A key issue is whether for *prudential purposes* there should be a "tax" proportional to deposits, or a "restriction" based on the bank's capital (the capital adequacy requirements, modeled in earlier chapters). Optimal prudential regulation involves a *portfolio* of instruments, as we shall discuss briefly in a later chapter.[7]

However, there is another reason that the government may impose reserve requirements, which is the focus of our concern here. Once we recognize that the bank need not limit its certification activities to the amounts it has on deposit, then there may be an imbalance between what individuals would like to save (at full employment) and what other individuals or firms would like to invest. For instance, if certifiers are highly optimistic about the returns to planting, they might be quite free in writing these certifications, demanding only low interest rates as compensation. As we have noted, it is not necessary that they actually have seeds to issue the certifications. As a result, unlike the corn model, if their willingness to supply certifications exceeds the supply of seed, banks are not forced to adjust the interest rates they pay depositors or charge borrowers. Rather, the problem in the banking market becomes reflected as a problem in the goods market, with an excess demand for goods (seed).

The certifications are denominated in dollars, with the repayment in dollars. In the model being explored here, borrowing and lending contracts are all denominated in dollars, so that the *real* price of borrowing and lending – the real interest rate – is based on expectations. Adjustments in the price level today – as a result of an excess demand for goods (seeds) today – need not be reflected in a corresponding adjustment in either the nominal or the real interest rate.[8] In short, the equilibrating processes of the economy may be weak, or even non-existent. The price system

the insurer the same level of expected utility (if the insurer is risk averse). The optimal contract then is the one which maximizes the expected utility of the insured. Obviously, the optimal contract will entail more reserves than the bank would have wanted, if it believed it could undertake more risk (more lending) without paying a commensurately higher premium.

[7] See also Stiglitz (2001).

[8] While borrowers obtain fewer units of seed, say, for each dollar, so long as they expect next year's price level to be the same as this year's, the return on planting is the same. So, the probability of default is the same, and there is no reason for the lender to adjust the terms of the contract.

(in the supply and demand of certification services, i.e. the interest rate) does not ensure the overall equilibrium of the economy, or at least that the equilibrium is attained quickly.

We return to the point emphasized in chapter 2: the credit market is not an auction market. The interest rate charged is not set in the classical way envisaged to equilibrate demand and supply, but rather is set by a particular set of firms – banks; and even if the cost of funds that they face (the deposit rate) is set in a manner that is well described by an auction market, the overall dynamics of the market are *not* well described by an auction model. Banks may be slow to adjust (either the nominal or real) interest rates that they charge, and there is no clear *signal* which provides banks with both the information and incentives to adjust quickly to ensure full employment of resources at stable prices.

However, there is a way by which government can relatively quickly "equilibrate" the system. For example, it can change the reserve requirements, thus making it less feasible and/or less desirable for the bank to provide certifications (loans), as we saw in chapter 3. In making these adjustments, the government is operating on aggregate information which may not be available to individual participants, and even were it available, would be of only limited relevance to their behavior.

They might know, for instance, that the aggregate supply of loans is such that there will be inflationary pressures on the economy, but that does not necessarily affect either the amount which they wish to lend or the real interest rate which they charge – or at least affect them in ways which lead to full employment of resources with stable prices. The clearest instances of this are provided by those situations where there is credit rationing; the bank may not change the real interest rate charged at all in reaction to inflationary pressures. Expectations concerning inflation affect similarly the real expected return on all financial assets – holdings of T-bills as well as loans. Lenders may believe that the inflationary boom will reduce the value of previous outstanding obligations of some firms (e.g. long-term corporate debt), thereby enhancing the attractiveness of lending to these firms. In such circumstances, banks might actually expand their lending activity, even if the (unanticipated) inflation slightly erodes their (real) net worth.

In the case of the non-competitive bank, it is also easy to see how there can be a shortfall in the supply of loans relative to deposits. The banks' optimal holdings of the safe asset (government securities)[9] may exceed the level of savings, so that the supply of loans (say, at full employment) is less than the (full employment) level of savings. Lowering the reserve requirement or lowering the interest rate on government bonds may make it less attractive for banks to hold government bonds and may increase households' willingness to hold demand deposits. However, banks may be so pessimistic about the returns to lending – they may perceive the default probabilities as so high – that, given their willingness to bear risk, they simply do not want to lend much. This is the *true liquidity trap*. It is not based on households' infinite elasticity of the demand for money, but rather on banks' inelasticity of lending with respect to the supply (cost) of funds. Providing more liquidity to the banking system does not generate more economic activity.

### Equilibrium analysis

We can now use the models presented in chapter 3 to analyze the equilibrium of the economy. The supply of loans is a function of the lending rate $r$,[10] the market interest rate $\rho$ on T-bills (which affects both the size of deposits as well as the allocation of the banks' portfolio between loans and government securities), the banks' capital stock $K$,[11] the firms' capital stock $K_f$, the state of nature $z$, which incorporates expectations about the future as

---

[9] More accurately, we should focus on *flows*, so that it is the *increase* in its holdings of T-bills with which we are concerned. We are comparing the increase in deposits plus the repayments on loans with the desired increase in T-bill holdings. The difference between the two is the supply of new loans.

[10] As the model of the corn economy should have made clear, the lending rate actually depends on the *size of the loan* (as well as any observable indicators for its riskiness). Here, $r$ can be thought of as a generic variable denoting the terms of the loan contract (like the variable $u$ in the corn model).

[11] As throughout this book, what matters is not just the *average* capital of the representative bank, but the entire distribution. Large losses in net worth by some banks will lead to greater contraction of the credit supply than corresponding gains in net worth by others. For purposes of this simplified analysis, we ignore these distributional concerns, which in practice may be of first order importance. Similar remarks apply to firm capital, $K_f$. See Greenwald and Stiglitz (1993c).

well, the reserve requirements (or other forms of the regulations) $q$, and the level of national income $y$, which is a flow variable and could be subsumed under the generic state variable $z$, but to highlight the parallels and differences with the standard *IS–LM* framework, we separate it out. Thus,

$$L_s = L_s(r, \rho, y; z, K, K_f, q) \qquad (6.1)$$

Note that we have asserted that the supply of funds depends not just on the banks' capital, but also on the capital of firms, $K_f$. This is because given $r$, the lower $K_f$, the higher the probability of default of the borrower, and hence the less attractive is lending. By the same token, in this simplified model, the demand for funds is a function of $r, y, z$, as well as the net worth of firms

$$L_d = L_d(r, Y; z, K_f) \qquad (6.2)$$

Banks and households have a demand for T-bills which depends on (among other things) the return on T-bills:

$$T = T(r, \rho, y; z, K, K_f, q) \qquad (6.3)$$

We have also expressed the demand for T-bills as a function of $\{K, K_f, r, q\}$, variables which affect banks. Bank holdings of T-bills will be affected by their willingness and ability to take risks, and these are among the variables which affect that. In the extreme case of the perfectly competitive depository bank, proposition 1 argued that banks will hold no T-bills, and in that limiting case, these variables will not appear in the T-bill demand equation.

In the case without credit rationing, market equilibrium is then determined by two equations, the loanable-funds market clearing condition

$$L_d = I_s \qquad (6.4)$$

and the T-bill market clearing condition

$$T(r, \rho, y; z, K, K_f, q) = T_s \qquad (6.5)$$

where $T_s$ is the supply of T-bills (controlled by government or the monetary authorities). We can solve (6.4) and (6.5) simultaneously for $\rho$ and $r$ as a function of $y$:

$$\rho = \rho\,[y; z, K, K_f, q] \qquad (6.6)$$

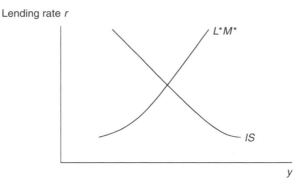

Figure 6.1 *Monetary equilibrium*
The equilibrium is the intersection of the *IS* curve and the $L^*M^*$ curve, the monetary equilibrium curve, which imbeds within it the changes in spreads.

$$r = r\,[y;\, z,\, K,\, K_f,\, q] \tag{6.7}$$

and then, substituting (6.6) into (6.4), we obtain the monetary equilibrium curve, which for simplicity is called $L^*M^*$ locus, much like the traditional *LM* curve (see figure 6.1).

There is an alternative formulation (more parallel to that of chapter 5), which highlights what is at issue. We again define

$$\xi \equiv r - \rho$$

as the spread between the lending rate at the deposit rate,[12] and solve (6.4) and (6.5) simultaneously for $\xi$ and $r$, giving (6.7) and

$$\xi = \xi\,[y;\, z,\, K,\, K_f,\, q] \tag{6.8}$$

While demand for funds depends on the loan interest rate, the supply depends on the deposit interest rate. By solving for the spread between these two interest rates, we can express everything in terms of the loan interest rate. Similarly, the *IS* curve can be generated, where again investment[13]

---

[12] There is a definition of spread which is perhaps more meaningful but less operational: the difference between the deposit rate and the certainty equivalent interest rate of a risk-neutral lender, as discussed in chapter 3. For this heuristic exposition, we ignore the issue.

[13] For empirical evidence of the importance of lending rates and the credit channel of monetary policy, see, Beckeni and Morris (1992), Bernanke and Blinder (1992), Friedman and Kuttner (1993) and Kishan and Opiela (2000). See also Blinder and Stiglitz (1983).

depends on the lending rate and saving depends on the deposit rate.[14]

While this formulation focuses on the relationship between the *lending* rate and the level of national income, one could just as easily have focused on the relationship between the deposit (T-bill) rate and national income – as indeed much empirical macro-work does. Note that in the case where banks hold no T-bills and households' demand for T-bills depends only on $\rho$ and $y$, the T-bill equilibrium equation might even enable us to solve for $\rho$ as a function of $y$, and we might therefore have thought that we could have defined an *LM* (monetary equilibrium) equation more simply, without all the trouble over loanable funds at all. The thrust of this entire book is to show why that is so misleading. What firms care about is not the interest rate that the government pays on its loans, but the interest rates that *they pay*, and the relationship between the two may differ markedly. Thus, investment does not depend on $\rho$, but on $r$ (and the availability of credit), and $r$ and $\rho$ do not necessarily move in tandem. That is the point of (6.8). Our generalized loanable-funds theory helps shift the focus to the variables that actually matter for the level of economic activity. While standard theory has obfuscated the difference between $r$ and $\rho$, we have argued that there is where the spotlight should actually be. While, as we saw in chapter 1, for long periods of time, the (real value of) $\rho$ changed little, the value of $r$ exhibited large secular and cyclical fluctuations.

Because of our focus on the variables that matter to firms – who, after all, make the decisions concerning output, investment, and employment – we prefer the formulation which relates the lending interest rate to the level of income.

## Why the fuss?

Up to now, we have worked extremely hard to derive an $L^*M^*$ curve that looks much like the *LM* curve that Hicks (1937) wrote

---

[14] Actually, as the analysis of the corn model should have made clear, saving decisions may also depend on $r$, especially when there is a margin of individuals who could either be savers or borrowers.

about almost three-quarters of a century ago. The reader may well ask: why all the fuss?

The answer is simple: as the economy goes into a recession, the $L^*M^*$ curve shifts, possibly markedly. By contrast, in the standard model, the $IS$ curve shifted as animal spirits changed expectations concerning investment opportunities, but the $LM$ curve was stable, since it was based on a stable relationship between income, interest rates, and the demand for money.

The $L^*M^*$ curve shifts because $\{K, K_f, z\}$ all vary with the business cycle. For instance, if banks become more pessimistic about the future, their willingness to lend (given everything else unchanged) will decrease, so the supply curve for funds would shift to the left. At the same time, if banks' pessimism is shared by firms, their willingness to borrow will change as well, which would cause the demand curve of funds to shift right. What happens to the interest rate – at any given $y$ – is thus indeterminate. The $L^*M^*$ curve, on these grounds, could shift either to the left or the right, to either $L_1^* M_1^*$ or $L_2^* M_2^*$.

Confounding the analysis is the fact that at the same time, as the economy goes into a downturn, both firm and bank capital

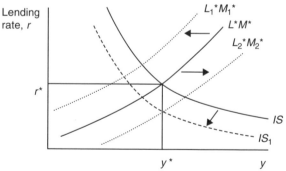

Figure 6.2 *Shift of IS–L*M* curves within business cycles*
There are shifts  in equilibrium as the economy faces a negative shock. In the new paradigm, both the $IS$ and the $L^*M^*$ curve shift. The direction of the shift of the $L^*M^*$ curve, however, is ambiguous, since both the demand and supply of loanable funds will be adversely affected at any level of income. The net effect on interest rates is, as a result, ambiguous.

may well decrease. Again, as $K$ decreases, banks' willingness (and ability) to lend decreases, while when $K_f$ decreases, firms' desire to borrow may increase or decrease. If the firms' working capital has decreased, firms' desire for borrowing may increase; but if the firms' working capital has remained unchanged, but, say, only the value of its land holdings has decreased, the firm may decide to reduce its production level, and it may decide that at the lower production level less working capital is required, so that its demand for funds from the bank for working capital may actually go down. Again, it is clear that what happens to the interest rate – at any given $y$ – is indeterminate.

Traditional monetary economics focused little on the spread between the T-bill rate and the lending rate. That approach makes sense in a neo-classical model, in which the economy fully divests itself of risk, and where there is perfect information (at least about risks) and hence there is no need for banks. In such a world, markets act in a risk neutral way, and the lending rate is just equal to the deposit rate, adjusting for risk[15] (and the – assumed insignificant – transactions costs). Borrowers, in such a world, see through the risk adjustment[16] and look at the underlying interest rate $\rho$, which turns out to be the only relevant interest rate because the spread between the effective (risk-adjusted) borrowing and lending rate is fixed by assumption.

In the model here, the spread is critical. Information is imperfect. Banks are thus performing a vital service. They cannot sell the service directly – who would believe their recommendations? It is because they are willing to back up their recommendations with their own money that their recommendations have meaning. However, this means the more loans (the more certifications) they offer, the greater the risk that the banks face. Banks must be compensated for bearing this risk, as they are if the spread is high enough.

As the economy goes into a recession, the capital stock of the banks may be eroded, and thus their willingness to bear risk is

---

[15] That is the *expected* interest payment received on funds lent differs from the interest paid depositors only by transaction costs.

[16] That is, borrowers do not look at the interest rate that they promise to pay, instead they care about their expected interest payments, the same variable that lenders look at.

reduced. At this point, even if expectations were restored, the banks' willingness to lend would remain limited. Only if the spread increases – and increases enough – will their willingless to lend be restored to the pre-recession level. A policy implication of this is that the T-bill rate must be reduced; and the reduction in the T-bill rate required to restore the economy to full employment is much greater than in the "risk neutral" case. The conventional analysis assumes that the spread is fixed, so that lowering the T-bill rate lowers the lending rate by an equivalent amount, stimulating investment. Here, we have emphasized that because of the increase in spread, the T-bill rate has to be lowered *just to keep the lending rate from rising.* A monetary policy which keeps real deposit rates fixed – or even lowers them slightly – can thus be contractionary.[17]

### Open market operations

While it is easy to see how changes in the reserve requirements affect bank behavior, it is also clear how open market operations affect the supply functions of loans, and in turn the equilibrium lending rate. In the restrictive banking model, open market operations affect the level of deposits (as T-bill rates change, deposits adjust), the implicit net worth of the bank, and the available opportunities of using funds (because deposits are affected). In the competitive banking model, it affects the costs of funds. In either case, an expansionary open market operation shifts the supply curve of loans to the right (as in figure 6.3), and thus the equilibrium lending rate is lowered.

[17] In part II we look at some instances where the failure of policymakers to take this into account had grave consequences. In 2000, the Fed, worried about inflation, raised $\rho$ in an attempt to slow down the economy. Some inflation hawks even criticized the Fed for not acting aggressively enough, observing that the increases in the nominal interest rate on T-bills were barely keeping up with increases in the inflation rate (though the inflation hawks typically focus on consumer inflation, not the inflation rates that are relevant for most domestic producers). The Fed failed to take into account the fact that changes in the economic environment had led to a large increase in the spread, so that borrowers were already facing higher interest rates. In that sense, the monetary policy was truly contractionary; and the contractionary policy contributed to the slowing down of the economy.

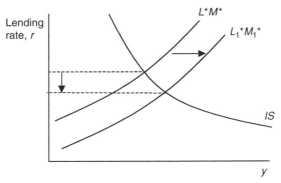

Figure 6.3 *Open market operations*
As in the traditional model, an open market operation can lead to a shift in the $L^*M^*$ curve to the right, and thus to a lower real interest rate and higher rate of real income.

## Comparison of the effectiveness of monetary policy in competitive and restrictive banking models

This section argues that as the economy moves into a regime of more competitive banking, the effectiveness of monetary policy may be greatly reduced. The essential reason for this is that in the current restrictive banking regime, there are potentially large wealth effects associated with monetary policy (including open market operations), and that monetary policy often exerts its effects through the force of *constraints*, rather than simply relying on *substitution* effects arising from changes in prices (interest rates). It is simply not plausible to believe that small changes in the intertemporal prices of twenty-five or fifty basis points could have the impacts as large as observed in the current environment. This is particularly the case in most countries nowadays, when interest rate changes are simply keeping pace with changes in inflationary expectations and thus changes in real interest rates are even smaller. Similarly, an increase in reserve requirements also is nothing more than a tax on deposits; it has a slight substitution effect.

Contrast these substitution effects with the effects that arise in the restrictive banking system, and where banks are sufficiently willing to bear risk (e.g. because they are optimistic about the economy) that they hold no T-bills in their portfolio, and so face real constraints imposed by reserve requirements. Higher reserve requirements force reduced lending. Similarly, a higher interest rate reduces deposits and lending is decreased accordingly. It is the *constraints* on lending, combined with wealth effects, that are driving the banks' behavior, not price effects. These effects may be far more powerful than substitution effects. Tightening the constraints is likely to have a far more dramatic effect in reducing lending. (In the extreme case where banks don't want to hold any T-bills, higher interest rates have no substitution effect; it is not because banks are induced to shift from lending to T-bills that monetary policy has its effects; banks are lending as much as they can, and continue to do so after the interest rate has increased. The effect of the increased interest rates arises *only* because of its impact on the banks' ability to lend.)

By contrast with its effectiveness in periods of boom – where the constraints are binding – monetary policy has often been described as ineffective in a recession. Attempts to stimulate the economy through lowering interest rates are described as "pushing against a string." Our analysis helps explain why – and in doing so, helps clarify why monetary policy in the future is likely to be less effective. The reason is that in a recession, the constraints are more likely not to be binding, and it is just the substitution effects which come into play – and these are simply not very strong.

Consider the restrictive banking system where banks do not *effectively* face constraints from reserve requirements, i.e. they voluntarily hold some T-bills in their portfolio. If they wish to lend more, they could simply sell some of their T-bills.[18] As noted earlier, an expansionary open market operation that leads to lower interest rates has a wealth effect as deposits are increased, which could be outweighed by the fact that the return on holdings of T-bills is decreased. At the same time, there is a substitution effect, which

---

[18] Obviously, in practice, matters are somewhat more complicated, because banks face a dynamic portfolio problem, and they may be holding T-bills, for instance, because the solution to the dynamic problem entails lending more in the not too distant future.

leads to more lending. But the limited wealth effect and the weak substitution effect simply are not strong enough to have much of an effect on lending. This is especially the case when banks are very risk averse – are virtually in a corner solution of no lending – or when there are dominant risky non-lending opportunities, such as holding long-term government bonds.[19] Even if the wealth effect is positive, the greater attractiveness of lending (relative to T-bills) may simply not be sufficiently large to move banks out of their "corner" solution; this is especially the case when, at the same time, a deteriorating economic environment increases the perceived risk associated with lending, so that the changes in monetary policy only (partially) offset these changes.

Under competitive banking, the wealth effects are likely to be smaller, so that the effectiveness of monetary policy will be even lower. In short, even when reinforced by wealth effects,[20] substitution effects do not seem strong enough to make monetary policy very effective in recessions. Wealth effects weaken, constraints become less important, and monetary policy has to operate through substitution effects. This makes it likely that monetary policy will have limited effectiveness, even when the economy is not in a deep recession.

These conclusions are reinforced once one recognizes that non-banking credit channels – which are not directly controlled by monetary authorities – are becoming more important. "Taxes" on banking (e.g. through reserve requirements) will have to be limited, else more credit activity will migrate out of the banking system. The existence of substitutes for bank credit (including overseas bank credit) will similarly limit the impact of actions

---

[19] As we note in chapter 9, p. 217, risk-adjusted capital adequacy requirements which treat long-term government bonds as if they are safe enhance the attractiveness of investing in such bonds, rather than lending.

[20] There are further reasons that the wealth effect may be limited. The gains to the banks occur at the expense of households and firms (depositors). Households may reduce their consumption as a result. Similarly, decreases in reserve requirements reduce the income of the central bank, which is passed on to the public fisc. If taxpayers see through this veil, again the gains to the bank are offset by losses to taxpayers, who thereby reduce their consumption. With imperfect information, there is not full "Ricardian equivalence"; there is no reason to believe that these effects fully offset the impacts on banks. Still, they serve to attenuate the overall magnitude of the wealth effect. See Stiglitz (1973, 1988a).

taken by domestic authorities to control the availability of credit through the domestic banking system.

## Why changes in nominal interest rates may matter

We are now ready to address one of the central puzzles posed in the beginning of this book: why is it that changes in the nominal interest rates matter? Given the appropriate intellectual frame, the answer is almost immediate: changes in nominal interest rates have real wealth effects whenever there is incomplete indexing. Those real wealth effects may alter both the supply of and the demand for loans. Earlier in this book, inflation rates (or expectations of them) were assumed to be fixed, so that changes in nominal interest rates translated directly into changes in real interest rates. Here we explore what happens when they are different. In order to highlight the difference between the two, we shall continue to denote the real interest rates by $\rho$ and $r$, and denote the nominal interest rates by

$$\rho_n \equiv \rho + i \text{ and } r_n \equiv r + i \tag{6.9}$$

where $i$ is the inflation rate.[21]

Let us begin by focusing on the supply of loans. Banks hold portfolios that consist of a whole vector of assets, i.e. we should think of the bank's original capital $K$ not as a single variable, but as a vector, denoted by $K \equiv \{K_1, K_2 \ldots K_n\}$ where $K_j$ is the holding of a particular asset $j$ (T-bills, long-term government bonds, mortgages, small business loans, etc.). Denote the value of $K$ by $W(K; r, \rho, i)$. $W$ will be a function of market interest rates, and *not* depend only on the real interest rate $r$.[22] The bank's liabilities are largely short-term deposits. A central function of banks is the maturity transformation – borrowing short and lending

---

[21] Since what matters for most economic decisions are expectations, we can think of $i$ as the expectation of the rate of increase of prices. The kinds of redistributive effects with which we are concerned in this section imply that actual, as well as expected, inflation matters. That is, differences between actual and expected inflation can have real consequences.

[22] Once we recognize $K$ as a vector, we have to modify some of the earlier equations. The amount that banks have to borrow to finance lending activity depends on their *liquid* assets. Bankruptcy becomes somewhat more ambiguous. A firm

long. Thus, an *increase in the nominal interest rate reduces the value of financial assets with fixed nominal interest payments, and accordingly has adverse effects on the real wealth of banks.* This is true whether the change in the nominal interest rate is accompanied by (or is the result of) an increase in the rate of inflation. This real-wealth effect will be less in banks which lend only short (so there is little maturity mismatch) or which lend only with variable rate loans (e.g. variable rate mortgages) where interest rates charged move in tandem with the interest rate that the bank must pay. The reduction in the wealth of banks leads, as we have seen, to a left-ward shift in the loan–supply curve.

These effects may be more limited, if current trends continue, in which more and more loans are indexed. (Note that in the nineteenth century, and in many developing countries even today, banks lent mostly for short-term working capital, e.g. financing inventories, in which case these effects will be relatively small. However, under these circumstances, banks play a relatively minor role in investment. The effects of the banking system are still felt through the extent to which and the terms on which they make working capital available.)

Even with ongoing changes in financial institutions, nominal changes in interest rates are likely to have *some* impact, though more through banks' increased efficiency in exploiting distortions and imperfections within the regulatory system, e.g. in the capital adequacy systems. For instance, some countries treat long term government bonds as safe, because bank regulators focus on credit risk, not market risk. With deposit insurance, banks have an incentive to borrow short-term (attract deposits) and invest the deposits in long-term bonds, especially when the interest rates on the two are markedly different. There is a presumption that the difference in interest rates reflects a compensation for the risk of a change in the

---

may seek bankruptcy protection even when the value of its total assets exceeds the value of its liabilities, if the value of its liquid assets fall short of its liabilities. At any moment of time, there are costs of selling non-liquid assets which can be significant. Hence, the dynamic optimization problem is far more complicated than depicted earlier. Still, the basic messages presented in this book are likely to remain valid in a more general model which takes all of these complexities into account.

asset value.[23] Therefore if the financial intermediaries' attitudes towards risk are similar to those of the rest of the population, there would be little reason for the bank to take a position. The fact is that some of the downside risk associated with holding long-term bonds – the risk that interest rates would rise and thus the value of the bonds would plummet – is borne by the government. It does pay off for banks under certain circumstances (especially if they are gambling on resurrection)[24] to hold positions in long-term government bonds. In that case, changes in long-term interest rates, which affect the value of those assets, will affect lending behavior.

Note again, however, that the effect of the long-term interest rates is not so much because it directly affects the costs of firms who raise capital through the long-term bond market – which is a relatively small source of funding for new investment[25] – but rather because it affects the lending behavior of banks.

Changes in nominal interest rates can, for quite similar reasons, affect the behavior of firms and households. A large increase in nominal interest rates may decrease the value of assets that the firm holds, and therefore make it more risk averse, less willing to undertake investments, or even production, and thereby decrease its demand for funds.

Moreover, increases in the nominal interest rate (keeping the real rate fixed) have the effect of shortening the duration of debt, forcing firms back into the credit market.[26] With credit rationing, serious cash flow problems – with real effects – can be generated.

---

[23] See the extensive literature on the term structure of interest rates, e.g. Meiselman (1962), Stiglitz (1970), Singleton (1980, 1988), Cox, Ingersoll and Ross (1985), Van Horne (1993), Duffie (1996), and Duffie and Singleton (1997).

[24] Kane (1985, 1990, 2000a, 2000b).

[25] Mayer (1990) found that on average, in several industrialized nations, approximately 70 percent of new investment into physical capital is financed by retained earnings, approximately 25 percent is provided by bank loans, and the rest by trade credits, equity issues, and bonds issues.

[26] That is, with a 50 percent inflation rate, even with a low 5 percent real interest rate, a borrower has to repay 55 percent of the amount borrowed at the end of the first year. Even if the total value of the project has, in nominal terms, increased on *average* commensurately in value, the project may well not generate sufficient cash flow to cover the interest payments. When the firm returns to the market to obtain the requisite finance, market views on the project may have changed, and it may not be able to obtain finance, or obtain it on as favorable terms.

Since different firms have different assets and liabilities, with their prices of inputs and outputs moving differently, different firms are affected differently; some gain at the expense of others.[27]

In short, changes in nominal interest rates (leaving real interest rates unchanged) have large redistributive consequences, which have large real effects, and expose borrowers to large risks. Distribution matters, especially because of the imperfections of information and the capital market imperfections mentioned in the beginning of this book. The redistributions may result in lower real net worth of firms and banks, and increased net worth of households. Should that not be a wash? The answer is clearly no, and at least part of the reason has to do with the equity constraints also mentioned earlier. If firms and banks have a lower net worth, they are less willing to engage in risky investing and lending. The cutback in those activities contributes to an economic slowdown.

If there were perfect information, the households could simply undo the changes that the market has wrought; that is, firms and banks could issue more equity. However, the very nature of the economic turmoil associated with large changes in market values is that such changes create large asymmetries of information. Investors may know what has happened on average, but in general, decisions are made about particular firms and banks. If they are going to buy more equity in a particular bank, say, they need to know the asset position of that particular bank, not how the average or representative banks' portfolio has been affected. And this is where the asymmetries of information come into play: investors will know that those banks most willing to restructure, to issue new equity, are those which are either in absolutely the worst shape – on the verge of bankruptcy, and so have no other choice – or those for which the market has assigned a value that is in excess of what the insiders believe or know to be correct. In either case, rational

---

[27] Of course, with perfect information and perfect risk markets, many of these effects do not occur. Presumably all contracts would be made in real terms, and (by definition) changes in inflation rates would have been perfectly anticipated. Thus, if firms were forced to reenter the credit market, that need would have been anticipated, and the availability of funds already contracted for. The fact is that we do not have, and are not likely to have in the immediate future, such perfect information or even contingent contracts that would eliminate these effects.

investors will be reluctant to provide new equity. They are willing to do so only if the terms are attractive enough – so attractive to the outsiders that the insiders are reluctant to make the deal.

More generally, periods of turmoil, with large changes in prices (interest rates, etc.) are associated with heightened problems arising from uncertainty, risk aversion, and asymmetries of information.

In part II, we will show how these same principles can be used to explain the successful recovery of the United States from the 1991 recession. We will also explore in greater detail some of the other policy implications of this model, but before doing so, we want to describe briefly the credit rationing regimes, and generalize the credit model.

## Credit rationing

In some ways, the credit rationing regime is easier to analyze. With the same notation as before, banks now set not only the amount of lending, but also the interest rate charged:

$$L_s = L_s(\rho, y; z, K, K_f, q) \tag{6.10}$$

$$r = r(\rho, y; z, K, K_f, q) \tag{6.11}$$

The demand for funds will exceed the supply if there exists credit rationing:

$$L_d > L_s \tag{6.12}$$

Investment is no longer determined just by interest rates (though interest rates will still be relevant, because they will affect the level of investment of those firms that are not credit constrained). Hence, we write

$$I = I(L_s(\rho, y; z, K, K_f, q), r(\rho, y; z, K, K_f, q)). \tag{6.13}$$

The important point to observe, however, is that monetary policy can affect investment, even when real interest rates themselves are not changed, as a result of its effects on the availability of credit. The analysis earlier in this chapter should have made clear that bank behavior – including the availability of credit – may be affected by changes in the nominal interest rate, as well as the real.

# SEVEN

# Towards a general equilibrium theory of credit

So far, we have argued that a central determinant of the level of economic activity is the supply of credit, which is different, in many ways, from the supply of ordinary goods and services, and that the most important institution in determining the supply of credit is the banking system. Credit is, however, a far more pervasive phenomenon in a modern society. Whenever one delivers a good to someone else without an immediate exchange of money or goods of full value, credit is extended. Traditionally, suppliers provide credit to their customers, who supply credit to theirs. In some cases, purchasers extend credit to suppliers, to enable them to produce the inputs that they wanted.

In each of these cases, the central question that the provider of credit has to ask is: What is the probability that the contract will be fulfilled? Will she be fully paid, or will the goods that have been paid for be delivered? Central to this query is information: information not only about the economic status of the party, but also about the incentive structures that the party faces. Every time, the party providing the credit has to ascertain both the risks involved and her ability and willingness to bear that risk. In effect, all of the questions crucial to modeling banks' supply of credit are relevant in determining the supply of credit by firms, households, or non-bank financial institutions.

## Why are there so many agents and institutions involved in the supply of credit?

Given these concerns, one might well ask, should there be more concentration in the provision of credit? Certainly, institutions like banks should be able to develop a comparative and absolute advantage in gathering and processing information. Large institutions should also have a greater ability and willingness to bear risks than households or small or medium size firms.

The reason that so many agents and institutions are involved in the supply of credit is simple. It relates to the distinctive attributes of information. Much of the relevant information is diffused throughout the economy, and is obtained as a by-product of other economic activity. In that sense, information that is relevant for credit is distinctly different, for instance, from information that is relevant for innovation. A firm knows a great deal about both its customers and suppliers as a by-product of their day-to-day interactions. A problem within a factory may be reflected in supply interruptions or a deterioration in the quality of what is produced. The firm may be able to hide these problems from its banker, but not from its customers. It would be expensive, perhaps impossible, for the bank to acquire information of comparable quality to that which is generated in the ordinary course of business.

In addition, incentives to pay may be greater when there is a customer–supplier relationship. Failure to pay will terminate the contract, which will impose huge costs on the firm. On the other hand, failure to make a payment to the bank may lead only to the firm not being able to get more loans from the bank – which the firm would not have been able to get in any case, even if it kept current on existing loans. (An extensive literature in development has explored the reasons for the interlinkage of product, land, and credit markets.[1])

---

[1]  See Braverman and Stiglitz (1982), Bardhan (1989).

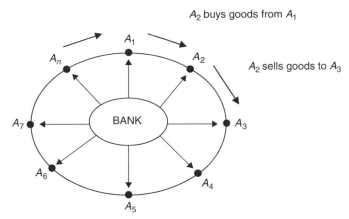

Figure 7.1  *General equilibrium credit relations model*
Each firm is both a borrower and a lender.

## Modeling general equilibrium credit relations

The specific nature of the information involved in providing credit means that any firm may be both a borrower and a lender; most firms are, in a sense, both producers of goods and financial institutions. A simple model illustrating this has firms arrayed on a circle as in figure 7.1. Each firm produces goods that are used as inputs to other firms. In this simple model, each firm uses as inputs goods produced by the firm to its left, and sells goods to the firm on its right. A joint product of these transactions is *information*, which is related to the provision of credit, so each firm borrows from the firm to its left, and lends to the firm on its right. While in equilibrium this might look like simply a wash, there is valuable service provided. There might in fact be several firms that could occupy each niche in the product space, some of which are nothing but charlatans, who will not repay the loans, but simply abscond with the funds. The screening services provided by each firm, in its role of producer-cum-financier, are critical for the efficiency of the economy.[2]

---

[2]  That is why so many firms seem to violate Polonius' charge to Laertes: "Neither a lender nor a borrower be . . ." (*Hamlet*) by becoming both borrowers *and* lenders.

To complete the model, we put a bank in the center of the circle, supplementing the credit provided by producers to each other, and we note that the firms produce not only for each other, but for customers; but these sales occur at the end of the period.

*These general equilibrium credit linkages may be every bit as important in determining the behavior of the economy as the linkages in goods and factor markets emphasized in traditional general equilibrium models.* However, the general equilibrium credit linkages are only partially mediated through the price system (i.e. adjustments in interest rates).

To observe the nature of these linkages, consider, for example, what happens if there is a shock to the system, such that some firm's net worth decreases. We assume that the firms in this economy are equity constrained, just as the banks were, as described in Greenwald and Stiglitz (1993a). As a result of the adverse net worth shock, their willingness to produce – and to finance – is decreased. The adverse shock has an impact on the product market in which it operates, but one might suspect that given the small size of the firm relative to the entire economy, it would have no impact on the capital market or labor market. The latter is true, at least initially; however, in the case of the capital market, matters are more complicated, because of the highly differentiated nature of credit. What matters is not the total supply of credit. Credit, as we noted in chapter 2, is not a homogeneous commodity, but is highly differentiated. Thus, the reduced willingness of firm $A_1$ to supply credit has an immediate and potentially large effect on its neighbor, the firm to which it provides credit, $A_2$. (Note too that the decrease in firm $A_1$'s net worth may also have had a direct impact on firm $A_0$'s willingness to lend to $A_1$, and the reduction in its supply of credit or the adverse change in the terms at which credit is provided would normally be expected to further accentuate the magnitude of $A_1$'s responses, including the reduction in its supply of credit to $A_2$.) But then this has an effect on $A_2$'s willingness to supply credit to $A_3$. The initial shock thus works its way around the circle. While the effects dampen out as one moves around the circle, what is clear is that the effects can be significant, on at least some firms. (Not only will the amount lent be reduced, but the terms at which funds are provided are changed adversely.)

## Bankruptcy

However, credit interlinkages become particularly important when the disturbances facing any single firm are large enough that they put the firm into distress, forcing it, for instance, into bankruptcy. Assume, as we postulated earlier, that there are large bankruptcy costs. Consider a firm facing a large negative shock that forces it into bankruptcy. Assume when that happens, bankruptcy costs are so large that the firm pays nothing to its creditor (to the left). Then that large adverse shock means that *its* neighbor may not be able to pay its creditors. A bankruptcy at one point in the circle can thus become translated into bankruptcies further along the circle. Orszag and Stiglitz (1999) have analyzed the determinants of the magnitude of these "bankruptcy chains." Clearly, if firms are highly levered, then a disturbance at one point can translate into a much longer bankruptcy chain.

However, there are adverse effects not only to the left, but to the right. The bankrupt firm cannot supply credit (or goods) to the firm on its right. It is costly for the firm to find alternative suppliers of goods, but even more difficult to find alternative suppliers of credit, because the credit suppliers have to obtain considerable information about the firm in order to be willing to supply credit (at least at reasonable terms). Thus, a bankruptcy at one point in the circle can lead to bankruptcies – or at least large negative effects – for firms that are its customers as well, and the customers of those customers (a possible bankruptcy chain to the right).

There is another mechanism through which the effects of credit linkages occur, and that is through the banking system. We assumed earlier that each firm received credit both from its supplier and from its bank. A bankruptcy thus has adverse effects not only on the supplier, but also on the bank. Some of the negative shock is absorbed by the bank, and its net worth is decreased. However, we have already analyzed the consequences of an adverse shock to the bank's net worth. The bank acts in a more risk averse manner, contracting its lending, and especially to what are viewed as its high-risk customers. Thus, the firms near the firm that has faced a negative shock (both to the left and the right) will face reduced supplies of credit and more adverse terms from their bank as well, exacerbating the downturn. However, even a firm at a large distance from the firm facing a shock will see its credit reduced. (Recall from our earlier discussion that even in economies in which there are a large number of banks, there are likely to be only one, or at most a few banks providing credit to any small or medium-sized enterprise (SME), because of the highly differentiated sunk costs associated with gathering the information required to assess credit worthiness. There are not a large number of other banks able to offset the credit contraction of the firm's principal loan supplier.)

The point is that a shock to any firm has large negative externalities to other firms in the economy, both to the firm's customers and suppliers, and to those firms' customers and suppliers. The fact that there are such large externalities provides, of course, an even stronger reason for firms to be careful in choosing the firms with whom they deal; they need to know, for instance, a great deal about the financial position of the firm, ascertaining how likely it is to go into bankruptcy. This provides a further stronger rationale for the interlinkages between credit and production.

### Credit interlinkages and confidence crises

The basic model of credit interlinkages can be used to show that there can be a financial collapse, even when the "fundamentals" are sound. If the banks come to believe that a particular borrower will not be able to repay them, then they will refuse to renew their loans to that firm; but then the firm's suppliers will also cut off credit; that firm's production will come to a halt, and the firm will go bankrupt. The banks' expectations will have been fulfilled. Credit interlinkages amplify what might otherwise have been a local disturbance, and there is a general equilibrium economy-wide collapse.

To simplify the analysis, we assume that there are three firms, located around the circle as before (see figure 7.2). Each firm lends a dollar to its neighbor to the right, borrowing a dollar from its neighbor to the left. In addition, it borrows $\alpha$ dollars from the

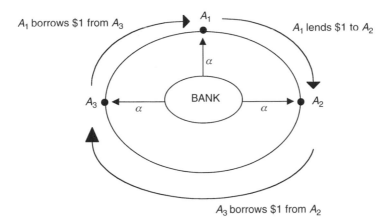

Figure 7.2  *Model of credit interlinkages with three firms*

bank. We refer to the bank as the "outside lender," and trade credit as "inside lending." Again, the reason that each firm is both a borrower and a lender, and that the bank is not relied upon as a sole source of credit, is the diffuse nature of information. Each of the firms can be thought of as representative of a large number of seemingly similar firms in a particular position in the economy. The other firms are not credit worthy. Individuals who lend money to firm $i$ are in a position to screen the firms in position $i$, and to ascertain that the firm to whom they have lent their funds is in fact credit worthy (or at least to ascertain with accuracy the probability that they will not be fully repaid). They cannot ascertain who is credit worthy in other positions. Each firm will presumably earn rents on its informational advantage; and it is these rents that make it attractive for firms to enter the lending business.

The interest rate charged by banks and suppliers for credit depends, of course, on their beliefs concerning the probability of bankruptcy. The essential idea behind the model is that if there is a common belief that the economy will be strong, then interest rates will be low, and there will be no bankruptcy. However, if there is a common belief that the economy may well go into trouble, then interest rates will be high, many firms will go bankrupt, and the expectation will be self-fulfilling. *However, the high rate of bankruptcy is a consequence of the high interest rates as much as a cause.*

To obtain these results we impose a little more structure on the model. We assume all loans are short-term.[3] Within the single period of the model, there are two production subperiods. In the first, output is $\beta$ ($\beta$ is observable). After observing $\beta$ and possibly some other signals, lenders must decide whether to renew their loans. If they do not, production is terminated, and output in the second period is zero. The creditors divide the output ($\beta$) among themselves. If they do renew their loans, the firm does not go bankrupt and output in the second period is $\gamma$. Lenders must *simultaneously* make decisions concerning whether to renew credit after observing $\beta$, and any other observable signal that they might observe. Assume, for instance, that a fraction $m$ of the time, they observe some signal. When they observe this signal, they lose heart, believe the economy is going to collapse, and accordingly, refuse to renew their loans. In this situation, investors each receive:

$$(\beta + \Lambda)/(1 + \alpha) = \Lambda \tag{7.1}$$

where $\Lambda$ is the payment (per dollar loaned) from any firm to its creditors. Solving, we obtain

$$\Lambda = \beta/\alpha \tag{7.2}$$

Thus, so long as

$$\beta/\alpha < 1 + R \tag{7.3}$$

where $R$ is the promised interest rate, the firm indeed goes bankrupt. This is an equilibrium: given that all individuals believe that other individuals will withdraw their loans, if the individual renews his loan, becoming then a junior creditor, he will receive zero.[4]

On the other hand, when the signal is not observed, they all believe there will be no bankruptcy. They renew the loans, and at the end of the period receive $1 + R$.[5] This is a consistent equilibrium, provided

---

[3]   It is possible to construct models showing why in fact the equilibrium loan contract will be short-term. See e.g. Rey and Stiglitz (1993).

[4]   Even if the rules allow the renewed loan the same seniority status as the original loans, if there is any cost of renewing the loan, it will not pay the lender to do so.

[5]   By assumption, the time elapsed between the loans and the output $\beta$ is much greater than that between the output $\beta$ and the output $\gamma$. These two production outputs can be thought of as occurring just a short time apart, so that we do not need to add an interest charge for the renewed loan.

$$\gamma > \alpha(1 + R) \qquad\qquad (7.4)$$

for if no firm defaults on its loans, each firm will be able to repay all of its creditors.

If the opportunity cost of funds in a safe investment is $r^*$, and investors are risk neutral, then $R$ must be set so that

$$1 + r^* = (1 - m)(1 + R) + m\beta/\alpha$$

or

$$1 + R = \{1 + r^* - m\beta/\alpha\}/(1 - m) \qquad\qquad (7.5)$$

Thus, for this to be a rational expectation equilibrium with bankruptcy when signal $m$ is observed, we need to combine (7.3) and (7.5) to get the condition:

$$\beta/\alpha < \{1 + r^* - m\beta/\alpha\}/(1 - m) \qquad\qquad (7.6)$$

and the return in the first period cannot be so large as to ensure the safe return regardless of the confidence crisis, i.e.

$$\beta/\alpha < 1 + r^* \qquad\qquad (7.7)$$

Combining (7.4) and (7.5), and then rearranging terms, we get the condition that the return in the second period must be large enough to stave off bankruptcy

$$\gamma/\alpha > \{1 + r^* - m\beta/\alpha\}/(1 - m) \qquad\qquad (7.8)$$

Notice that the signal is, in a sense, completely extraneous to the economy; yet if all other individuals choose to co-ordinate their behavior on that signal, it is rational for each to do so. Given the complicated nature of the world, it may be difficult for the individuals to be sure whether any particular signal is or is not extraneous. Are the announcements of money supply extraneous information? Do they have effects only because individuals and firms believe that they have effects?

We have thus constructed a simple model of a confidence crisis leading to a credit collapse. We call it a confidence crisis because there is no underlying real event (other than the co-ordinating signal) that touches it off.

### Real credit crises

By contrast, we now consider *real credit crises,* in which bad outcomes lead to a general credit collapse. The objective of the model is to show that the interdependence of credit can lead to a general credit collapse, even though only a single (class of) firm(s) has a fundamental problem. As before, each firm borrows at interest rate $R$ one dollar from its neighbor and $\alpha$ from the bank. The outside creditor (bank) has seniority relative to inside (firm) creditors.[6] We assume that the investment project of each firm $i$ yields a return of $x_i$, which can be either low, say $\varepsilon$, or high, say $\gamma > \alpha(1 + R)$. The repayments firm $i$ makes to firm $i + 1$, denoted $\Lambda_i$, can be described (in the absence of bankruptcy costs) by the following three equations:

$$\Lambda_1 = \min\{\max\{0, x_1 - \alpha(1 + R) + \Lambda_3\}, (1 + R)\}$$
$$\Lambda_2 = \min\{\max\{0, x_2 - \alpha(1 + R) + \Lambda_1\}, (1 + R)\} \quad (7.9)$$
$$\Lambda_3 = \min\{\max\{0, x_3 - \alpha(1 + R) + \Lambda_2\}, (1 + R)\}$$

Now we will derive the conditions under which the failure of one firm leads to a general credit crisis in which all firms go bankrupt. Suppose firm 1's project yields the low return of $\varepsilon$ and this is not enough to pay back the bank's loan, so that firm 1 defaults and the bank receives all of its assets, i.e. $\Lambda_1 = 0$. This is the case precisely if

$$x_1 + \Lambda_3 < \alpha(1 + R) \quad (7.10)$$

Firm 1's default bankrupts firms 2 and 3 if

$$x_2 < (1 + \alpha)(1 + R) \quad (7.11)$$

and

$$x_3 + \Lambda_2 < (1 + \alpha)(1 + R) \quad (7.12)$$

Note that $\Lambda_2$ and $\Lambda_3$ are both strictly positive because we assumed $\gamma > \alpha(1 + R)$, and $\Lambda_2$ and $\Lambda_3$ are less than $(1 + R)$ because

---

[6] Given the differences in seniority, outside and inside loans should carry different interest rates. We ignore this distinction; it would complicate the calculations without altering the conclusions. Later, we shall provide a more complete analysis for the case where there are bankruptcy costs.

we assume that all firms go bankrupt. Plugging the expressions given in (7.9) into (7.10) and (7.12), we can rewrite the system of equations with the conditions under which all firms will go bankrupt as

$$
\begin{aligned}
x_1 + x_2 + x_3 &< 3\alpha(1 + R) \\
x_2 + x_3 \quad &< (1 + 2\alpha)(1 + R) \\
x_2 \qquad &< (1 + \alpha)(1 + R)
\end{aligned}
\tag{7.13}
$$

The first condition specifies that total income must be less than total obligations to outside creditors. The second and third conditions require that the income for the second firm be insufficient to cover its debt obligations, and the income of the second and third firms in total be insufficient to cover the debt obligations of those firms, under the assumption that their debtor, firm 1, completely defaults.

We can now show that there may be multiple equilibria, in one of which real credit crises will occur with a given probability, while in the other of which real credit crises will not occur. For simplicity, assume that there are two states of nature: one with probability $\mu$ in which one (type of) firm has the low return $\varepsilon$; and the other in which no firm has the low return; lenders cannot tell *ex ante* which firm will have the low return.

(i) *The no bankruptcy equilibrium.* Then $R = r^*$. This is an equilibrium provided $\varepsilon > (1 + r^*)\alpha$

Given the low interest rate, the firm can meet its debt obligation, even in the bad state.

(ii) *The bankruptcy equilibrium.* Given that all firms go bankrupt with probability $\mu$, the required return on loans must be adjusted upwards. Let $c$ be the transactions costs involved in a bankruptcy.

There are a variety of bankruptcy patterns, depending on the bankruptcy costs. For simplicity, we assume that these costs are sufficiently large that, if bankruptcy occurs, the inside lenders get nothing, and outside lenders get all the residual, net of transaction costs. We assume that the interest rate on inside loans, $r_i$, is set so the expected return equals $r^*$, i.e.

$$(1 - \mu)(1 + r_i) = 1 + r^* \tag{7.14}$$

In the bankruptcy state, the outside loan to the firm with a high return of $\gamma$ gets $\gamma - c$; that to the firm with the return of $\varepsilon$ gets $\max\{\varepsilon - c, 0\}$. The interest rate $r_o$ on these loans is set so the expected return also equals $r^*$:

$$\alpha(1 - \mu)(1 + r_o) + \mu(\max\{\varepsilon - c, 0\} \tag{7.15}$$
$$+ 2\gamma - 2c) = 1 + r^*$$

For consistency, we require here that even the good firms cannot meet their debt obligations in the bad state, i.e.

$$\gamma < (1 + r_i) + \alpha(1 + r_o) \tag{7.16}$$

and that indeed, in the bankruptcy state, they cannot even meet their full obligations to the outside lender

$$\gamma - c < \alpha(1 + r_o) \tag{7.17}$$

It should be clear that for $c$ sufficiently large, these inequalities can easily hold.[7]

It is thus apparent that if lenders believe there will be a general real credit crisis, they will set interest rates sufficiently high that firms cannot meet their debt obligations in the bad state, and a real debt crisis will occur whenever any firm has a bad outcome. However, if lenders do not believe there will be a real credit crisis, interest rates will be set sufficiently low that there will be no bankruptcy. (It is also clear that there might be other equilibria, entailing some but not all firms going bankrupt.)

### Monetary policy

Monetary policy operates directly upon banks. However, its effects can be amplified through the effects on the risk averse, equity constrained producers-cum-financiers. A reduction of credit to a firm or an increase in the interest rate charged affects the willingness

---

[7] If $c > \gamma$, then in the event of bankruptcy, the outside lenders get nothing as well, and $r_i = r_o$.

and ability of that firm to supply credit to its customers. As its customers are adversely affected, they transmit the monetary contraction on to their customers, and so forth around the economy.

However, the impacts do not stop here. The higher interest rates charged by suppliers imply higher bankruptcy probabilities for these firms (even when they adjust their production optimally), and this in turn induces other suppliers of credit (e.g. banks) to cut back on their credit.

The process continues until a new equilibrium has been attained, with lower levels of credit by both inside and outside creditors, and a lower level of economic activity. In a sense, we are arguing here for a new form of *credit multiplier*. Traditional monetary economics assumed, in effect, that the only source of credit is banks, and that banks are constrained in their lending by the magnitude of base money. Our analysis has challenged both assumptions. In many cases, banks hold government securities; how much they lend is thus a choice variable. It is not simply determined by constraints. The objective of monetary theory, in this context, is to understand how those choices are affected by monetary policy. And secondly, much of the credit in the economy is mediated not through banks but through firms. Our analysis has shown how the choices of credit supply by both banks and firms are interrelated. While the initial impact of monetary policy is on bank behavior, we show the interactive play between the choices made by banks, the choices made by firms in their role as providers of credit, and the choices made by firms in their role as producers. The initial actions of the monetary authorities are amplified through the system through the interlinkages among firms and banks.

# PART TWO
# Applications of the new paradigm

In part I, we explained the deficiencies in the standard monetary paradigm, as we perceived them. We argued for a shift in focus from money to credit, and from thinking about the interest rate as determined in the money market, by the demand and supply for money, to an examination of the determinants of credit. In a sense, while we are arguing for a return to the pre-Keynesian emphasis on "loanable funds," there is a basic difference between this new approach and the older one: we focus on the ways in which credit is different from other commodities, the central role of information in the provision of credit, and the institutions – banks and firms – which obtain that information and bear the risk associated with the provision of credit. We have also focused on the important limitations that capital market imperfections – themselves derived from limitations on information – play in limiting the ability of banks and firms to divest themselves of the risks associated with the provision of credit. We investigated how those limitations, in conjunction with the costs of bankruptcy, are critical in determining both the level and changes in the level of credit provided and we examined the role of monetary policy in affecting the amount of credit that is available and the terms at which it is available, thereby affecting the level of economic activity.

Some might ask, even if the micro-foundations of the old trans-actions-based approach to money (or even the portfolio approach) were suspect, didn't the model do well enough? What does one get out of all of these refinements? The question is similar to that posed by the monetarists twenty years ago: did one really need any micro-foundations? There was an empirical regularity – the constancy of velocity. There might be innumerable reasons for that constancy, but the reason was not important: it was important is to recognize this empirical regularity, and to take it into account in deriving policies. The problem was that just as monetarism became fashionable, the grounds on which it rested began to shake: the empirical regularity on which it was based no longer seemed valid, as figure 1.3 illustrated.

So too here. The usual relationships work well most of the time, but in times of crisis – when the consequences of policy mistakes can be particularly severe – they often do not hold. As Greenspan repeatedly lowered interest rates in the 1991 recession in the United States, the economy failed to respond in the way he (and many of the standard models) predicted. And the recovery from that recession also seemed to be more robust than he (and many of the standard models) predicted. Only as the economy finally emerged from the recession, in his Humphreys–Hawkins testimony[1] before Congress in February 1993, did he publicly admit that there had been large changes in the underlying relationships.

In this part, we want to highlight some of the more important – and in some cases surprising – policy implications of the new paradigm, focusing in particular on situations where the standard theory produced misleading and, in some cases, disastrous results. Part II is divided into seven chapters. Chapter 8 deals with the role of monetary policy in the new paradigm; chapter 9 with its implications for regulatory policy; chapter 10 puts its focus on the implications for certain aspects of the liberalization of financial markets; chapter 11 considers banking

---

[1] The Full Employment and Balanced Growth (Humphrey-Hawkins) Act of 1978 required the Federal Open Market Committee to report to Congress and release a report on the economy and monetary policy semiannually, in February and July. The original act expired in mid-2000, but the Fed chairman has continued the practice since.

sector restructuring, and chapter 12 with the implications for regional growth and stabilization policies. Chapters 13 and 14 take up two important recent episodes, viewed through the lens of the new paradigm, the 1997 crisis in East Asia, and the 1991 US recession, and the subsequent recovery and boom. The final chapter 15 explores some of the implications of the "New Economy" for monetary policy, as seen through the lens of our new paradigm. Chapter 16 draws conclusions.

# EIGHT

# Monetary policy

A central reason for interest in monetary theory is that monetary policy remains one of the most effective means by which the government can control the level of the economy's activity, *at least at certain times*. It is by now well recognized that the mechanisms for self-adjustment of the economy are at best imperfect; that the economy, on its own, may have extended periods of underemployment or inflation. Traditional monetary theory has government controlling the money supply, which affects interest rates, which in turn affect the level of investment. Under the new paradigm:

(1) What affects the level of economic activity is the terms at which credit is made available *to the private sector*,[1] and the *quantity* of credit, not the quantity of money itself.

(2) The relationship between the *terms at which credit is available* (e.g. the loan rate) and the *T-bill (or deposit) rate* may change markedly over time.

(3) Similarly, the *supply of credit* may not change in tandem with the money supply; and changes in the relationship between money and credit may be particularly marked in periods of crisis.

---

[1] As opposed to credit conditions for the government, which are reflected in the T-bill rate.

154

(4) The terms at which credit is made available and its quantity are determined largely by *banks*; their ability and willingness to lend are affected by the T-bill interest rate, but in ways which depend on economic conditions; changes in interest rates affect the net worth of firms, and the net worth and opportunity sets of banks. Large changes in interest rates may affect the degree of uncertainty on the part of lenders about the credit worthiness of borrowers.

(5) Monetary authorities and regulators can affect *bank behavior* not only through changes in the T-bill rate, but also by altering constraints (e.g. reserve requirements, capital adequacy standards) and incentives; obviously, impacts on bank behavior of changing constraints are likely to be greater when constraints (e.g. reserve requirements) are binding than when they are not (there is "excess liquidity"); in some extreme circumstances, there may even be a liquidity trap, in which easing of monetary policy has no significant effect on lending.

(6) Monetary policy affects economic activity not only through its effect on *demand* for credit (e.g. for investment) but also on *supply* (e.g. when there is credit rationing, it is impacts on the supply of credit that matter); by the same token, monetary policy has impacts on aggregate supply and on aggregate demand which are often intertwined.

(7) Typically, the supply-side and demand-side effects reinforce each other, e.g. in leading to a contraction of the economy; but the supply-side effects may in fact be larger than the demand-side effects, in which case tighter monetary policy may actually be *inflationary*.

(8) In small open economies, the dominant effect of monetary policy is through *supply-side effects*, since the country may face a close to horizontal demand curve for its products.

(9) Monetary policy affects bank and firm (and household) behavior not just through intertemporal substitution effects (changes in the real interest rate), but also

(and in many cases more importantly) through *real-wealth and cash flow effects.* These may be particularly pronounced in open economies where they induce changes in exchange rates, when banks and firms have a foreign exchange exposure.[2]

(10) *General equilibrium effects* arise through a variety of channels besides those emphasized in the traditional literature and the credit interlinkages focused upon in chapter 7. Higher interest rates affect asset values and risks, both the uncertainties associated with asset values and with default. They affect the relative attractiveness of lending vs. holding long-term government bonds. These effects may be magnified when the regulations for capital adequacy require inadequate risk adjustment for particular types of assets (e.g. long-term government bonds); behavior is distorted.[3]

(11) The effects of monetary policy are *long lived.* An increase in the interest rate today which is subsequently reversed can have effects long after the initial impacts. There can be important hysteresis effects.

(12) Monetary policy is highly *distortionary* in its impact on the economy and these distortions must be taken into account in balancing off the advantages of monetary policy vs. other stabilization instruments. There are ways by which the distortions can be mitigated, but they in turn may reduce the effectiveness of monetary policy.

(13) While the immediate impact of monetary policy is on the banking system, its full effects are distributed through the economy as a result of the network of *credit interlinkages.*

(14) Increases in the *competitiveness* of the banking system, eliminating or significantly reducing the profits which accrue from the difference between lending and deposit rates, are also likely to reduce the effectiveness of monetary policy.

---

[2] These effects play a large role in the discussion of the East Asia crisis in chapter 13.
[3] See chapter 9 for a more extended discussion of regulation.

(15) Other *changes in financial structure*, such as the growth of commercial paper and bond markets and the enhanced global integration, are likely to affect, but not eliminate the effectiveness of monetary policy.

## The basic framework

In chapters 3 and 4 in part I we laid out the basic framework, focusing particularly on how changes in interest rates, reserve requirements, and capital adequacy standards affected the opportunity set of banks, both under highly competitive and imperfectly competitive regimes, taking as given the characteristics (mean and variance) associated with the loan portfolio. But monetary policy has several other impacts, which can take on first-order importance, and which we shall explore in this chapter. These include

(1) Monetary policy induces changes in the value of assets, and thus the net worth position of banks *and* firms (we call this the *asset value effect*).

(2) Large changes in interest rates have large effects on these asset values, but since outsiders are unlikely to have detailed knowledge of the asset structure, such changes enhance *uncertainty*, both concerning risks associated with outstanding loans and new loans.

(3) Changes in interest rates and credit availability (now and expected in the future) change the expected present discounted value of profits of banks and firms, and therefore affect the cost of bankruptcy (we call this the *franchise value effect*).

(4) Changes in existing risk exposure (which we will call the *portfolio risk effect* of monetary policy) and the *portfolio wealth* effect may be stronger than the *intertemporal substitution effect* on which traditional theory has focused.

(5) There are similar effects on firms, and they affect the actions undertaken by firms, and thus both the risk associated with existing loans and that associated with new loans (we call these the *firm risk effects*). There is some ambiguity in the *direction* of these effects – whether

they reinforce or reduce the first-round impacts – but especially in severe economic downturns, they are likely to reinforce the negative impact of measures designed to tighten monetary policy, while in better times they are likely to mitigate the effects.

(6) Thus, monetary policy affects the lending behavior of the bank by affecting the level of its current wealth, the risk that it is currently bearing, the risks associated with new loans, and the return to remaining in business; as a consequence, attitudes towards risk are changed, and the opportunity set is altered in far more complicated ways than depicted in part I.

(7) If there were a perfect market for loans previously made, then the behavior of the bank could be summarized in terms of impacts on wealth, preferences (willingness to take risks), and risks associated with new loans, i.e. risks associated with old loans would matter only to the extent that they affected market prices. But capital markets for "used" loans are far from perfect, because of large asymmetries of information, and thus for many categories of loans, only if the bank is in quite bad shape will it turn to selling its existing portfolio of loans, and in that case, it is unlikely to be making new loans. Hence the risk associated with the bank's existing loan portfolio affects its willingness to undertake new loans. And monetary policy affects that, through the channels described above.

Before turning to a more detailed explication of several of these points, we need to re-emphasize the importance of general equilibrium effects, upon which we touched only briefly in part I.

## General equilibrium effects

In part I when we contemplated changes in monetary policy, e.g. an increase in reserve requirements, we traced out the consequences assuming that deposit rates remained unchanged, that is, we undertook a *partial equilibrium* analysis. Clearly, when all banks simultaneously face, say, higher reserve requirements there are general equilibrium effects (indeed, that is precisely the point of increasing the reserve requirements). These second-round repercussions, however, are not likely to reverse the impact effects that we described earlier. While we could go through the analysis for all four principal cases (competitive and restrictive banking, with and without credit rationing), we shall limit ourselves here to the case of restrictive banking. Similarly, while we could go through the analysis for each policy instrument, we shall limit ourselves here to the case of increasing reserve requirements. As mentioned before, it will be important to distinguish between those cases where the bank has excess liquidity (holds government bonds) and where it does not.[4]

We begin with the case where banks do not hold government bonds; banks are fully lent out, so that an increase in reserve

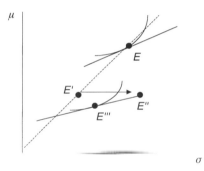

Figure 8.1  *General equilibrium effects of an increase in reserve requirements*
(With restricted banking and credit rationing; the bank holds no T-bills.) The partial equilibrium effect moves the opportunity set in proportionately to the reduction in the bank's available capital (i.e. deposits plus net worth), equilibrium shifts from $E$ to $E'$, with homothetic preferences. The general equilibrium effect – lower national income leads to increased possibility of default – shifts point $E'$ to the right, to $E''$. Increases in interest rates charged have a larger *marginal* effect on risk, so that the slope of the opportunity locus is flatter. Lower wealth of banks may make them more risk averse, making the indifference curve steeper. Hence equilibrium is to the left of and below $E''$ – at $E'''$.

[4] We do not, of course, identify all the general equilibrium effects, e.g. on relative prices. We focus on the macro-economic effects – the contractionary impact on the economy and the implications for bankruptcy risk. Monetary policy also

requirements reduces the banks' lending portfolio directly. Figure 8.1 shows the case where there is credit rationing. The first-round effect has each bank's opportunity set shrinking proportionately to the bank's available capital. If a bank's risk preferences were homothetic, then it would choose the point $E'$, along the ray through the origin from the original equilibrium $E$. At $E$ the loan rate may be the same as at $E'$.[5] But the reduced loan supply will be associated with a reduced level of economic activity, and thus there will be greater risk of default:[6] $E'$ shifts to the right, to $E''$ in figure 8.1; the opportunity set flattens out. Moreover, as we noted, increased reserve requirements act like a tax, making the bank poorer. Because the bank is poorer, it is less willing to accept risk. We can represent this as an increase in the slope of its indifference curves – the bank insists on a larger increment in mean return to offset any increase in risk. The two effects together imply that the equilibrium will be to the left of and below $E''$, entailing less risk. Banks' increased unwillingness to take risk *may* thus be *reflected in an actual lowering of loan interest rates, though the supply of loans is reduced.* (We emphasize this point because one of the puzzles presented in chapter 1 was the cyclical pattern of interest rates. There seems to be no clear pattern of the relationship between lending and interest rates; the model just presented provides one of the reasons why this may

affects the price *level*; what matters are impacts on the real credit supply. Throughout, we assume that prices do not increase proportionately to the increase in credit supply. For simplicity, we assume prices are rigid. For a theoretical discussion in the context of the theory of the risk averse firm with imperfect information, see Greenwald and Stiglitz (1989b, 1990a, 1991a, 1991b).

[5] The relationship between the interest rates charged at the two points is complex. If all projects were identical (so that we are concerned only with adverse incentive effects as interest rates increase), then choosing a portfolio with the same coefficient of variation would imply choosing the same interest rate. However, if there are adverse selection effects, matters are more complicated. Figure 8.2 shows the adjustment of the average interest rate charged in response to tightening credit in the presence of an adverse selection effect. The expected return to loans is a function of interest rate charged for two classes of borrowers. Let $R_a^*$ and $R_b^*$ be the maximum expected return for each class, with corresponding interest rates $r_a^*$ and $r_b^*$. As credit gets tightened, the bank may decide to lend only to type a. But if the interest rate on type b was higher than on type a (because it was the higher-risk loan), as the high risk–low return class is excluded from the market, the average interest rate charged actually falls.

[6] Assuming that the initial situation is one where there is rough macro-economic balance, in particular no strong inflation pressures, and there already are some problems of under-utilization of assets.

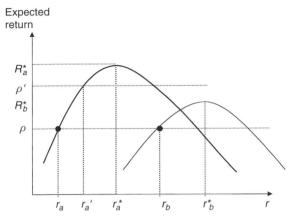

Figure 8.2 *Impact of higher opportunity cost of funds (expected rate of return on lending rates charged)*

Average interest rates charged may decrease as credit gets tightened with adverse selection. At low cost of capital, the bank lends to both type a and type b borrowers. The interest rate charged equates the expected return. Type b is charged a higher interest rate. When the required expected rate of return is high (tight monetary conditions) then the bank lends only to type a. The interest rate charged under tightened monetary conditions (high $\rho$) is lower than the *average* interest rate charged when $\rho$ is lower.

be the case.) Since by assumption there is credit rationing, actual lending activity is dictated by the supply of loans. And the supply of loans has been *directly* affected by the increased reserve requirements.

At first blush, one might ask, how does the change in reserve requirements affect T-bill rates? After all, banks are not holding any T-bills; hence there is no effect on the demand for T-bills. But general equilibrium theory teaches us that all markets are interconnected. The reduced availability of loans means that some entrepreneurs will not be able to get the capital they would have liked. They are *forced* either to reduce their scale of operations, or to increase the amount of self-financing (or both). If a significant number of firms increases the extent of self-financing, it will imply that there will be a reduced demand for T-bills by households (entrepreneurs). For the demand and supply of

T-bills to equilibrate, their price has to decrease, which implies that the interest rate on T-bills has to increase.

But note the markedly different *causal* story we have just told. It is not that the increased T-bill interest rate has led to a contraction in the economy; or even that an increase in the T-bill rate has induced banks to lend less. It is that reduced lending by banks has reduced the demand for T-bills, and led to an increase in the T-bill rate.

Moreover, the reduction in the level of economic activity will be related only loosely to the magnitude of the increase in the T-bill rate. Assume the only holders of T-bills are entrepreneurs. Then in aggregate, entrepreneurs cannot sell their holdings of T-bills; they cannot shift resources into their corporations. But they will try and in doing so they will bid up the interest rate until it reaches a level at which it is no longer attractive for them to invest. Hence the reduction in the  level of economic activity is determined by the contraction in bank lending. The increase in the interest rates is determined solely by the interest rate at which entrepreneurs are indifferent between holding more T-bills and putting more money into their firms. If they are optimistic about the prospects of their own firms, the requisite increase in the T-bill rate may be very high. But the high T-bill rate has not *caused* the decrease in economic activity; but rather the high T-bill rate is the *result* of the optimism of entrepreneurs.[7]

### General equilibrium effects when there is excess liquidity

Figure 8.3 considers the same case where banks are so risk averse that they hold some excess liquidity. Now they also care about

---

[7] Traditional models have a number of mechanisms through which entrepreneurs seek to mitigate the impact of the reduced availability of credit, but many are unpersuasive in the context of the models developed here. If there are some non-entrepreneurial households, one might be tempted to argue: the entrepreneurs will sell their T-bills to the non-entrepreneurs, and with the money thus received continue to finance the activities of their firm. But recall, money and T-bills are, in our model, for all intents and purposes the same; the line of credit – the total amount that the entrepreneur is allowed to spend – is presumably based on his total asset position, and the bank will be indifferent as to whether his liquid funds are held in the form of T-bills or CMA accounts. Thus, selling T-bills would seem to do little good.

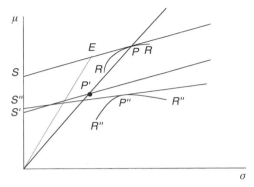

Figure 8.3 *Impact of increased reserve requirements, credit rationing with excess liquidity*

(With restricted banking and credit rationing; the bank holds T-bills.) The general equilibrium effect now includes an increase in interest rates as a result of lower demand for T-bills by banks, a flatter opportunity locus, higher interest rates charged on loans, smaller deposits, and thus greater substitution and wealth effects through second-round general equilibrium impacts. (Higher interest rates imply that, in equilibrium, households hold more T-bills, so banks hold fewer T-bills, so lending is reduced by less than the reduction in the banks' total of lending *plus* T-bill holdings.)

Collateral might be thought of as providing another avenue of adjustment. But recall, we are in a credit rationing regime, and we postulate that the individual has already used up all his available collateral, or there is some adverse signal associated with the willingness to provide more collateral. (This is important, since otherwise, banks could, by increasing collateral requirements, at any given interest rate, increase their expected return, and they could do so until the demand for funds equaled the supply – there would be no credit rationing; see Stiglitz and Weiss (1986). Bester's (1985) critique of Stiglitz and Weiss (1981) is misguided on precisely these grounds.)

When we are not in a credit rationing regime, readjustments among the portfolios of entrepreneurs and non-entrepreneurs may, however, reduce the impact of monetary constraints. The entrepreneurs may have other assets, which they may be willing to put up as collateral. While, by assumption, the total amount that the bank can lend (in aggregate) is fixed, taking into account the general equilibrium effects, the amount of credit that the system as a whole is willing to extend can thereby be increased – the total credit multiplier is increased, though the borrowers, in doing so, have left themselves more exposed. The higher interest rates also induce non-bank suppliers of credit to increase the amount of credit they make available. With more credit available, the interest rate falls (though presumably not to the level that existed prior to the tightening of monetary policy), and the amount of lending increases – the initial impact of the credit reduction by the banks is mitigated, to some extent, by increased credit availability elsewhere in the system.

what happens to the interest rate on government bonds. The first-round effect has their opportunity locus shrinking in as before, and with homothetic preferences, the demand for T-bills is reduced proportionately. (In the figure, this is represented by the move from $SP$ to $S'P'$. For simplicity, we do not show the whole opportunity locus nor do we illustrate the indifference curves. The initial equilibrium is shown as the point $E$.) This means that for the demand and supply of T-bills to equilibrate, T-bill rates have to increase. This in turn means that demand deposits decrease, and hence under restrictive banking, $S'$ and the locus $RR$ shift in even more. $S''$, the bank's income if it puts all of its money into T-bills, may lie above or below $S'$; in the case illustrated it lies above. In either case, the opportunity set moves from $S'P'$ to $S''P''$; it is flatter, and the optimally chosen loan portfolio, on that account, is riskier. In addition, as noted in the case without excess liquidity, reduced lending has a general equilibrium effect in increasing risk, thereby changing the shape of the $RR$ curve, typically making it flatter. Again, the net effect on the lending rate appears ambiguous.

The analysis of the effect on the amount lent is somewhat more complicated. The first-round effect of moving their opportunity locus inwards normally leads to reduced lending, so long as there is decreasing absolute risk aversion. With decreasing relative risk aversion, even the proportion of the smaller bank portfolio which is lent out may be reduced. The second- and subsequent-round effects are more complicated. The increase in T-bill rates has an

---

In the longer run, there are other channels through which the initial impact of monetary tightening is reduced. Assume, more generally, there are some non-entrepreneurial households, who respond strongly to higher interest rates by saving more, and who, with higher T-bill rates, are willing to hold more T-bills. Then, as T-bill rates increase, households are willing to hold more T-bills. The households buy T-bills from the entrepreneurs, who use the money to provide funds to their firms. The problem with this argument, however, is that it mixes *flows* and *stocks*. In any *short* period of time, the flow of savings is small relative to the stock, and hence the effect just described will be negligible.

In the older theories, there was a *stock* version of the same story. Households used their money to buy T-bills; they exchanged demand deposits for T-bills. The higher the interest rate, the more they exchanged. With more demand deposits, they could provide more funds to the firms. But in our theory, T-bills and money are perfect substitutes – and so this exchange does not affect the total amount that creditors are willing to extend to the firm.

income and a substitution effect: banks may be either better or worse off (than they would have been had T-bill interest rates remained unchanged). The lower level of deposits makes them worse off, the higher T-bill rate makes them better off. If they are worse off, which will be the case if the elasticity of demand for T-bills is large, or even if it is small, if they hold relatively few T-bills in their portfolio, then the wealth and substitution effect both lead to reduced lending. If they are better off, which they may be if they lend little and if the elasticity of demand for T-bills is low, they are willing to take more risk, i.e. lend more, and hold fewer T-bills. But because T-bills have become relatively more attractive, they wish to lend less. On the face of it, the net effect seems to be ambiguous. But we can work our way through the possibly conflicting income and substitution effects by observing that the increased interest rates on T-bills will normally lead to increased holdings of T-bills by the non-banking sector, so that *in equilibrium* the holdings of the banking sector are reduced. And indeed, ignoring for the moment the impact of the changes in interest rates on the overall value of the portfolio, households' reductions in demand deposits equal their increased holdings of T-bills.[8] But the reduced demand deposits reduce the banks' overall lending plus T-bill portfolio by only a fraction of the reduced demand deposits, because of reserve requirements. Some of the reduction in banks' overall portfolio is absorbed in reduced holdings of T-bills: hence, even when lending is reduced (which would be the normal case), it will be reduced by less than the reduction in bank liquidity. The converse may be even more important: increases in the *capacity* of banks to lend, as a result of reduced reserve requirements, may lead to proportionately smaller increases in lending. (For the extreme case where the increase in lending may be negligible, see the discussion on p. 189 below on liquidity traps.)

Diagrammatically, the flatter opportunity locus means that the tangency of the opportunity locus and the indifference curve shifts

---

[8] The higher interest rates lead to a lower overall value of the portfolio, which would normally be associated with lower total holdings of T-bills *plus* demand deposits; hence the reduction in deposits will be slightly greater than the increased holdings of T-bills.

to the left, that is, even with constant relative risk aversion (where loans and T-bill holdings would have been reduced proportionately) the bank shifts to a portfolio which is more weighted towards T-bills than it was in the original situation. But the fact that the bank's loan rate has increased – and hence each loan is riskier – means that to obtain a given level of risk, the bank needs to make fewer loans. Hence, the number of loans[9] is reduced even further. (This is seen by observing that the point $P'$ moves to the right.[10])

## General equilibrium effects in the absence of credit rationing

The non-credit rationing case is only slightly more difficult. If banks are fully lent out, then the supply of funds is fixed (at the given deposit rate), and the intersection of the demand and supply for funds determines the loan interest rate. An increase in reserve requirements shifts the loan supply curve to the left. The second-round adjustments (resulting from the higher T-bill rate that follows from tighter monetary policy, and the resulting reduction in deposits) reinforces the first-round adjustment. But even if the bank is not fully lent out, there will be a leftward shift in the loan supply curve. We can break down the effect of an increase in the reserve requirement into several steps. The first-round effect is to shift the opportunity locus of the bank down proportionately, reducing lending and the purchase of T-bills. In the second round, the lending rate increases to equilibrate the demand and supply of loans; the T-bill rate increases to

---

[9]  Or more accurately, the amount of lending. One of the decision variables of the bank is the size of each loan. In this book, we have not analyzed how the size of the loans changes with changes in, say, monetary policies. We might normally expect that some of the reduction in lending will take the form of smaller loan sizes, particularly since a reduction in loan size will help mitigate the adverse risk effects of higher interest rates.

[10]  If $\sigma^*$ represents the risk of an all-loan portfolio, the risk of a portfolio in which a fraction $\alpha$ of the dollars is invested in risky assets is $\alpha\sigma^*$, so that if the overall level of risk were kept constant, at $\sigma'$, then $\alpha = \sigma'/\sigma^*$, so that an increase in $\sigma^*$, keeping $\sigma'$ constant reduces $\alpha$, the number of dollars lent. If $\sigma^*$ remains unchanged but, say, the mean of the risky portfolio is reduced, then $\alpha$ remains unchanged along a vertical line in the diagram. Thus, as the bank's wealth is reduced, its holdings of loans of unchanged risk would remain unchanged only if the equilibrium point $E$ moved directly down.

equilibrate the demand and supply of T-bills; and deposits are reduced, as the opportunity cost of holding money increases. Thus, the bank's opportunity locus again shifts in, but whether the slope of the opportunity locus changes depends on the relative size of the increase in the lending rate and the T-bill rate. (In addition, the tighter monetary policy leads to a contraction in economic activity and hence to an increase in the riskiness of lending and a lowering of the mean return. Moreover, the higher lending rate itself leads to more risk.) Again, in equilibrium, so long as the T-bill rate increases, household holdings of T-bills increase, so bank holdings must decrease, so that the decrease in loan supply is less than it would be if there were not this "buffer" provided by banks' holdings of T-bills.[11]

All of this (both in the case of credit rationing and no credit rationing) has ignored the asset and franchise effects mentioned above, and to be discussed in greater detail on p. 175 below. They may easily be incorporated into our analysis. Assume, for instance, the bank has long-term government bonds, which, as a result of the increase in the interest rates are worth less. The bank's opportunity set then shrinks down on this account. (These effects are described at greater length below.) There are further effects. The higher return on long-term bonds[12] is likely to shift banks towards long-term bonds *within* their risky portfolio – and therefore towards less lending; and the slowdown of the economy induced by the higher interest rates may lead to increased bankruptcy rates, thus increasing the riskiness of the loan portfolio and new lending. The former effect (the higher return on long-term government bonds) further shifts the trade-off towards

---

[11] Diagrammatically, the sequence of shifts parallel that of the credit rationing case, except while in the latter, the point $P$ or $P'$ is *chosen* as the tangency of the line through $S$ or $S'$ with the loan opportunity locus ($RR$ or $R'R'$), now, it is chosen as the tangency of the line through $S$ or $S'$, with the locus $rr$ or $r'r'$ (the loan opportunity locus with interest rate fixed, at the market clearing rate), and the shift from $rr$ to $r'r'$ represents not just a change in wealth plus deposits, but also a change in the equilibrium loan interest rate. The increase in the loan interest rate partially offsets the direct adverse impact on lending of the reduced funds available for lending and the increased returns to holding T-bills.

[12] The long-term bonds have a higher yield to maturity, but the expected return in the short-term may or may not be higher, depending on expectations

holding long-term bonds within the risky portfolio, and the latter effect (the increased risk of bankruptcy) induces a shift towards a safe portfolio – larger holdings of T-bills (lowering T-bill rates *from what they would have been otherwise, though not necessarily relative to the level ex ante*), larger holdings of long-term government bonds,[13] and *lower* interest rates[14] on the loans they make.[15]

### Asset price effects

In our earlier analysis, we took the bank's initial assets, $a_t$, as given and unaffected by monetary policy. In fact, the bank has a large variety of assets, from long-term fixed interest and variable interest rate loans, to holdings of buildings and other real estate. While it is obvious that changes in economic circumstances may affect the value of those assets, it is also the case that changes in monetary policy can do so. For instance, an increase in the short-term interest rate is likely to be accompanied by an increase in the medium- and long-term interest rates, resulting in a decrease in the value of fixed interest rate obligations. If the bank holds long-term

concerning *future* movements in long-term bond prices. We assume that the fall in bond prices does not result in an expectation of further bond price declines, so that the expected return on long-term bonds is indeed increased, even taking into account changes in bond prices. It is, of course, possible that the greater uncertainty about future price movements so increases the variance of the return on long-term bonds that they become less attractive, and banks shift their portfolio towards T-bills.

13  Keynes' liquidity trap essentially argued that as interest rates became lower, long-term bonds became so risky relative to money (T-bills), that the demand for money became infinitely elastic. Conversely, consistent with the above analysis, as interest rates increased, long-term bonds became relatively more attractive. Keynes did not, however, pay particular attention to the *regulatory* incentives for banks to hold long-term bonds when interest rates are high, which plays a large role in the analysis here, nor did he have (as we have already noted) a consistent theory of the determination of the price of long-term bonds relative to short-term ones.

14  Though to reiterate, not lower than the interest rate *ex ante*, before the increase in reserve requirements.

15  Diagrammatically, these changes represent a shift in the risky investment locus $R'R'$ or $r'r'$ and hence in the point $P''$ to the right and down. There are further general equilibrium effects which can be traced out: there are also asset price effects on households, which may lead them to reduce their demand deposits even further, shifting the opportunity locus still further in towards the origin.

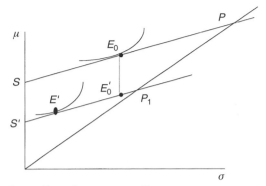

Figure 8.4 *Asset effect of monetary policy*
An increase in interest rates reduces the value of $a_t$, and hence leads
to less lending. Not only has the opportunity set shrunk, at the lower
level of wealth, the bank is less willing to bear risk. $E_0'$ represents the
point with the same level of lending activity as $E_0$.

government bonds in its portfolio, there is an immediate and direct impact on the bank's net worth (see figure 8.5).

The value of the bank's loan portfolio is also likely to decrease,
but the analysis is considerably more complicated. As usual, we
need at this juncture to separate our analysis of the case where there
is credit rationing from that where there is not. When there is not
credit rationing, the general equilibrium analysis presented earlier
makes clear that normally, there will be an increase in the lending
rate. The increase in the lending rate (the return received on loans)
offsets the increase in the discount factor *for loans with variable interest rates*. But our earlier analysis left out several other effects
which may be important. For highly leveraged firms (with short-
term or variable rate debt, where the higher interest rate leads
quickly to increased payments to creditors), an increase in interest
rates, particularly if large, significantly increases the probability of
non-payment (default), and hence will decrease the value of those
assets (though because they are typically not marketed, the magnitude of the decrease may not be apparent),[16] and because banks
are not required to mark-to-market, the decrease in value may not

---

[16] Most firms have some amount of short-term debt, so increases in interest rates
affect their viability.

show up on the bank's books. Thus, an increase in the interest rate will, through the channel just described, lead to an instantaneous decrease in the bank's net worth, and (provided the decrease is not so large that the bank starts "gambling on resurrection") induces still more risk averse behavior.[17]

If the bank has some long-term fixed interest rate loans to firms, then the adverse effects on the bank are even more marked. It does not benefit from increased interest payments, but the higher interest rate leads to those interest payments being more heavily discounted, so the value of those loans decreases. Moreover, if the firm also has some long-term variable rate loans, the probability of default on all the long-term loans increases, further decreasing the value of the fixed interest rate loans.

In the case of credit rationing, the lending rate may or may not change, even when loans are short-term so that the bank has the discretion of changing interest rates. The key issue is what happens to the mean–standard deviation locus associated with lending and investing in long-term government bonds.

The diagrammatic analysis is exactly as in figures 8.1 and 8.3, except the changes are exaggerated: there is a larger shrinking in the opportunity set because of the asset price effect. The curve *RR* (which we will now refer to as the *investment opportunity locus*, since it includes both investments in long-term government bonds and loans) changes shape, as the two asset classes are likely to be affected differentially.[18]

### The risk effect of changing interest rates

Moreover, if, as is likely to be the case, the bank is imperfectly informed concerning the economic position of its borrowers, it will know that the increase in the interest rate has affected some more than others; but there may be a great deal of uncertainty about exactly how much the probability of default has increased. Thus, the bank will perceive itself as facing greater

---

[17] This assumes that the bank has decreasing absolute risk aversion.
[18] A similar analysis applies to competitive banking, with one modification: now, there is no deposit effect.

risk.[19] If all the assets of the bank were readily marketable, then the increase in risk would have the effect only of decreasing their market value (assuming the market acts in a risk averse manner, or that the risk is perceived to be correlated with market risk) more than just the direct effect discussed earlier.[20] But loans are not perfectly marketable. If the bank attempts to sell them, it must undertake a loss. The reason for this is the large asymmetries of information; buyers of the loan portfolio will presume that the bank will be selling those loans which are least likely to pay (conditioning on the readily observable information).[21]

Moreover, the risk associated with *new* lending has also increased, because of increased uncertainty in evaluating the borrower's financial position. On three accounts – the greater risk aversion from the lower net worth, the greater risk already embedded in the portfolio, and the greater risk associated with new lending – banks are likely to be less willing to engage in lending.

These supply-side effects are further exacerbated if the bank believes that the consequence of the increase in interest rates is a macro-economic slowdown, since then on that account alone there will be an increased probability of non-performance.

These effects are illustrated in figures 8.5 and 8.6. Figure 8.5 assumes that all of the bank's assets are fully marketable, so that the increased risk associated with the interest rate increase moves the opportunity set in (relative to that depicted in figure 8.3), and the increased riskiness of the new lending is reflected in a rightward shift in the loan portfolio curve. Moreover, the overall economic slowdown is reflected in a downward shift in the expected return. There are thus three effects, all of which lead to less lending: the decreased asset value leads to a wealth effect which is associated with less lending; the increased riskiness and reduced

---

[19] Note that what matters is large increases in interest rates; it is *changes*, not levels, that give rise to these uncertaintives. Over time, information about the net worth of the borrowing firms, at the new level of interest rates, will be acquired, if the economy settles into a new equilibrium.

[20] That is, the certainty equivalent of the future (random) income streams is reduced by more than just the reduction in the present discounted value of the expected returns.

[21] See the literature on the problems of used loan markets. This is just a standard application of Akerlof's (1970) "lemons" model.

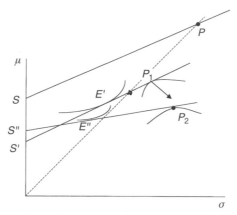

Figure 8.5 *Risk effect of monetary policy, loans marketable*
A large increase in interest rates increases the risk associated with existing loans, and this shrinks the opportunity set in further. At the same time, new loans become riskier, and this shifts the opportunity locus to the right. The higher probability of default associated with the worsening economic conditions is reflected in a movement in the loan portfolio curve down and to the right. The wealth and substitution effects both lead to less risk-taking, which implies less lending. The effects are thus reinforcing.

returns on lending are associated with a substitution effect. And the increased riskiness of any given loan means that to obtain the same risk profile, fewer loans need to be given.[22]

Figure 8.6 considers the case where the bank cannot market its existing loan portfolio. (Outsiders will assume that the bank will try to sell off its worse performing loans, or, more accurately, those loans where the true value, based on its inside information, is most markedly below what would be the market value, based on more widely observable characteristics. Knowing this, buyers of loans from the bank will subject them to a discount, called the "lemons premium."[23]) The point $S$ then represents the mean and standard deviation that the bank would face if it took all of its new funds, and put them into T-bills, the point $P$ the mean and standard

---

[22] Moreover, the flatter slope of the line from $S$ to the opportunity locus implies choosing a loan portfolio to the right of the original point, which is normally associated with greater risk, as we noted earlier. At a higher level of risk of each loan, the number of loans to obtain a given level of risk will be lower.

[23] See Akerlof (1970) and Greenwald (1986).

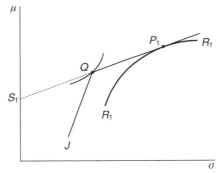

Figure 8.6 *Risk effect of monetary policy, no secondary market for loans*
An increase in interest rates lowers asset values and increases uncertainty (risk). Given the changed environment, the quantity and the
characteristics of the loans held at point $Q$, which were carried over
from past periods, would no longer be optimal, if markets for used
loans were perfect (e.g., if there were no information asymmetries
between the bank originally making the loans and others). However,
if the bank wanted to sell some of its risky assets and increase its
holdings of T-bills at this point, it could not, or it could only do so by
selling loans at a large discount. Hence the bank's opportunity locus is
$JQP_1$ (in the figure, only the new loan opportunity locus $R_1R_1$ after the
increase in risk is depicted). Under these circumstances, no additional
funds would go into risky assets, i.e., no new loans would be made.

deviation that the bank would face if it took all of its new funds
and put them into loans (in an efficient portfolio). There is a kink
in the opportunity locus at $S$: the bank can reduce its holdings of
risky assets only by disposing of its current assets, at a "lemons
premium." An increase in the interest rate moves the whole curve
over. Now, the increased risk associated with the current portfolio
has an even greater adverse effect on the lending of banks. Indeed,
the bank might have liked to have sold some of its portfolio of existing loans, were it not for the "lemons premium" (see figure 8.6).
Instead, it stays at the kink, putting any new deposits into T-bills.

## Summary

In short, higher interest rates affect not only the demand for loans,
but also the supply, through effects on asset values through several

channels: (1) direct impacts on the value of long-term debt instruments held in the bank's portfolio; (2) decreases in the value of loans, as a result of increased probability of bankruptcy as a result of increased firm payments to creditors on short-term loans; (3) decreases in the value of loans as a result of increased probability of bankruptcy, as a result of changed behavior of borrowers, resulting from their lower net worth and higher interest payments[24]; (4) increased uncertainty associated with the banks' existing portfolio, resulting from imperfect information concerning each borrower's asset position; and (5) increased risk associated with new lending.

### Franchise value effects

Banks (like all firms) are affected by the prospect of continuing in business. Part of the cost of bankruptcy is the loss of the present discounted value of future profits. Increases in interest rates typically reduce the expected present discounted value of future profits – and thus reduce the cost of bankruptcy, and thus lead to increased risk taking on the part of firms. The impact on banks (and on bank lending) on theoretical grounds is ambiguous: the induced risk taking on the part of firms means that the riskiness of the banks' existing portfolio has increased; and there is also an increase in the risk associated with new lending. This by itself should lead to less lending. But the effective reduction of the cost of bankruptcy of the bank (since the losses in future profits it encounters were it to go bankrupt are correspondingly smaller) means that it is willing to undertake greater risk. We suspect that the former effect would normally dominate the latter, so that the *net* franchise value effect is to reduce lending activity.

### Summary of effects of monetary policy on the supply of credit

Traditional monetary policy emphasizes the impact of monetary policy on aggregate demand, through impacts on investment induced through changes in interest rates, as indicated by changes in T-bill rates. We noted in part I that this is less than half the story:

---

[24] E.g. of the kind that Stiglitz and Weiss (1981) emphasized.

monetary policy also affects the *supply of funds* available for lending, and with credit rationing, it is this effect alone, not changes in interest rates on T-bills, which matters. Even if there is not credit rationing, the spread can change, so that the impacts on borrowing, e.g. for investment purposes, may be greater or less than what we might have expected from changes in T-bills alone. In this chapter, we have amplified the discussion of the substitution and wealth effects of, for instance, a change in reserve requirements, by taking into account the general equilibrium impacts, through changes in the relative attractiveness of T-bills, long-term government bonds and loans, caused by changes in interest rates, perceived risk, and franchise value; and by changes in the level of deposits and asset values induced by the changes in interest rates (and thus in the wealth and availability of funds for lending of banks). While the latter effects augment the first-round impacts (tighter monetary policy leads to higher interest rates which reduce asset values and levels of deposits), the former effects are more ambiguous. Consider the impact of tighter monetary policy. In equilibrium, bank holdings of T-bills decrease with higher interest rates, thus buffering the direct impact, but there may be an increase in the relative attractiveness of long-term government bonds, which increases the direct impact. Spreads will adjust to accommodate these changes. Because asset price and deposit effects can be large, the general equilibrium effects can be substantially larger than the first-round effects, but the magnitude depends on the particular circumstances of the banking system.

## Monetary policy and the theory of the firm

So far, we have analyzed how monetary policy affects the supply of credit – both its availability and its terms. There is an equally fundamental question: how does credit affect the level of economic activity?

### Credit rationing

In the case of the credit rationing regimes, the answer is obvious. Firms are unable to obtain the funds that they would like either to finance production or investment; hence they must curtail one or the other, or both. While traditional monetary analysis has focused on the impact of monetary policy on aggregate demand, it has failed to discuss the important effects through *aggregate supply*, which are likely to dominate in small open economies; and it has also failed to take note of the impacts on demand resulting from the increased probability of bankruptcy.

If firms cannot obtain the credit they need to finance expansion of production, or even current levels of production, output (and presumably employment) will be lower than it otherwise would be. Small open economies in principle face a horizontal demand curve for their products (once the exchange rate is fixed appropriately), so they should not face any aggregate demand problems. Economic fluctuations, at least over the intermediate term, should be related to problems on the supply side.

## No credit rationing

But even when firms can get as much finance as they want, changes in the terms at which credit is made available seem, at times, to have large effects. In some cases, this seems anomalous. Given the uncertainties about costs and benefits, is it likely that a change in twenty-five or fifty basis points will shift many projects from being profitable to unprofitable, especially in a world with highly imperfect information, where judgments about the desirability of projects are not that fine-tuned? Some of the observed effects are related to concomitant changes in credit availability, the effects of which are clearly palpable. It should also be noted that even if credit constraints are not currently binding, the possibility (or probability) that they may be binding in the not too distant future will affect firm behavior. But there are other reasons why increases in interest rates may discourage production (and investment).

The reasons for these supply-side problems follow closely our analysis of bank behavior. In neoclassical models, production is simply a matter of engineering. Firms produce up to the point where the wage is equal to the value of the marginal product of labor, and similarly for any other factor. We argue that because of lags of production and incomplete contracting, there is always risk in production. Perfect risk markets do not exist for the absorption and distribution of these risks. While widely held shares in major corporations do a reasonably good job of distributing risk, even then there are limits. As mentioned before, even large firms rely relatively little on new equity issues for finance. For small or medium-sized firms, risk divestiture is even more incomplete. As a result, firms are sensitive to the risk consequences of their actions. The more they produce, the greater the risk they bear. Higher interest rates have adverse effects on firms' cash flow, implicitly increasing the likelihood of bankruptcy (at any given level of production and other parameters). The reasons stated earlier explain why firms cannot simply undo the damage caused by monetary authorities by recapitalization.[25]

If firms are (or act) risk averse, an increase in the interest rate today can have larger effects if it is expected to persist. (This is in contrast to the substitution effects; a temporary lowering of the interest rate may lead to larger intertemporal substitution effects than a longer-term change.) If there is uncertainty about the length of time that the interest rates will remain high, and if there is no fixed date of termination, if the market believes the reversal of the high interest rate will follow a Poisson process, then not only will the initial impact be large, the wealth effects will become larger as time goes on. (With a Poisson process, the expected future duration, given that the high interest rate policy is in force today, is the same as it was when it was originally announced.) By contrast, if individuals believe that the high interest rates will prevail for, say, two years, then there will be an immediate *firm* wealth effect, depressing production and investment immediately, with consequences persisting long after interest rates have been increased, and possibly even after they have returned to their normal level. There are, in short, large hysteresis effects.

---

[25] There are further effects which we have also described in the context of banking: asset value and franchise effects. The firm may have assets (like land) the value of which decreases as the interest rate increases; hence the value of these assets as a source of collateral decreases; hence the amount of credit that the bank is willing to extend decreases (and/or the terms at which it is willing to make the credit available worsens).

This latter point is important: changes in prices (interest rates) in neo-classical models have impacts on periods before and after temporary changes go into effect; production or demand is moved out of (or into) the periods from adjacent periods. As a result, the total impact – looked at over a longer horizon – may be relatively small. The policies may nonetheless be highly desirable, if in one period the economy is facing an excess demand and another a shortage of demand.

But in the model here, the impacts, through the *firm* wealth effect, of interest rate changes out of the period in which they are imposed are not only persistent, but reinforcing. The recognition that the firm's real wealth will be (or is likely to be) eroded in the future by high interest rates discourages production and risk taking today; and after the firm's net worth has been eroded by high interest rates, the effects are persistent, lasting long after interest rates have decreased to normal levels. There are adverse effects both directly (through increased payments to the creditors), and indirectly through the resulting reduced level of production and thereby lower expected level of profits.

This highlights one of the contrasts between our analysis of the risk averse economy, and the standard neo-classical model. There, wealth effects do not matter; they simply reflect a redistribution – higher interest rates mean creditors receive more, debtors pay more; but distribution does not matter. In our analysis, these redistributions do matter; the increased expenditure on the part of the gainers does not offset the reduced expenditures on the part of the losers.

A focus on risk also highlights several other unintended adverse effects of high interest rates, affecting both aggregate demand and aggregate supply. On the demand side, we observed in the previous section that much trade occurred accompanied by finance. An increase in a trading partners' bankruptcy probability (as result of the higher interest rates) makes him a less reliable trading partner, not only because of the higher likelihood that he might not repay the loan, but equally important, because other terms of the contract may not be fulfilled. This became dramatically clear in the East Asia crisis, where in spite of the marked change in exchange rates, accompanied by falling domestic prices, export sales did not boom, at least to the extent expected. In some cases, the explanation proffered was that importers worried about delivery: the high interest rates and other adverse economic conditions had sufficiently raised bankruptcy probabilities. A firm worrying about a delivery for a Christmas season would not place an order, even if the price advantage was substantial.

We noted earlier that changes in interest rates have variable effects on different assets, but that outsiders might have a difficult time ascertaining how each firm's balance sheet was affected. Thus large changes in interest rates will be accompanied by large increases in uncertainty about the wealth of different firms. This increased uncertainty may both lead to a cutback in credit and an increase in interest rates charged. Risk averse banks will require higher spreads to compensate them for the increased risk.

## The many aspects of the risk averse behavior of firms

We have argued so far that firms act in a risk averse manner, that they may be credit constrained, that cash flow and net worth effects can be important, and that changes in monetary policy can affect firm behavior through making them more risk averse, through increasing the risk associated with particular activities (e.g. producing at a given level), and through adverse effects on cash flow and net worth.

Every element of firm behavior can thus be affected by monetary policy. In a series of papers, we have explored the implications for employment, price determination, wage setting, investment, and inventories.[26] We do not want to repeat the arguments made there, except to highlight some of the channels through which monetary policy exerts its influence in our general theory of risk averse and credit constrained firms.

Assume that tighter monetary policy reduces the availability of funds to a firm. It may not have enough cash (credit) to maintain

[26] See Greenwald and Stiglitz (1987a, 1989a, 1989b, 1990a, 1990b, 1991c, 1993a, 1995), Greenwald, Kohn and Stiglitz (1990), and Greenwald, Salinger and Stiglitz (1990).

working capital at its previous level, i.e. to purchase inputs to maintain its previous level of production. There is a large increase in the implicit cost of capital. The firm will be induced to reduce its inventories, as a way of obtaining quick liquidity. Inventories may be highly sensitive to monetary policy, not so much because of the changes in the real interest rates charged on the loans that are made available, but because of the reduced availability of funds.[27]

Similarly, consider what happens as the economy goes into a recession, when the monetary authorities do not take quick enough action. The unanticipated slowdown in the economy means that prices are lower *than they were anticipated to be* (that is, there may still be positive inflation, but the inflation rate is lower than it otherwise would have been). Thus, the real payments of borrowers (whose debt, remember, is not indexed) to creditors has increased, and borrowers (firms) are accordingly worse off. They wish to shed risk, to hold less of all risky assets, including inventories. Standard theory argues that firms ought to increase inventory accumulation as they go into a slowdown– it enables production smoothing, which lowers long-run production costs. The empirical evidence suggests the contrary.[28] Our analysis provides an explanation for why that might be so. And it explains why looser monetary policy *may* be able to offset these effects, not just through the greater availability of credit to finance inventories, but through the higher rate of inflation (lower rate of deflation), induced through greater credit expansion – and through the real wealth effects on firms that that generates.

Similarly, standard neo-classical theory suggests that as firms contract production, moving along a given production function, the real wage should increase, and significantly so. The evidence

---

[27] Empirically, it is often hard to distinguish among these different hypotheses. Those who are skeptical of the role of credit rationing might claim that the real problem is that borrowers simply were not willing to borrow at the interest rates at which the bank would have been willing to lend, given the risk that the bank perceives. There has, in fact, been a plethora of literature verifying that credit rationing is an important phenomenon, especially for SMEs, and it is these enterprises which account for a disproportionately large share of economic fluctuations. For a sampling of the empirical research in this area, see Calomiris and Hubbard (1989), Mayer (1990), and Hubbard (1998).

[28] See Blinder and Maccini (1991).

is that it does not, and again, our theory provides an explanation. Competition is imperfect, and firms use low prices as a way of recruiting customers. They wish to spend more on this risky investment when the shadow price of capital is low. As the economy goes into a recession, the shadow price of capital increases, as we have seen, and firms are less willing to make these investments, i.e. they increase mark-ups, implying that real wages fall *relative* to marginal productivities. What happens to actual real wages is ambiguous, since marginal productivities are rising simultaneously.[29]

The effects which we have just described can be illustrated using the familiar heuristic from elementary textbooks of aggregate demand and supply.[30] Figure 8.7 shows a standard aggregate demand and supply curve with output on the horizontal axis and the price level on the vertical axis.[31] Panel a shows a first-round effect of monetary policy, shifting the aggregate demand curve to the left (the standard effect emphasized in traditional economics) *and* shifting the aggregate supply curve to the left. The impact on output is unambiguous: tighter monetary policy leads to a reduction in output. But its effect on the price level (or inflation) is more ambiguous, depending on the relative strength of the effects on aggregate demand and supply. Panel b shows some second-round effects as the higher interest rates stay in place: higher rates of bankruptcies shift the supply curve further to the left, and the increasing unreliability of suppliers shifts the demand curve further to the left as well. Again, the net effect is a further decrease in output, with a stronger presumption of adverse effects on prices (on the price level or inflation; that is, the supply-side effect is likely to be larger than the demand-side effect). Panel c shows the case of a small, open economy which faces a close to horizontal demand curve for its products. The entire impact on the economy is thus felt through the supply- side effects.

[29] For more extensive discussion of the concept of "customer markets," see Phelps and Winter (1970) and Phelps (1986).
[30] Since we are using the diagram only for illustrative purposes, we will not delineate precisely the assumptions which are required to define these curves.
[31] Many modern renditions of aggregate demand and supply put the rate of inflation (or the rate of wage increase) on the vertical axis. We slide over these distinctions here. See e.g. Stiglitz and Walsh (2002).

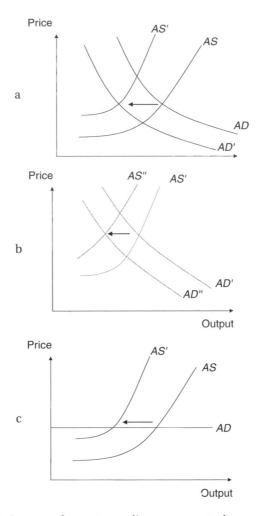

Figure 8.7 *Impacts of monetary policy on aggregate demand and supply*
   a   Tighter monetary policy
Reflected not only in a shift to the left of aggregate demand, but also of aggregate supply.
   b   A second-round effect
Further shifts in aggregate demand (as more firms become bankrupt, firms are viewed as less reliable suppliers) and aggregate supply.
   c   A small open economy
Impacts on monetary policy are mainly felt through a shift in the aggregate supply curve.

### Exchange rate effects

The discussion so far has analyzed how monetary policy affects firm behavior through a variety of channels – not just through the cost of capital, but through its availability, not just through changes in intertemporal prices, but through changes in firm wealth, not just directly, but indirectly, through impacts on the *uncertainty* associated with the value of a firm's net worth, and thereby on the availability of credit and its terms. We have noted that changes in monetary policy have marked effects not just on *interest rates*, but on *asset prices*, and these asset price changes have first-order consequences.

Monetary policy affects a whole variety of other *relative* prices, and these changes in turn have direct and indirect consequences. Among the most important of these changed prices in open economies are *exchange rates*. When there is a mismatch between liabilities and assets – when the liabilities of a firm are denominated in one currency while future revenues are denominated in another – then changes in exchange rates can have marked effects on balance sheets of firms, with all the firm wealth effects described earlier.[32] (There can be a similar impact on households and government.) Thus, monetary policy needs to be attentive to these consequences as well. If, as is usually presumed to be the case, increases in the interest rate lead to currency appreciation, then firms that are net foreign debtors are better off. Since in many developing countries, many firms are net foreign borrowers (and relatively few are net foreign creditors), these exchange rate induced wealth effects will attenuate the magnitude of the economic slowdown from raising interest rates. Peculiarly, some have argued that these *exchange rate* wealth effects not only dominate

---

[32] In principle, risk averse firms should purchase insurance against this risk. In practice, they often do not. The reason for this failure is a matter of some controversy. In part, it is because many firms *believe* that the government will act to maintain the exchange rate, particularly if there are enough firms who are highly exposed. IMF bail-outs, and the rhetoric that has been used to justify these bail-outs, has helped reinforce these beliefs. Imperfections of capital markets also play a role: the cost of "insurance" often seems high. Irrational expectations must surely play a role: the cost of insurance often seems especially high relative to the perceived likelihood of a devaluation.

the direct *interest rate asset* effects but are so large that they may actually offset the adverse direct effect, so that raising interest rates actually has a positive effect on the economy. The relative importance of these wealth effects played a significant role in the debate over monetary policy in the East Asia crisis, discussed later in chapter 13. In that episode, high interest rates were deliberately used to try to strengthen the exchange rate. It was argued that a continued weakening of the exchange rate would hurt firms greatly, more than offsetting the stimulation that lower exchange rates would have on exports. It turned out that the direct asset price effects and the other adverse effects were so large, and so adverse, that they absolutely dominated the exchange rate effect; indeed, in some instances, they were so large that the normal exchange rate effect did not even seem to be present.

### Monetary policy and credit interlinkages

Monetary policy operates directly upon banks. But its effects can be amplified through the effects on the risk averse, equity constrained producers-cum-financiers. A reduction of credit to a firm or an increase in the interest rate charged affects the willingness and ability of the firm to supply credit to its customers. As its customers are adversely affected, they transmit the monetary contraction on to their customers and so on around the economy.

But the impacts do not stop here. The higher interest rates charged by suppliers imply higher bankruptcy probabilities for these firms (even when they adjust their production optimally), and this in turn induces other suppliers of credit (e.g. banks) to cut back on their credit.

The process continues until a new equilibrium has been attained, with lower levels of credit by both inside and outside creditors, and a lower level of economic activity. In a sense, we are arguing here for a new form of *credit multiplier*. Traditional monetary economics has assumed, in effect, that the only source of credit is banks, and that banks are constrained in their lending by the magnitude of base money. Our analysis has challenged both assumptions. In many cases, banks hold government securities; how much they lend is thus a choice variable. It is not simply determined by constraints. The objective of monetary theory, in this context, is to understand how those choices are affected by monetary policy. And secondly, much of the credit in the economy is mediated not through banks but through firms. Our analysis has shown how the choices of credit supply by both banks and firms are interrelated. While the initial impact of monetary policy is on bank behavior, we show the interactive play between the choices made by banks, the choices made by firms in their role as providers of credit, and the choices made by firms in their role as producers. The initial actions of the monetary authorities are amplified through the system through the interlinkages among these choices.

## Monetary policy, households, and government

While we focus our attention in this book on the impact of monetary policy on the supply side of the economy through its impact on firms, we should also note that there are effects on households and government, and that our focus on *credit, balance sheet* and *cash flow* effects extends to these as well, though in the short run their impact is realized more through demand-side impacts than through supply-side effects. For instance, increased interest rates increase the incomes of households, but to the extent that they lead to lower asset prices, reduce their net worth, and in many circumstances the latter effect predominates: households will accordingly consume less. Lack of availability of credit will have an especially large effect in curtailing investments in consumer durables, like cars and houses.

The distinction we made earlier between the T-bill rate and the lending rate plays out here as well, though in different ways. Raising the T-bill rate increases incomes of retired individuals dependent on returns on their investment (especially since older people are likely to have a large fraction of their portfolio invested in bonds). This leads to higher consumption, partly offsetting the adverse impact on aggregate demand from reduced investment.

If the spread decreases, and if the interest elasticity of investment is low, it is conceivable that raising the deposit rate/T-bill rate may actually stimulate the economy.[33] More generally, interest rate changes can have markedly different effects on different households. To look at the matter from the converse side: very low interest rates can put great strain on households that derive their income from T-bills, and have large positive wealth effects on households that have invested in long-term bonds and stocks that increase in value. The adverse impact on consumption of the former may outweigh the positive impact on consumption of the latter, especially if the former are cash constrained.

Governments in developing countries (or even states in the United States) may face severe constraints on their ability to borrow.[34] These constraints may arise either because lenders are unwilling to lend, or for political or constitutional reasons. Cash flow effects and credit availability effects of monetary policy may again take on first-order importance. For instance, higher interest rates for governments with large amounts of short-term debt outstanding crowd out other forms of expenditure. Even were the government to maintain the overall level of expenditure, the net effect on aggregate demand could be negative. The decline in aggregate demand in turn may lead to a decline in aggregate income, with a concomitant reduction in tax revenue. If the government then has to reduce expenditure (or increase taxes) to avoid an increase in the deficit, the induced *fiscal* effect of tight monetary policy exacerbates the contractionary impact.

More generally, in developing countries, there is evidence that fiscal policy is pro-cyclical.[35] It is not because government officials, however, do not understand the basics of macro-economic policy. Rather, it is because they are credit constrained. When they go into an economic downturn – and need deficit financing to stimulate their economies – private lenders reduce the availability of funding. They are, in effect, forced to reduce their deficits, exacerbating the economic downturn. While monetary policy may not be able

---

[33] Thailand, in spring 2001, used arguments similar to this in increasing interest rates.
[34] See Eaton and Gersovitz (1981).
[35] See Gavin et al. (1996); Easterly, Islam and Stiglitz (2000a, 2000b).

to undo fully these effects, it is important that the monetary authorities be aware of them, in formulating their economic forecasts and in estimating the overall impact of their policies.

*Expectations* on the part of lenders can play an important role in determing the magnitude of these effects. We noted earlier that an increase in interest rates facing firms with high levels of indebtedness increases their probability of default; lenders respond by reducing the availability of funds and/or increasing the interest rate charged still further. So too for governments. As monetary policy tightens and governments have to pay higher interest rates, market judgments of the likelihood of a default increase. Hence, creditors reduce the supply of credit and increase the interest rates charged. A vicious downward cycle is started – one which may make the worries self-fulfilling. The induced *fiscal* effect described above leads to a slowdown of the economy and increased deficits, enhancing the likelihood of a default.

Market responses to the large increases in interest rates following Brazil's devaluation in January 1999 illustrate the contrasting strands. The IMF pushed Brazil to have higher interest rates, claiming that the high interest rates would restore confidence. (Their analysis of market psychology did not seem to run much deeper than that.) Many analysts, especially in the West, reacted in a quite contrary way: the immediate impact of the high interest rates was to increase the size of the government's deficit, which had become emblematic of the nature of the country's problems. The high interest rates, from their perspective, weakened confidence. On the other hand, many investors in Brazil were particularly worried that the devaluation would set off an inflationary episode, and they saw the high interest rate as a signal that that would not be the case. For them, the high interest rate did help confidence. Some of the economists at the World Bank had urged upon Brazil an alternative strategy: adopt an inflation-targeted monetary policy. Given the low level of inflation and high unemployment, this would have allowed a lower interest rate – reassuring those who focused on the size of the deficit – at the same time as providing reassurance to those who worried about inflation. This is the policy which Brazil eventually adopted.

## Monetary policy and the liquidity trap

One of Keynes' fundamental insights was the ineffectiveness of monetary policy in stimulating an economy in a deep depression. Part of Keynes' argument rested on the liquidity trap. As interest rates fell, the precautionary demand for money increased, since investors worried more and more about an increase in the interest rate, which would decrease the value of long-term bonds. The consequence was that the monetary authorities might find it difficult if not impossible to push interest rates down. More generally, the inefficacy of monetary policy in a deep recession (in contrast to its ability to slow down an economy facing inflation) was highlighted by an analogy: it was like pushing on a string.

The diagrammatic depiction of Keynes' idea was simple enough: there was, in effect, a horizontal demand curve for money at a particular interest rate, so that no matter how much liquidity was pumped into the system, households would be willing to hold it, so long as interest rates remained below a threshold level (figure 8.8). The intellectual foundations of Keynes' argument for a liquidity trap have long been questioned, especially once it is recognized that even if one worried that the price of long-term bonds might fall, one can hold on to T-bills, rather than money. (Questions were also raised about the underlying expectation foundations; if individuals expect the short-term rate to rise next period,

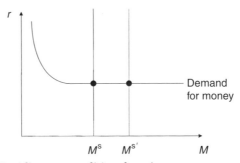

Figure 8.8 *Liquidity trap, traditional version*
With a horizontal demand curve for money (in the relevant region), increasing the money supply has no effect on interest rates.

then this will be reflected in today's long-term rate, which should simply be equal to the average of the short-term rates.)

Our model provides another explanation for the inefficacy of monetary policy in the face of a recession. If banks are pessimistic about the returns to loans, or if they face (or worry that they will face) problems in meeting capital adequacy requirements, they may decide to hold government bonds rather than loans; an easing of monetary policy may not result in more lending, simply more holding of long-term government bonds or T-bills. Some would argue that this is precisely what happened to Japan in the 1990s. Monetary policy affects the economy through the ability and willingness of banks to make loans. It is banks' unwillingness to make additional loans, even in response to lowering government T-bill rates or reducing lending constraints (e.g. associated with reserve requirements, which in many cases are simply not binding), which gives rise to the ineffectiveness of monetary policy, a form of liquidity trap. Figure 8.9 illustrates a case where the wealth effect of lower interest rates offsets the substitution effect for banks, so that no additional lending occurs. As depicted, this may be an unusual case where the elasticity of demand for money is relatively low and the bank originally held much of its assets in T-bills. But there are a number of further factors, several

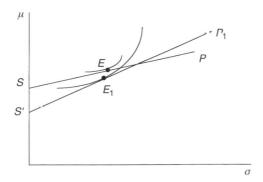

Figure 8.9 *Liquidity trap, new version*
With banks holding on to large amounts of T-bills, lowering interest rates does not necessarily lead to more lending. The wealth effect from lower interest rates may offset the substitution effect.

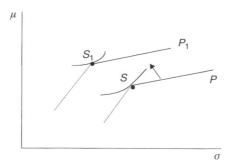

Figure 8.10 *Liquidity trap, corner solution*
  In the situation depicted in figure 8.6, banks would like to sell some
  of their existing loan portfolio, but cannot, or the discount that they
  receive if they do so makes it unattractive for them to do so. Lowering the interest rate on T-bills still leaves them in the corner solution.
  (In the figure, lower interest rates shift the opportunity locus up because there is a large elasticity of demand for deposits. The analysis
  does not depend on this or on whether the opportunity locus shifts
  to the left or right.)

of which we have already discussed, which make such an outcome, where lending is not increased, more likely.

Part of the underlying problem arises from the fact that it is
hard to force interest rates to be negative; people can hold cash
rather than T-bills or demand deposits with negative nominal
rates. But this means that if there is deflation, T-bills yield a positive expected return, even if the nominal interest rate is zero;
and this positive expected return may be sufficiently high to
induce banks simply not to lend, given their perceived risks of
lending.

The problems can be particularly severe if regulatory authorities
do not treat long-term government bonds as risky – simply because
there is no credit risk. Even when T-bill rates are forced down close
to zero, long-term rates may remain high. When banks face problems with capital adequacy constraints, holding long-term bonds
becomes a particularly attractive way of risk taking. The bank earns
a spread between the deposit rate and the rate on long-term bonds,
which it gets to book as income – even though the return, in part,
is compensation for the risk of a loss in capital value.

For banks that already have large amounts of long-term bonds in their portfolio, lowering interest rates – including the long-term interest rate – has ambiguous effects. Sometimes the effects may be very weak – a form of liquidity trap. But at other times the effects can be quite strong.

Figure 8.10 repeats figure 8.6, with the bank at a corner solution, wishing to sell some of its existing portfolio of loans, if only it could do so without paying a "lemons premium." Lowering government interest rates shifts the opportunity locus as depicted. In this case, the bank is assumed not to have many long-term bonds, so that the negative income effect of lower returns dominates any positive effect from increased asset values. The bank continues to operate at the kink: no new lending occurs.

Figure 8.11 shows a case, however, where lowering interest rates does work. To the extent that the bank has long-term bonds, the lowering of interest rates has a positive wealth effect, and this effect may predominate – as it did in the 1993 recovery in the US. Even if the bank was originally at the kink, it is induced to move markedly away from it.

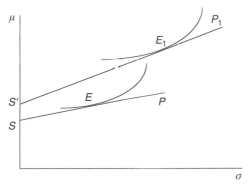

Figure 8.11 *How lowering interest rates can sometimes have large positive effects*

If banks have large portfolios of long-term government bonds, which increase in value as interest rates on government bonds fall, then the positive wealth effect reinforces the substitution effect, leading to marked increases in lending.

## Why monetary policy?

The theory of monetary policy that we have presented here provides part of the explanation for why governments do, and should, rely so heavily on monetary policy for stabilization; but it also highlights the costs and limitations of doing so.

One major advantage, in comparison with direct government expenditures, is that it imposes far lower informational burdens on the government. It uses market mechanisms – banks – to allocate the additional expenditures necessary to correct the under-employment of the economy's resources.[36] It thus employs their wealth of information and their incentives to ensure that the additional investments are allocated efficiently.[37]

A second major reason for using monetary policy is that there may be large, and at times, highly predictable multipliers. An increase in base money leads to a multiple credit expansion. And, at least in the model of restrictive banking where banks enjoy profits from the difference between lending and deposit rates, the effects can be realized even if banks hold T-bills in their portfolios. For the increased net worth of the banks induces them to lend more. Especially when credit is constrained and firms are cash constrained (as they may be when the economy is emerging from a recession), the expansion of credit can have large multiplier effects, not only on aggregate demand but also on aggregate supply, and not just through the interest rate channel (as we have just seen).

These supply-side effects are particularly worth drawing attention to, because they imply that economic activity can be increased without the threat of inflationary pressures (or, in any case, with less of a threat). Indeed, as we have noted, in small open

---

[36] One should not make too much of this point: in many cases, under-investment in public assets is sufficiently great that there is ample room for increased expenditures yielding high returns, often far in excess of that obtained at the margin in the private sector.

[37] But one also needs to bear in mind that credit markets are not auction markets; banks do not ask: what investment projects yield the highest social returns? They look only to their repayments, ignoring the surplus that accrues to equity owners. In general, the resource allocations are not even constrained Pareto-optimal. See Greenwald and Stiglitz (1986a).

economies, weaknesses in economic activity may be more related to supply-side problems than to demand-side problems, so that accordingly, it makes sense to focus on policies which operate on the supply side – and which operate in the short run.[38]

But these advantages are mirrored in the limitations. One we have already discussed: monetary policy may be ineffective, because of the liquidity trap that arises if banks simply hold more T-bills; monetary policy then becomes like pushing against a string.

However, there are two further problems: monetary policy is distortionary, and the impacts of monetary policy are not always predictable. The distortionary nature of monetary policy has become more and more important as financial markets have developed. In standard theory, interest rates are just intertemporal prices; for some reason, markets do not set these intertemporal prices at the "right level," and somehow monetary authorities are able to control these intertemporal prices, setting them at the right level. Thus, when done properly, monetary policy, through the use of market mechanisms, not only ensures full employment, but also the efficient allocation of resources intertemporally. (To be sure, in all of this, there is a certain amount of hand-waving. After all, there is *some* market failure(s) that gave rise to the need for government macroeconomic intervention – often asserted to be rigidities in wages and prices. No pretense is usually made that monetary policy corrects the *original* source of market failure. Thus, we are, by definition, in the world of the second best. But normally, there is also even no pretense of trying to establish that monetary policy is the optimal second-best policy, or even of showing that, given the market failures, monetary policy results in efficient

---

[38] Thus, traditional supply-siders have focused on policies designed to increase investment; these have supply-side effects which are significant in the long run. Some supply-side economists have focused on labor, but there is little evidence of large elasticities, either in the short or long run. Note that increased *public* investment, too, can have large long-run supply-side effects. There are, however, also fiscal policies which can have supply-side effects in the short run, e.g. government orders accompanied by finance, which simultaneously provide funds to firms and reduce the risks associated with production. These policies were important in the Second World War.

intertemporal allocation of resources. These issues are simply not raised.)

Our analysis has begun with the observation that intertemporal resource allocation is not done through the normal price mechanism (analogous to auction markets). Financial institutions, and especially banks, are involved in the allocation of credit – in screening, monitoring, and enforcement. But not all credit is mediated through banks, as we have noted several times. Monetary policy has its most direct and largest impacts on sectors (firms) that rely on banks as a source of funds; thus monetary policy induces more variability in economic activity – and therefore greater costs – among say, SMEs, in industries like construction, that cannot tap into commercial paper and medium- and long-term bond markets. Moreover, if there is credit rationing, then higher-risk loan categories may be completely excluded from the market, as discussed in part I.

By contrast, large international firms can switch their funding from one country to another. To be sure, the larger such shifts are, the less the impact on SMEs from any credit contraction, but so too the less overall impact will the contraction of the domestic credit supply have. As financial markets develop, the smaller the multipliers (the less effective monetary policy) and thus the larger the actions required to obtain a given effect, the greater are the distortions associated with the use of monetary policy.

In short, there are real costs to relying on monetary policy; these costs may be especially marked in economies facing high volatility and weak securities markets, and they may be even greater in the long run than in the short because a high variability of interest rates and credit availability makes borrowing very risky, inducing firms to have lower debt–equity ratios. In the absence of good securities markets, this forces firms to rely more on self-financing. Thus, economies which rely more on monetary policy for macro-stabilization, and hence have more variability in interest rates and credit availability, may be characterized by less efficiency in the overall allocation of capital – greater disparities between the marginal returns to investment in different firms. (It is unlikely, for instance, that Korea or the other economies in East Asia could have achieved growth anywhere near what they did had firms had to rely on their own funds for expansion.[39])

### Exchange rate policy

But as bad as these distortionary effects of monetary policy are, they are exacerbated when monetary policy is used to maintain exchange rate stability; for such usage entails raising interest rates to extremely high levels when the economy faces a currency crisis; since such crises typically are followed by an economic downturn, interest rates thus move in a pro-cyclical rather than countercyclical way, forcing firms with even moderate levels of short-term or variable interest rate debt into bankruptcy, which in turn has both high private and social costs, not only the direct costs of the bankruptcy proceedings, but the larger costs associated with the destruction of informational and organizational capital. And again, risk averse firms in open economies which rely on such mechanisms will have even greater incentives to limit their borrowings – and their growth.

It might be argued, won't failing to stabilize the exchange rate have similar adverse effects, and doesn't one therefore face a trade off? The answer is, "not necessarily," and if there is a trade-off, greater weight needs to be attached to the costs of interest variability than has been the case in the past. *In the short run*, an increase in interest rates may not strengthen the exchange rate, if it induces a more than offsetting increase in default probabilities.[40] And a weakening of the exchange rate may have minimal effects on economic activity, if firms have engaged in prudential borrowing policies, obtaining cover for exchange rate risk to the extent needed; export firms, of course, automatically have partial

---

[39] The growth literature of the 1960s explored the dynamics of economies in which firms were restricted to their own retained earnings for expansion (the so-called Rosa Luxemburg model). See, for instance, Dobell (1968).

[40] The discussion above explained why an increase in interest rates increases the default probability. Even if the actions of the borrower were to remain unchanged, there would be a higher probability of default, and there are real costs to default, so potentially fewer resources left over for lenders. In addition, however, borrowers' behavior may be affected (the adverse incentive effect) in ways which result in lower returns to creditors.

cover, since their revenues (in terms of domestic currency) rise when the exchange rate falls. To be sure, to the extent that governments bear risk, e.g. associated with bank failures, there will be inadequate incentives to obtain such cover, but the appropriate response is to recognize the danger, and design appropriate regulations (as Malaysia did), not to reinforce the "bad" behavior (as the IMF has repeatedly done) by bailing out those who have failed to obtain cover.[41]

In the long run, however, the argument is even more compelling. For firms need not have foreign exchange exposure. They can obtain cover. Artificially supporting an exchange rate – especially when the ostensible reason is to protect firms who have uncovered positions – induces a moral-hazard problem, that is, reduces the incentives to obtain cover and increases the incentives to have an exposed position. When firms collectively have such an exposure, and government policy responds by protecting the exposed firms by raising interest rates to high levels, there is a clear externality – a cost borne by all those who have borrowed, including those who have chosen not to have foreign exchange exposure. There is a discrepancy between *social* and *private risk*. By contrast, the only way for firms to protect themselves against highly variable interest rates and credit availability is not to borrow, or borrow as much, and this imposes large economic costs, given the imperfections in equity markets which exist in all economies, even the most advanced (and are themselves explained by informational imperfections, as we showed), but are especially important in developing countries.

Some of the adverse effects of monetary policy can be offset by targeted lending programs, e.g. for small businesses or agriculture. In the case of interest rate policies used to shore up exchange rates, these special credit windows may not have a significant adverse effect on the efficacy of the policy itself; that is, to the extent

---

[41] Remarkably, for long periods of time, the IMF reinforced the conviction that there would be a bail-out, by emphasizing the necessity to avoid the fall in exchange rate *because firms had not obtained adequate cover for their exchange rate risk.* In effect, it told those in the country, if enough of you do not obtain cover, we will provide public funds for an intervention that will maintain the exchange rate, or at least reduce the magnitude of its fall! They thus helped coordinate an equilibrium in which most firms did not obtain cover.

that the high interest rate policy is intended to draw new capital into the country and prevent capital flight, it can still do so. Indeed, by reducing the adverse macro-economic consequences, it may lessen the probability of default, thereby increasing the effectiveness of the policy. It is simply misguided to argue against such policies on the grounds that they introduce a distortion in the allocation of capital. On the contrary, such special windows reduce the distortion that arises from the use of monetary policy, given the imperfections of information that force certain categories of firms to rely more heavily on short-term debt finance. It should be noted, however, that when the object of monetary policy is to contract the level of economic activity, while such special windows may reduce the distortions associated with such policies, they may also reduce the efficacy of monetary policy. It is precisely because credit is mediated through banks that monetary policy has such large effects, and alternative sources of credit (whether domestic financial markets, foreign banks, or special government windows) accordingly weaken its effects.

### Distributional impacts

Because the impacts of monetary policy are concentrated in certain sectors of the economy, those in those sectors bear the brunt of the costs of adjustment. And often, these are among those less able to bear those costs; typically, they cannot obtain *insurance* against the risks which high interest rates present to them. Small businesses and farms, for instance, must rely on bank finance, and they thus bear more of the brunt of high interest rates.

To be sure, any price change has distributional as well as allocative effects. But given how credit (capital) is allocated, the distributional effects perhaps should be given more weight, especially since the distributional impacts can have such allocative consequences. To give but one example: the huge increases in interest rates in the United States in the late 1970s and early 1980s decreased the value of the assets of the S & Ls; it led many to have negative net worth. The negative net worth in turn had large implications for their behavior – it induced them to undertake many risky investments, eventually culminating in the S & L bail-out. It was not just the huge costs to taxpayers: resources had been badly allocated. And all of this can be traced to the high interest rate policies. (To be sure, there were ways that these effects could have been mitigated, through either tightened regulation or subsidies.[42] But both of these have their costs, and need to be included as part of the cost of using monetary policy instruments.)

### Summary: the adverse distributional and distortionary impacts of monetary policy

In short, while under certain circumstances monetary policy can be a powerful instrument for stabilization (and under other circumstances it may be ineffective), even when it is effective, governments need to be aware of the high economic costs associated with the excessive reliance on this instrument. By the same token, to criticize measures that are intended to mitigate some of its worst distortionary impacts (and some of its impacts with the most adverse distributional consequences) as interfering with the efficiency of the market mechanism is simply wrong-headed: it demonstrates a lack of understanding of the nature of the credit allocation mechanism.

There is an important link between the problem first discussed, the lack of efficacy, and the problems just discussed, the distortionary and distributional consequences. There was always an easy answer to the charge that monetary policy was *relatively* ineffective. So long as it had some effect, it could still be used. Indeed, some might even say it became a better instrument for fine-tuning. If slight changes in interest rates or money supply led to huge changes in the level of economic activity, monetary policy would not be a good instrument for fine-tuning. If the effects are weak and one wants to have a large effect, then one simply spins the dial some more.

But if changes in interest rates have distributional and distortionary consequences, then large changes are likely to have large adverse effects. We have seen this repeatedly – and will discuss this

---

[42] Note that an up-front subsidy might have been far less costly than the bail-outs.

at greater length in chapter 13 (on the East Asian crisis). Large changes in interest rates force firms into bankruptcy, and thus have impacts that are long-lived. They impose real damage on the economy, and large hardship on many of the poorest in it. And when used repeatedly and regularly as instruments of macro-economic control, they force firms to increasingly rely on self-finance, and weaken sectors that traditionally rely on bank finance.

### Predictability and irreversibility

Two final cautions[43] against excessive reliance on monetary policy as a mechanism for controlling the economy are the lack of predictability of its effects and their irreversibility. One of the reasons that monetary authorities were attracted to monetarism is that it was a theory that contended that the effects of monetary policy were highly predictable and easily reversible. All one needed to control the economy was to control the aggregate supply of money. There was a simple relationship between the money supply and the level of nominal income. Increase the money supply and GDP increases proportionately; reduce it, and it is reduced proportionately. But even more broadly, the traditional approach to monetary economics suggested that its effects were highly predictable: the demand curve for money was stable, implying that there was a stable *LM* curve. If money (as conventionally defined) was what mattered, presumably it would be only the aggregate supply of money that mattered. But even as monetary economists have moved away from monetarism, partly because of the observed instability in velocity, they have continued to focus on simple metrics, like "the" interest rate (the T-bill rate or discount rate), and "the" intertemporal price.

But credit, as we have argued, is highly differentiated. A line of credit to one individual is a far from perfect substitute for a line of credit to another. Money is anonymous. Credit is clearly not. If one bank has free reserves, and another does not, the free reserves cannot simply be transferred from one to another; and an increase

---

[43] This list is not meant to be comprehensive, only to emphasize some aspects of monetary policy that have not been adequately discussed elsewhere, at least in the policy literature. For instance, monetary policy often operates with long lags.

in, say, reserve requirements, which if all banks were identical (and therefore each had a pro rata share of the free reserves) would have no effect on loan supply, will in the case where some banks are fully loaned up and others not, have a marked effect.

We have noted that in economic downturns associated with a financial crisis, not only may it be difficult to induce banks to lend more, but also how much additional lending may be generated from a given expansion in the monetary base may be highly uncertain. This is in part because the impacts depend not only on what has happened to banks in general, but also on the distribution of the wealth changes. There may be marked differences in losses incurred by different banks. Differential information imposes a further problem: banks may have a better view of their *expected* losses than does the central bank, and individual banks have good reasons to hide what information they have.

### Predictability and measuring the impact of policies

Because of the long lags between monetary policy changes and the full impacts being realized by the economy, monetary authorities focus on intermediate variables. (If the links were instantaneous, then the monetary authorities would simply set the policies to attain the desired level of inflation or employment or growth.) In earlier decades, they focused on the money supply; more recently, on changes in the T-bill rate. As we have repeatedly emphasized, the links between money supply and credit, or between T-bill rates and lending rates, are weak. They may move in tandem "normally"; but it is when matters are *not normal* – when the economy is facing a crisis or an episode of inflation – that macro-economic policy becomes important. It is just at those times that the usual relationships break down. It is the supply of credit and the terms on which it is available which matter for the level of economic activity. Focusing on T-bill rates or the money supply may do in normal times; but not when a shock has changed the underlying structural relationships. Compounding the problems facing policymakers is the fact that even the average *lending rate* may not provide a good measure of the "cost of capital"; for if lending rates rise simply because of an increase in risk *and* information were symmetric and lenders and borrowers risk neutral, then higher lending rates would not be contractionary. The problem is that it is difficult to ascertain the extent to which an increase in spreads is due to an increase in risk or in risk aversion (or an increase in asymmetries of information or differences in beliefs).

### Predictability, non-linearities, and irreversibilities

The problems of *unpredictability* interact and, in some cases, compound the problems noted in the previous subsections. One of the sources of unpredictability arises from the non-linearities in the impacts: they become very large when interest rates become so high that firms are forced into bankruptcy. Even the nature of the effects may change: while small increases in interest rates, which leave bankruptcy rates relatively unaffected, may induce capital to move into a country, large increases in interest rates, which vastly increase bankruptcy rates, may induce capital to leave a country. But monetary authorities may lack the kind of information on the basis of which to know the critical level of interest rate. Similarly, to assess the impact of interest rate changes, both directly and indirectly through the impacts on exchange rates, one has to know not just the "average" balance sheet, but which firms are likely to encounter problems[44] – the kind of micro-economic data that macro-economic authorities typically have not collected. Many of the IMF's mistakes in monetary policy in East Asia can be traced to their seeming[45] failures even to take note of these micro-economic details.

---

[44] It makes a difference, for instance, whether the firms that are likely to encounter problems are those which already are shutting down: the marginal impact then may be small, at least in the short run. In Thailand, with the collapse of the real-estate bubble, there was huge excess capacity. Construction had virtually stopped. In those circumstances, policies which had an adverse effect on the construction industry thus had little *marginal* effect in the short run on the level of aggregate demand.

[45] The failure was greater: in virtually none of the discussions on policy were these considerations even raised, let alone given weight. For a more extended discussion, see chapter 13 and Furman and Stiglitz (1999); Stiglitz (1999, 2000b).

There is some uncertainty associated with any policy. Good policy instruments are those where any mistakes can be quickly detected, and quickly and easily corrected. If there are long lags in detection and correction, and/or if there large irreversibilities, then the instrument needs to be used with caution. The IMF, when it imposed the huge interest rates in East Asia (nominal interest rates in Indonesia of 60 percent or more, real interest rates in Korea of 25 percent or more) said that *if these were excessive, it would reverse the policy.* But the high interest rates forced thousands of firms into bankruptcy. Lowering interest rates did not unbankrupt them. Even if firms were not forced into bankruptcy, their net worth was depleted. Lowering interest rates did not immediately undeplete the net worth of these firms. The farmers who could not afford to buy seed and fertilizer for their crops, given the high interest rates, and whose children as a result suffered from malnutrition, could not go back and replant, when the interest rates came down; nor was the damage caused by malnutrition undone even if they eventually were able to get enough food to live on; and, all too often, educations that are interrupted will not be restarted.

# NINE

# Regulatory policy and the new paradigm

Traditionally, monetary policy and financial regulatory policy are treated as distinct subjects. One is, fundamentally, a branch of macro-economics, the other a rather applied branch of micro-economics. One is concerned with *money* supply, the other with the *safety and soundness of banks.* In part I, however, we argued that monetary policy affects the level of economic activity through its impact on the supply of credit, mediated through the banking system. We analyzed how changes in policy – from open market operations to reserve requirements to capital adequacy standards – affected banks' incentives to lend and the constraints they face (their opportunity set). We showed that both traditional monetary instruments *and* regulatory provisions affected the incentives and constraints of banks. Monetary policy and financial regulatory policy are intertwined: both are relevant both for the level of aggregate economic activity *and* for the safety and soundness of the banking system. And just as monetary policy often went awry because of its failure to focus on how monetary and regulatory policies affected bank behavior, so too, as we shall see in this chapter, has regulatory policy often been misguided. The analysis of regulatory policy must begin with an analysis of how various regulations affect banks' behavior, and that must rest on an analysis of how the incentives and opportunity sets (constraints) are altered.

While the analysis of part I showed how both traditional monetary instruments and regulatory constraints affected the level of lending – the supply of credit – in this chapter we focus on bank risk taking. While monetary and financial regulatory policy are intertwined, both resting on the theory of banking and credit, the former focuses on the level of credit, the latter on the *quality* of credit, on the amount of risk taking. To be sure, in part I, we repeatedly noted how changes in policy affected the level of risk undertaken by banks, including their impact on the probability of bankruptcy, but that was more incidental to the focus on the impact on the level of credit. Here, we focus explicitly on the risks undertaken.

Our objective is to explain why the approach which has all too often dominated public discourse – a focus on capital adequacy standards combined with "liberalization" or "deregulation" which strips away other forms of control – is seriously misguided and to provide an alternative approach to regulation. A second objective is to emphasize some of the general equilibrium aspects of regulatory policy, aspects which too have received insufficient attention.

While we focus on the structure of *regulation*, it should be clear that just as regulation affects the supply of credit, traditional monetary instruments affect the safety and soundness of the banking system, and one ignores these considerations at one's peril. Raising interest rates suddenly can decrease the value of a bank's assets (which are often long-term – or at least longer-term than the maturity structure of its liabilities), markedly decreasing its net worth, putting the bank into a precarious position. Moreover, the high interest rates may lead to distress or worse among the bank's borrowers who have short-term debts, the carrying cost of which suddenly increases to a far higher level than was anticipated; and this too will have an adverse effect on the bank's balance sheet.[1]

---

[1] One might have thought that banks, as creditors, would gain from high interest rates, in ways which largely offset the losses they bear as borrowers. But different banks are in markedly different positions, and thus even if *on average* banks are better off, particular banks can be much worse off, and the additional lending of those who are better off will not offset the reduction in lending of those who are worse off. More importantly, with bankruptcy costs, the changes are not "zero-sum."

While monetary policy can, and often has, had marked effects on the safety and soundness of the banking system, the impact of regulatory policies on macro-economic activity is even more significant. Much of the volatility in the level of economic activity–the financial crises that mark the history of capitalism – can be traced to *bad* lending practices. The real-estate booms and busts have been fed by excessive speculative lending to that sector – the crises in Thailand and Scandinavia being only the most recent episodes; and margin lending is widely believed to have played a central role in the stock market crash of 1929. Thus, economic stability, no less than the safety and soundness of individual banks, is at stake in the design of good regulatory structures.

Awareness of these issues is hardly new: it is well recognized that the origins of the US Savings and Loan (S & L) *débâcle* can be traced to the *combination* of sudden increases in interest rates (to fight inflation) under Volcker and deregulation under Reagan.[2] The problems festered for years, hidden from widespread view, but in 1989, they could be hidden no longer. The rapid tightening of regulation in 1989 contributed to the macro-economic downturn of the early 1990s.

At times, it has seemed that the US Treasury and IMF had an almost perverse desire – they wanted the developing countries to learn for themselves the lessons which the United States had learned, with such pain, in its experiment with high interest rates and financial market deregulation in the 1980s, culminating in the S & L *débâcle* of 1989! If their objective was this experiential learning, they succeeded; unfortunately the developing world lacked the resources, the institutions, and the safety nets, to deal with the resulting predictable, and predicted, crises.

Nowhere has this been more evident than in East Asia, where it is now widely recognized that the policies of financial and capital market deregulation played a central role in the crisis that began in 1997 (see chapter 13). Consider, for instance, the case of Thailand. In the 1970s and 1980s, it had relatively good financial regulation. Banks faced limits on the amount of speculative real-estate

---

[2] To be sure, with the magnitude of the losses increased as a result of the policy of forbearance – through the creation of "artificial capital."

lending they could engage in. This was partly because the regulators realized that throughout the world, real-estate booms – and busts – had been a source of economic volatility, and that these booms and busts were fed by bank lending. They also realized that they needed investments to provide jobs for their growing population, and to realize the rising aspirations of their people. Empty office buildings, as gleaming as they might appear, were hardly the basis for sustained economic growth. But they were told – encouraged, forced – to liberalize, to take down these limitations to speculative real-estate lending, to let the market decide on its own. If the market wanted to build empty office buildings, who were government bureaucrats to interfere with these choices? The potential impact on others – should the real-estate bubble burst – was never mentioned. The dogma was that the investors bore the costs and reaped the rewards.

Part of the deregulation initiative was a focus on *capital adequacy standards*. It sometimes seems that those advocating the sole reliance on capital adequacy standards have a hidden agenda. They really believed in free banking – as disastrous as that has been, and as universally rejected as it is. To those of this persuasion, reliance on capital adequacy standards seemed a second best. *All* the government needed to do was to ensure that the capital adequacy standards were satisfied.

The earlier discussion of part I should have made clear the dangers of that approach. It is not just that the theoretical foundations underlying capital adequacy standards are absent. Because there are, to put it mildly, imperfect adjustments for risk, banks have an incentive to go for the riskiest assets within any risk category. But matters are even worse, as we shall show later in this chapter. The net result may be that risk is actually increased.

### The rationale for regulation (or deregulation)

Throughout the world, governments regulate financial institutions; their regulatory role in this sector goes beyond that in virtually almost any other sector of the economy. The natural question to ask is: why? We have already hinted at the answer: banking systems have repeatedly failed; the failure has imposed large costs on society, both through the macro-economic disturbances to which they give rise and through the bail-outs at the public expense which almost inevitably follow. Bad lending practices are at the root of these failures, whether they arise out of seemingly well-intentioned behavior, incentive structures that lead to excessive risk taking, or out of seemingly fraudulent behavior, the "looting" of banks at the expense of the public. And indeed, it is often hard to distinguish between the three, which is why convictions for fraud have succeeded in only a minority of cases. Is a bank which lends at interest rates which seem too low, given the risks, "looting" or making bad business judgments? (Part of the answer, of course, depends on whether there is a quid pro quo, but those engaged in fraudulent behavior have learned the tricks of masquerading the quid pro quo.) In the subsequent analysis, we assume honest banks, and focus on the simple question: why might they undertake excessively risky lending?[3]

The answer to this question, too, is not hard to find: the private costs borne by banks are less than the social costs – when there is a failure, society bears both the macro-economic costs and the bail-out costs. To be sure, the bank, too, faces costs should it go bankrupt[4]; but the question is: are incentives aligned *at the margin*? And the answer is clearly "no."

The argument for intervention can be put in two ways. There are externalities associated with these bad lending practices, and as usual when there are externalities, there is a role for government, to help align private and social costs.

The alternative perspective focuses on the role of government as insurer. Governments typically provide deposit insurance.[5] All

---

[3] For a discussion of looting, see Akerlof and Romer (1993) and the discussion below.

[4] Thus, the argument put forward repeatedly by IMF officials concerning the moral hazard associated with their repeated bail-outs, that the lenders typically did bear *some* costs (they were not fully repaid, or were repaid only with a delay) misses the point: the question is not whether they bear some costs, but whether the private costs they bear are equal to the social costs. The bail-outs open up a wedge.

[5] Even when such deposit insurance is not explicit, governments typically bail out banks, either when the bank is large, or when several banks go under simultaneously.

insurance leads to moral-hazard problems – because of the insurance, the insured do not bear the full costs of their risk taking. Insurance companies thus seek to mitigate the risks. They do this partly by limiting the extent of insurance, but there is a large cost to doing so – the insured have to bear more risks. As a result, they attempt to *regulate* the behavior of the insured. Fire insurance companies require commercial buildings to install sprinkler systems. Such regulations are part of the risk-mitigation system, ways of reducing the moral-hazard problem which inevitably arises as part of insurance.

Critics of financial regulation, imbued with a perspective that sees all government regulation as intrusive, have sought to minimize its scope, failing to realize that as insurer, it is doing no more than any other insurer would do – trying to mitigate the risks which it faces. The focus of financial market deregulation should have been to minimize the risks faced by the government, or more accurately, to balance off the benefits in terms of risk mitigation with the costs; instead it was focused on narrowing the scope of regulation. The result was predictable: the government, and society more broadly, ended up bearing enormous costs from the excessive risk taking.

Nowhere is the misunderstanding of financial regulation more evident than in the excessive reliance on capital adequacy standards. But before turning to a consideration of capital adequacy standards, we need to set out some of the general principles of regulation.

### General principles of bank regulation

If the government could perfectly monitor every bank, perfectly insuring that it makes only "good loans," then of course the government would itself have (at least) the same information that banks have. Ignoring for the moment the incentives of the bank regulator, the natural question is: if government has all the relevant information, and the right incentives (to make only good loans), then why not simply have the government make loans itself?

Regulation thus must be based on the premise that there is some differential information, as well as some differential incentives. That is, while the regulator is less well informed (at least about some of the key pieces of information), the regulator has some incentives (imperfect as they may be) to correct (at least partially) for some discrepancy between social and private returns. In the case of banking, the discrepancy is clear: if a bank goes bankrupt, its owners do not bear the full costs. The government does, through implicit or explicit deposit insurance.[6] Moreover, when many banks go bankrupt (or a large bank goes bankrupt) there are macro-economic consequences affecting the whole economy, not just the owners of the bank. The regulator is thus presumed to have some (albeit possibly imperfect) incentives to prohibit banks from engaging in excessive risk taking, which enhances the likelihood of bankruptcy.[7]

Given that the regulator has imperfect information and can control only indirectly the bank, the theory of bank regulation is a classic principal–agent problem[8]: the regulator (the principal) tries to *control* or *affect* the behavior of the bank (the agent), to make the bank act *more* in accord with social objectives. Various control mechanisms have their advantages and disadvantages: some

---

[6] Because of their large systemic effects, even when governments do not provide explicit deposit insurance, they almost always bail out banks, at least when they are large and/or a significant number of depositors have their money at risk. See Stiglitz (1993b, 1994). Jerry Caprio (1996) has put the matter forcefully: "There are two kinds of governments, those that have [explicit] deposit insurance, and know it, and those that have [implicit] deposit insurance, and don't know it".

[7] We ignore here the corruption which is prevalent in many countries, which entails connivance between bank regulators and private bankers, and which partly explains why the record of bad lending for private banking in many less developed countries is worse than that for public lending. State banking is subjected to more intense scrutiny than private banks. In other countries, corruption itself provides part of the explanation for the bad record on state lending: political connections rather than credit worthiness has been a principal determinant of who gets loans.

[8] Principal-agent considerations are also important in the design of the institutional structure of regulation. Many countries (including the United States) have multiple regulators. Such multiple regulation has been criticized for its inefficiency, in imposing excessive costs both on the government (as regulator) and on the banks. But there may be distinct advantages of having multiple regulators, though some of the arguments put forward by the regulators (such as Federal Reserve Board Chairman Greenspan) in resisting regulatory consolidations that would undermine their role are, to say the least, specious.

have greater costs (either in terms of explicit costs, such as the pay of supervisors, or in terms of *distortions*), and some work more or less imperfectly. Regulations, for instance, that are intended to discourage bad lending may, at the same time, have the effect of prohibiting some good lending. Restrictions on insider lending are an example. Problems of asymmetric information (between the borrower and the lender) are less with insider lending; but moral-hazard problems – incentives to make bad loans, or loans at terms that are not commensurate with the risk – are greater; and the latter danger is almost universally agreed to be the dominant consideration. But restrictions on insider lending may, at the same time, rule out some "good" loans; and because of asymmetries of information, the good loans may not be picked up by other banks.

The general presumption in the theory of regulation is in favor of *price-based* mechanisms that directly address the source of the problem, the discrepancy between social and private returns. Thus, *if* the probability distribution of total returns to the bank's portfolio could be easily observed, then there would be a "tax" imposed on bankruptcy which would increase with the probability of bankruptcy and the severity of losses in the event of bankruptcy. But, as noted in the beginning of this chapter, part of the problem arises from the fact that the government (the regulator) does not have information about the risk characteristics of each loan, let alone information with which to make informed judgments concerning the variance–covariance matrix, required

---

If the regulated can choose their regulators, competition among regulators *may* result in greater efficiency in regulation, but it is more likely to result in greater laxness in regulation, a race to the bottom in minimal enforcement of onerous rules and regulations, regardless of their social benefits or the magnitude of the discrepancy between social and private costs (unless there are ways of making the regulator bear those costs). More relevant is the observation that there are high costs associated with *not* detecting and prohibiting excessive risk taking, and while the approval of multiple regulators may result in some sound lending practices not being undertaken, the resulting losses may be far smaller than the losses that result from allowing unsound lending practices being undertaken. For a broader discussion of these issues, see Sah and Stiglitz (1985, 1986, 1988). The virtues of having multiple regulators are increased when there is a risk of corruption, of particular concern in many developing countries; it is typically considerably harder to bribe several regulating agencies than one.

to assess the overall probability of returns. In an ever-changing environment, such probability judgments are, in any case, highly subjective. What the government can easily observe is the actual event of bankruptcy (or indirect, and imperfect, indicators of stress, like the number of non-performing loans). The problem is that once the bank goes bankrupt, it is too late to impose the tax: there are often insufficient funds to pay off depositors, let alone pay a penalty to the government.[9]

In the absence of the ability to address directly the source of discrepancy between social and private returns, in general, it is desirable to use a variety of instruments, to use both price- and quantity-based interventions. (Indeed, the distinction between price and quantity interventions is often artificial; non-linear price interventions are often desirable; only in limiting cases are "pure" (linear) price or strict quantity interventions desirable.) There is no single, dominant instrument. There are desirable interventions that focus on inputs, on outputs, and on processes – the processes of production that convert inputs into outputs.[10] Yet, much of the discussion of regulatory policy has focused on capital adequacy requirements, and the deregulation movement has stressed reducing the scope for other interventions. We shall shortly show why these approaches have been so misguided – and why they have led to such disastrous results. But first, we wish to put the issue of prudential regulation within a broader context.

In this chapter, we focus on prudential regulation, directed at enhancing the "safety and soundness" of the banking system, and more broadly, of the financial system. There are, in fact, several

---

[9] In some cases, there is a residual value to the owners of the bank, particularly if the bank is terminated for failure to have adequate capital, rather than because it is actually bankrupt. In such situations, it does make sense for the government to impose a penalty on the bank; such penalties would, *ex ante*, reduce the risk of excessive risk taking.

[10] Consider one of the principal contexts in which principal–agent theory originally developed – sharecropping in agriculture (Stiglitz, 1974b). The landlord was assumed not to be able to control (observe) directly labor input. Interventions included those related to inputs (specifying amounts of fertilizer, or subsidizing fertilizers), processes (what crops were to be grown, when they were to be planted, if that was observable), and outputs (Braverman and Stiglitz, 1986). Other markets, such as capital markets, were interlinked, at least partly because of the principal–agent problem (Braverman and Stiglitz, 1982).

other objectives of regulatory policy, addressing other market failures: (a) competition, especially in lending to small and medium size businesses,[11] is often limited, and consolidation of banks, with the associated reduction in competition, is one way of enhancing bank profits; there is an important role for government in maintaining a competitive banking system; (b) consumers (borrowers) are often uninformed, and lenders (banks) often try to exploit their limited information; government has assumed an important role in *consumer protection*; and (c) there are often certain groups in the population that seem underserved by the market; this may be because of red-lining – we noted earlier that when there is credit rationing, some groups may be completely excluded from the market; banks do not lend to those for whom the social return is highest, but rather those from whom they can extract the highest returns, and there may be a marked discrepancy between the two.[12] The last concern has given rise in the United States to the Community Reinvestment Act (CRA 1995), which has encouraged (forced) banks to lend more in inner city areas.

That there are conflicts among objectives should be clear: we know how to create a banking system that would (almost) never go bankrupt, simply by requiring it to invest all deposits in government T-bills. But such a bank would not be performing the essential functions of a bank, providing credit to the private sector. Similarly, by reducing competition, we can enhance bank profits and thereby reduce the probability of bankruptcy (enhance the safety and soundness of the banking system).

Thus, while we focus on prudential regulation, we cannot ignore the broader purposes of the banking system and the other

---

[11] Note that competition on the depository side is often keen; but the critical role of banks that we have emphasized is that of providing credit. The fixed costs of obtaining information about potential borrowers (their likelihood of repaying) and monitoring them means that, inevitably, there will be limited competition in the supply of loans to any particular borrower, even if there are many banks providing loans in general. See Stiglitz (1975b), Jaffee and Stiglitz (1990).

[12] This is related to the fact that the credit market is not an auction market, as emphasized in chapter 2. In general, markets with asymmetric and costly information are not constrained Pareto-efficient, and this is just one manifestation of such inefficiency. See Greenwald and Stiglitz (1986).

reasons for government regulation. Keeping this in mind, we turn now to a more detailed analysis of what has been, for a long time, the central focus of prudential regulation, capital adequacy standards.

## The theory (or lack thereof) of capital adequacy standards

Putting aside the notion that the true motivation for the sole, or excessive, reliance on capital adequacy standards is as a second best to free banking, two alternative rationales are proffered, and it is important to distinguish between them, because they have markedly different policy implications. The first is capital adequacy as a *buffer* – the more capital the bank has of its own, the less money that the government may have to put out in the event of a failure. The second relates to *incentives*: the more capital the owners have at risk, the less likely it is that they will undertake undue risk. A central result of part I was that when the net worth of a bank falls below a critical level, the bank shifts from being risk averse to being a risk lover. By ensuring that the owners have enough net worth at risk, one can at least ensure that the bank will act in a risk averse manner.

The differing policy implications of the two theories are illustrated by proposals to require banks to have a publicly traded tranche of uninsured capital. Such capital provides a buffer, but may not affect incentives, since the amount of funds that the bank has at risk is not increased.[13]

Keeping clear the *objectives* of capital adequacy standards is important, because all too often policymakers propose ways of meeting the capital adequacy standards which do little either to provide additional buffer or to improve incentives. Consider a not-uncommon situation where a country faces a financial crisis, private providers of the additional equity to meet the

---

[13] To be sure, if the uninsured tranche is relatively short-term, then if the bank engages in excessive risk taking, *and it becomes known that it has done so*, then it will have to pay high interest rates (reflecting this risk) to obtain the capital. The incentives of the bank will accordingly be affected. See also the discussion on p. 219.

capital adequacy standards cannot be found, and the social costs of a contraction of the credit supply are so great that the government provides the capital required to meet the capital adequacy standard. Putting up capital *before* the crisis does not, of course, provide additional protection for the government; indeed, it may stand to lose even more. To see how this can happen, assume the government injects new capital, equal in amount to the value of the original capital, so that it is given a 50 percent stakeholding for an investment of $500 million. Assume subsequently that as more loan losses accumulate, the bank is shut down, and, after selling off assets, there are $1000 million to pay off depositor liabilities of $600 million. The government, as a 50 percent equity owner, gets back $200 million – for a net loss of $300 million. Had the government simply waited, the bank would have gone under, and to be sure, the government would have been left with large payments to depositors. Without the $500 million equity injection, the net worth of the bank at termination would have been, say, $500 million, and the government would have had to put up $100 million. Still, the amount that it loses is only a third of what it would otherwise have lost. *Government-financed equity injections to meet the capital adequacy standards do not provide additional protection to the government, and indeed, if they are not well structured,*[14] *may even expose government to higher losses.*

On the other hand, government equity injections to meet capital adequacy standards have a limited effect on the *incentives* of the bank, unless government takes an active role in management. For the amounts that the original owners have at risk are not changed, and there is no obvious reason why they should worry about the losses that the government-as-owner faces any more than they worried about the losses that the government-as-insurer faced. Indeed, the previous paragraph made clear that with a straightforward equity injection, the amounts the original owners have to risk should the bank go out of business are *less*

---

[14] That is, the equity injection has to be designed in such a way that the old equity owners bear disproportionately the risk of failure.

than without the injection, so that the owners might be induced to engage in riskier behavior.[15]

There is an answer: the government must simultaneously tighten regulation. But there is a deeper question raised by this answer: what can the government-as-owner do that the government-as-regulator cannot do; and if the government-as-regulator can avoid excessive risk, what *additional* role is provided by a government equity injection?[16] Indeed, if the analysis above is correct, the government equity injection may make the government-as-regulator's job more, not less, difficult.

### How much capital should be required?

Later, we shall explain some of the further problems with capital adequacy standards, having to do with (inevitable) imperfections in risk adjustments and asset valuation – problems which imply

---

[15] Actually, the impacts on risk taking are ambiguous. The government ownership share reduces the gains from large risk taking, at the same time it reduces the losses, so long as the losses are not so large as to leave nothing over even with the government equity injection. But as the above example illustrates, if the bank's assets are more than $600 million, the old shareholders get one half of the residual, which is increased as a result of the equity injection by the government.

If $Y$ is the income of the bank, $W$ the net worth (capital) before the equity injection, $2W$ after, then the value of the original owners' shares after the equity injection is

$Y/2 + W$ if the bank does not go bankrupt

max $\{0, Y/2 + W - c\}$ if it does, where $c$ is the bankruptcy cost, while before the equity injection, the original owners' shares would have been

$Y + W$ if the bank does not go bankrupt and

max $\{0, Y + W - c\}$ if it does.

Assume the bank has a range of policies, indexed in terms of riskiness $\omega$, (Rothschild and Stiglitz, 1970), with a return of $Y(\omega, \ldots)$. Recall from part I that $F$ represents the probability of default, which can be expressed as $F(\omega, a)$, where $a$ is the initial net worth of the bank ($a = W$ before the equity injection, $a = 2W$ after). Then the first-order condition for $\omega$ is

$EY_\omega = cF_\omega$

The equity injection leads to an increase in risk taking provided $F_{\omega a} < 0$, that is, an equity injection will always lead to a reduction in the probability of bankruptcy, but whether it leads to an increase in risk taking depends on its impact on the *marginal* probability. It is plausible, but not inevitable, that it should do so.

[16] Though the question is posed as if it were purely rhetorical, in practice, in many cases the government-as-owner has access to information that the

that they may be counterproductive. But before turning to these problems, there are some more fundamental objections, having to do with the assessment of the amount of capital that is required. The central questions are: what is the probability of the bank's capital being inadequate to meet its obligations to its depositors, should the bank cease to operate, and what is the magnitude of the losses that the government might have to bear, should that happen? The answer to these questions, as we have seen, depends on the probability distribution of the total return on the bank's portfolio, which the bank regulator cannot typically directly assess. Capital adequacy standards turn to a *third-best* approach – looking at each asset in isolation, ignoring the correlations among the returns to different assets. And historically, capital adequacy standards focused only on credit risk, not market risk (e.g. the risk associated with the decrease in value of a long-term government bond[17]); but even as more comprehensive definitions of risk are embraced, capital adequacy standards based on the risks of individual assets still do not take account of the correlations between credit and market risks, correlations which played a critical role in the global financial crisis of 1997–1998. More generally, even when banks (and corporations) believe that they have obtained cover for the risks they face, there is *counterparty risk* – risk that those providing the cover will not be able to meet their obligations – precisely at the times when the cover is needed. For the times when banks are most likely to face severe problems are those when there is a macro-economic shock, a shock which simultaneously affects not only the value of the assets of one bank, but of all banks.

The problem is that focusing on each asset in isolation not only does not give a good picture of the overall risk facing the bank, it affects bank behavior in ways which may not significantly reduce risk, which may even increase it, and which, at the same time, interfere with the efficient allocation of credit.

government-as-regulator does not. The government-as-owner can replace management, and this can obviously affect the extent of insider lending.
    Even if the government-as-regulator has no more information than the government-as-owner, it still pays to have a separate government regulatory agency to prevent insider lending (corruption) on the part of those entrusted to manage the bank.

[17] See chapter 14.

*The risks of imperfect capital adequacy standards*

In part I, we saw for instance how risk-adjusted minimum capital adequacy ratios affect the admissible portfolio allocations of banks. In a world with just loans and T-bills, they may force a bank which has a limited amount of capital (which it cannot increase) to have fewer loans and more T-bills than it otherwise would. In a world in which there are, in addition, long-term government bonds, we saw that if market risk is ignored in capital adequacy standards – and attention is paid only to credit risk (the probability of default, assumed to be zero for the US government) – then an increase in the capital adequacy ratio *could* reduce lending, increasing holdings of long-term government bonds, and actually increase the riskiness of the bank's portfolio.[18] More generally, the reduction in risk is less than what might at first blush appear to be the case.

It is also easy to see that *the degree of imperfections of information may itself be endogenous.* Assume, for instance, the regulators can observe asset values only upon the completion of a transaction, e.g. upon the sale of the asset.[19] Then a bank facing a

---

[18] When the restrictions are binding, they move the bank's opportunity locus down. We might normally think that they would also flatten the mean–standard deviation trade-off: the additional constraint implies that the marginal increase in mean return as a result of increased risk bearing is lowered. These two effects would be expected to lead to less overall risk taking. But there are two countervailing effects. The first arises if there is a limited number of good projects. Then as the bank would have borrowed more, it would have shifted more into long-term government bonds in any case (since there are no diminishing returns). Beyond some point, the bank is also engaging in more lending to diversify the risk of holding government bonds. Then the imposition of capital adequacy requirements may actually increase the slope of the opportunity locus, leading to more overall risk taking, with the substitution effect dominating the income effect. More importantly, the *franchise value effect*, described earlier, implies that the bank's indifference curves become flatter (it becomes more willing to accept risk). This point is elaborated on at greater length below.

[19] In the case of a loan, the problems of valuation are even larger, as evidenced by controversies over when to declare a loan non-performing. Clearly, once a creditor emerges from bankruptcy, the "transaction" is completed, with the creditor receiving so many cents on the dollar. At that point, we can value the asset (though even then there are problems, because the creditors may be awarded not dollars, but shares in the firm, upon which the Court may have placed a value, in order to implement the bankruptcy, but those values may or may not be identical, or even approximately equal, to what the shares might fetch in the market). But short of the full resolution of bankruptcy, valuations are even more difficult. Standard procedures focus on non-performing loans, i.e. loans that have not fulfilled their contractual obligations over a certain period of time. But

capital adequacy constraint (or the threat of one) has an incentive
to sell assets which have increased in value, in order to realize the
capital gain, and retain those which have decreased in value. These
"valuation benefits" – reducing the bindingness of the capital adequacy constraint – must be set off against any marginal costs, e.g.
in reduced mean return or increased variance (or increased probability of bankruptcy). It is easy to see that banks may be induced
to take portfolio decisions which actually increase their true riskiness, though their *measured* riskiness goes down. There is an increase in the gap between measured and true value.

But matters do not stop here. A bank not today facing a capital adequacy constraint knows that there is some probability in
the future that it will do so. It wants to have the *option* of engaging in the *valuation obfuscation* exercise described in note 19.
If it buys assets with highly variable prices, there is a larger probability that some of those assets will have decreased markedly in
value, and some increased markedly in value; there is thus a
higher probability that it can increase its measured valuation by
a given amount by selling the asset(s) which have increased in

not all non-performing loans are identical; in some cases, the bank will receive
full payment, in others only a fraction of what is due. But even more problematic is the fact that banks can stop the loans from being non-performing, at least
for a long time, simply by lending the firm money in order for it to keep up its
payments. It may even be optimal for the bank to do that to obfuscate, because
there are adverse consequences of a loan being declared non-performing for
both the bank and the borrower. Both have an incentive to hide the true condition of the firm. But the incentives to do so on the part of the bank are increased
when it faces capital adequacy constraints. Then the costs go beyond simply the
costs of the provisioning requirements.

Statistical models may be used to assess the actuarial value of the repayment,
given a particular history of non-repayment, but two complications make the
use of such models problematic, especially in times of crises. The first is the
fact, just noted, that whether a borrower is not repaying a loan is as much a result of a decision of the lender as of the circumstances of the borrower; it can
be simply the consequence of a decision to roll over a loan or not. (Nowhere is
this more evident than in the case of IMF loans. Russia did not default on its
loans to the IMF even when it defaulted on loans to other creditors, because
the IMF simply rolled over those loans, even though that country failed to live
up to the conditions that the IMF normally imposes.)

But there is another reason that such statistical models are problematic, especially in times of crises, and that is because many borrowers become what is
called *strategic non-performers*, that is, when there are sufficiently large num-
bers of firms in distress, there is a belief that there will be a partial bail-out of
debtors "who cannot pay," and they wish to benefit from such a bail-out. Thus,
it pays them, as it were, to become non-performing.

value and retaining those which have decreased in value. *Ex ante,* capital adequacy standards induce banks to have a more risky portfolio than they otherwise would (on this account alone – the direct effects *may* work the other way) because such a portfolio has a greater opportunity for increasing the disparity between measured and true value.

But matters do not even stop there. If the value of all assets were easy to ascertain on the market, then the regulator, recognizing the danger just described, could see through the actions of the bank; presumably, if the regulator could do so, he could also take actions (design regulations) to offset these perverse incentives (though in practice, it might be hard to do so). But there are some assets (like marketed securities) for which it is easy to ascertain market value, and other assets (like real estate, especially real estate like commercial office buildings and land) where valuations are particularly difficult (reflecting in part the high volatility of these asset values). Banks have an incentive to invest a larger fraction of their portfolio in these hard-to-value assets, thereby increasing the information asymmetry between the bank and the regulator.[20]

### *Further perverse impacts on incentives of increased capital adequacy requirements*

Hellman, Murdoch and Stiglitz (2000) have shown that sole reliance on capital adequacy standards is Pareto-inefficient (provided restrictions on deposit rates can be enforced), whether there is or is not deposit insurance. In fact, they establish that increasing capital adequacy standards can lead to less prudential behavior because it may actually adversely affect incentives. Incentives are affected by the banks' total capital, the part that is counted in the capital adequacy standards as well as the franchise value, the present discounted value of future profits. Equity is high-cost capital – far higher than the cost of deposits. Indeed, the very fact that the government has to impose capital adequacy

---

[20] For a general development of this point, see Edlin and Stiglitz (1995).

standards is evidence that banks are being forced to hold more equity (or whatever is counted as capital for regulatory purposes) than they would like. This cost is reflected in a decrease in the franchise value of the bank – its value as an ongoing concern to its owners. This indirect effect can be greater than the direct effect; but even if that is not the case, the net benefit from increased capital adequacy standards may be limited.

### Further reasons for the failure of financial market deregulation: problems of transition[21]

The movement towards financial (and capital) market deregulation – focusing on capital adequacy standards – is now recognized to have played a central role in the financial instability which has characterized so much of the developing world for the past quarter century.[22] Part of the problem was the absence of a theory of bank behavior on which to build a theory of regulation; but part of the problem was the lack of attention to the problems of transition.

Deregulation had two contrasting effects on the franchise value of banks. One was that it opened up new opportunities (for risk taking, as well as profit making), and this increased profitability; but it also led to more competition, and this reduced profitability. In the long run, the latter effect often seems to dominate, and thus the franchise value of banks is decreased. In that case, deregulation both increases the *incentives* and the *opportunities* for risk taking. Indeed, *announcements* of future deregulation initiatives will increase the incentives for risk taking, even before it increases the opportunities.

At the same time, deregulation has typically reduced the regulators' abilities to monitor banks, both because it has increased the complexity of the task (the range of actions which the bank can undertake is increased) and because in the early stages of deregulation, the regulatory authorities often lose many key employees – they simply cannot compete with the new

---

[21] For a more detailed elaboration of these points, see Hellman and Stiglitz (2001).
[22] See Caprio (1997), Demirgüç-Kunt and Caprio (1997), and Demirgüç-Kunt and Detragiache (1998a).

private entrants. This is a particular problem in developing countries, where the supply of trained personnel is limited. Just at the time when the need for enhanced oversight is greatest, the regulatory authorities' abilities are weakest.

In the East Asia crisis, there was an attempt to shift much of the blame to the countries themselves, saying that the problem was their weak institutions, in particular their inadequate institutions for financial regulation. The lesson that was drawn was that countries should have better "institutions." While no one could object to what seemed an almost obvious point, there was no obvious recipe for how to obtain better institutions. It was seldom noted that countries with *seemingly* strong institutions – the countries of Scandinavia – were the last set of countries that had had major financial crises; either strong institutions were insufficient to inoculate against a crisis, or the developing countries had a virtually impossible task ahead, if even advanced industrial countries with good and transparent governance structures were unable to establish strong institutions. But there was a deeper point: some of the countries had had strong institutions. Thailand's Central Bank was viewed as one of the strongest in the developing world in the 1980s, with good regulatory structures and practices. In effect, the process of liberalization had led to the weakening of this central institution. It is not enough to make sure that there are good institutions in place *before* liberalization; they have to be strong enough to withstand the almost inevitable weakening that will occur as a part of the liberalization process, and the liberalization process has to be conducted in a way to minimize that damage. Unfortunately, in the past, little attention has been paid to these issues.

Even when regulatory authorities are aware of these problems and therefore propose a process of gradual liberalization (resisting international pressure for rapid deregulation), their task is not easy: for as we have noted, the incentive for greater risk taking is increased as soon as the program of liberalization is announced. In effect, a process of regulation must begin with tightened supervision *even before* regulations begin to be stripped away.

*Risk assessment methodologies*

As a result of the growing recognition of the inadequacies of capital adequacy standards, there has been an emphasis on assessment of a bank's risk assessment methodologies, methodologies which presumably take account of the correlations among assets. Yet, even in the more advanced industrialized countries, these methodologies have not really been tested. Implementation in developing countries may be particularly problematic; not only may there be a shortage of the requisite skills, but also they require data which simply may not be available. We know that the risks facing developing countries are markedly different from (and in many cases, significantly larger than[23]) those in more developed countries, so that it is clearly inappropriate simply to borrow parameter estimates; and we know that the risk may vary markedly with changing policies: any analysis based on data collected prior to capital market liberalization would be of limited value after capital market liberalization, given the huge risks to which capital market liberalization exposes a country. Thus, while it is clear that banks should develop risk assessment methodologies, and regulators should assess those methodologies, there is no reason to have confidence *at the current time* in such an approach: it seems clear that a bank that wanted to engage in risk taking activity – that the regulators might have disapproved, were it to be fully apprised of what was going on – could develop a *methodology* which gave it considerable discretion to do what it pleased and still please the regulators.

## The portfolio approach to regulation[24]

There is an alternative approach to regulation that follows from the models presented in part I, which we call, for want of a better name, the *portfolio approach to bank regulation*. The approach has three key features:

(1) a recognition that any theory of bank regulation must begin with a *model* (or theory) of bank behavior;

---

[23] See Easterly, Islam and Stiglitz (2000a, 2000b).
[24] Caprio, Honohan and Stiglitz (2001); Stiglitz (2001).

(2)  a recognition that the government can only imperfectly control the actions of banks;

(3)  that therefore it must take a variety of actions, which affect both the *incentives* of banks and the *constraints* that they face (or otherwise affect bank behavior).

In part I, we described how banks make their decisions, maximizing their expected utility or expected profits, taking into account bankruptcy costs. The choices banks make depend on their opportunity sets and their preferences. The regulator can take actions to affect both the opportunity set and preferences. It does so very imperfectly, as we shall see.

### Imposing restrictions

There are a variety of restrictions that affect the riskiness of the bank's portfolio. The most well known are restrictions on real estate (or even more specifically, land) holdings and holdings of equities. Thailand in the 1980s had such restrictions, which, as we have already noted, it imposed for two reasons. First, it knew that a large number of instances of economic downturns were caused by real-estate booms that crashed, and such booms were typically fed by collateralized lending. Banks are willing to lend because they believe (falsely) that they are secure, since the value of the collateral is, say, 120 percent of the value of the loan. Only if market prices go down by 20 percent will the bank be at risk – and such declines are relatively rare. The willingness of banks to make such loans helps feed the bubble. But every such bubble does eventually break. And when it does, prices can fall far more than 20 percent. And of course, it is precisely when the collateral declines in value that borrowers have a strong incentive not to repay. And since the declines in market values on different real-estate assets are correlated, many loans go bad, posing a real threat to the viability of the bank. As a bank's net worth suddenly collapses, it has to decrease its lending, possibly even calling in some loans. The credit contraction (especially to the real-estate market) thus exacerbates the decline.

Secondly, Thailand believed that, as a developing country, its scarce funds should be invested in employment generating investments rather than in speculative real estate. Many of the successful East Asian economies engaged in directed lending (though there is some controversy about the extent to which their rapid growth can be credited to that). The restrictions on real-estate lending can be viewed as "negatively directed credit" – not telling banks where to lend, but where not to lend. In retrospect, it appears the economic returns to investing in manufacturing are likely to have been greater than what emerged after these restrictions on lending to real estate were abandoned – the construction of empty office buildings.[25]

A second set of *constraints* relates to insider lending.[26] Here, the problem is a mixture of incentives and opportunity sets: there is likely to be a larger discrepancy between social and private risks with insider lending. While presumably banks may have better information about projects undertaken by connected parties, this advantage is more than offset by the fact that the bank officers stand to gain more from the upside potential (because of their implicit or explicit equity stake), and these private gains may offset the downside risks that the bank (or even more, the government) faces should the project turn out to be unsuccessful.

A third set of constraints has to do with bank exposure, e.g. to foreign short-term indebtedness, a mismatch between the currency in which its assets are denominated (in which, for instance, loans are due), and the currency in which its liabilities are denominated. Such exposure implies that large changes in the exchange rate can force a bank into financial distress. In the aftermath of the East Asia crisis, many countries are imposing such

---

[25] To be sure, one of the reasons put forward for the abandonment of such restrictions is that they are ineffective – non-bank banks can engage in such lending. Such possibilities provide the rationale for broader regulation of financial markets, and the overall regulation of holding companies which include banks and other institutions. The critical issue is insuring that those institutions for which there is implicit or explicit deposit insurance and/or which can give rise to systemic risk are brought under the umbrella of any regulations imposed on "banks."

[26] A related set of restrictions concerns entry: those who have a history of fraud or other "bad behavior" are thought to be more likely to engage in excessive risk taking (perhaps because they are less averse to "bankruptcy") and are therefore prohibited from owning banks.

constraints on their banks. A few countries (such as Malaysia) have extended the constraints further, to embrace the exposure of the firms to which banks lend money. Malaysia's imposition of such constraints was one of the factors that resulted in its over-all foreign denominated short-term indebtedness being less than that of other countries in the region.

These restrictions on the foreign exchange exposure of banks can serve to illustrate the close link between macro-economic and financial regulatory policy. Financial regulatory policy can affect the range of feasible macro-economic policies, or in any case, their consequences. Consider, for instance, the debate dur-ing the East Asia crisis over whether the East Asian countries should allow their currencies to depreciate. The fact that some of the countries had a large foreign exchange exposure put them in a bind: part of what they gained from increased trade from devaluation they lost on their balance sheets.

The S & L crisis illustrated another exposure risk, that arising from a mismatch between the maturity of assets and liabilities. But this maturity transformation is one of the main functions of banks, i.e. to borrow short-term and lend long-term. Banks could, of course, hedge themselves against a risk of a change in the term structure of interest rates through the use of derivatives. To our knowledge, however, no government has attempted directly to impose con-straints on the extent of the (uncovered) maturity mismatch, per-haps because derivatives which make obtaining such a hedge easy have been available for only a relatively short period of time

A fourth set of constraints has to do with "speed limits" – the rate at which banks can expand their deposit base or lending portfolio. There is evidence that there is a close connection between the rapid expansion of a bank and the likelihood of a problem. There may be a variety of explanations for this empir-ical observation. Banks that expand very rapidly may not be able to increase at a commensurate pace their capacity to monitor and screen loan applications effectively. As a result, there is a de-terioration of the loan portfolio. In some situations, such as the S & L crisis in the United States, the banks that expanded rapidly did so on the basis of deposits that they garnered by offering higher interest rates. The only way that it could be profitable for them to pay such high interest rates is for them to undertake greater risk. And greater risk implies a higher probability of a problem down the line. With deposit insurance, there is a kind of Gresham's law at work. Bad – or risky – banks drive out good, or safe banks. Depositors do not care about the risk, since the government absorbs that. All they care about is the promised return. A third possible explanation has to do with what might be thought of as fraud. In some cases, rapid expansion is a hidden form of a pyramid scheme. The new deposits are used, in effect, to pay interest promised on the previous deposits. (Like all pyramid schemes, those based on bank expansion inevitably eventually collapse.)

A final set of constraints relates to interest rates paid on deposits or charged to borrowers. If the government succeeds in forcing deposit rates below the market equilibrium rate, it has the effect of lowering one of the "costs of production" – what the bank has to pay for its funds. This increases the bank's profitability – its franchise value (the present discounted value of the bank as an on-going concern). And the increase in profitability increases prudential behavior, i.e. the constraint leads to altered incentives.

A limit on the interest rate charged also alters incentives. Banks will have diminished incentives to make highly risky loans, since their compensation for these high-risk loans will be limited. Such risky lending is characterized by a large discrepancy between social and private risk, since it is precisely when the bank goes bankrupt that the public (through deposit insurance) has to pick up the costs. The argument against such restrictions – that they interfere with banks' decision making – is thus turned on its head: it is precisely because it interferes with banks' lending decisions in those circumstances where banks would not be lending if they bore the full costs of their decisions that such restrictions are desirable.

The general equilibrium response to such constraints may be different than the partial equilibrium; in some cases, the general equilibrium response reinforces the argument for the constraints, in others, it diminishes it. For instance, in a monopolistic competitive equilibrium model, banks have an incentive to raise deposit rates to try to steal depositors away from other banks. The social benefit of increasing the interest rate may be limited (e.g. the higher interest rates may not induce any more aggregate lending, if the interest elasticity of savings is low) while the private benefits may be significant. On the other hand, entry may dissipate the benefits that would have emerged from the increase in franchise value had entry been forestalled; then the deposit rate restrictions simply lead to more expenditures on fixed costs, and are more likely to be inefficient. Similarly, restrictions on deposit rates may be circumvented through other non-pecuniary benefits to depositors. But it is certainly conceivable (indeed likely) that even though there is some circumvention, it is also the case that these non-pecuniary benefits are not perfect substitutes, and therefore it is possible (and perhaps even likely) that franchise value will nonetheless be increased.

### Incentives

Regulators attempt to affect *incentives* facing banks through several channels. The most important is through capital adequacy requirements. We have already discussed the (sometimes perverted) incentives provided by capital adequacy standards.

As noted earlier, imperfect risk adjustments in capital adequacy standards may induce banks to undertake the riskiest activities within any "risk class." The recognition of this has led to calls for better risk adjustments. But the fundamental problem is that risk is a property of a portfolio, not of an individual asset. To be sure, the probability of bankruptcy, or the variance of returns, is a property of a particular asset. But what matters to regulators is not the variance of an individual asset or the probability of a particular loan going bad, but the riskiness of the portfolio, the probability that the government will have to bail out the bank, and the costs of doing so. A security which has a large variance may, if it is negatively correlated with the rest of the portfolio, actually reduce overall risk. The whole theory of the valuation of risky assets, the CAPM, is based on this premise, and has the strong implication that, for the economy as a whole, the only aspect of risk that matters is covariance with the market as a whole. Thus, the principle underlying risk adjusted capital adequacy standards is fundamentally flawed.

That is why regulators in more advanced countries have placed greater emphasis on banks putting in place risk management systems, that allow the bank (and presumably its regulators) to identify the magnitude of the overall risk facing the bank. But as desirable as these systems may be in principle, they are problematic as a basis of regulation. First, relatively few financial institutions in developing countries have the capacity to develop and use sophisticated risk management systems adapted to the situations that they face. Moreover, for these models to work effectively the firm must have data on the variance–covariance matrix; it is difficult enough to estimate the variance – especially since the risk (e.g. the probability of default) is likely to vary with circumstances, the identification of which in an econometric model may be extremely difficult. Bankruptcies of individual firms and "extreme" outcomes which could lead the bank to be in distress are small probability events – the tails of distributions of the random variables affecting firms and banks. There is a wide-spread view that these tails are "thicker" than would have been predicted by normal distributions; in any case, the failure of standard risk management models to work well in the 1987 and the 1998 crisis raises questions about the excessive reliance on such models by banks, let alone by regulators, whose main concern is these low-probability outcomes.

Matters become even more complicated once one recognizes that what matters is not just credit risk, not just market risk, but the interrelations among them. And while derivatives may have proven useful to some banks as a mechanism for managing their risk, they are particularly troublesome for regulators. For instance, in the Korea crisis, many Korean banks believed that they had "cover" for their foreign exchange exposure. But when the crisis struck, the firms providing the cover went bankrupt, leaving Korea with an exposed position. For regulators to evaluate the risk position of the banks would have required the regulators to be able to evaluate the risk position of the firms providing cover. More generally, there are often important interactions between credit and market risk – a point reinforced by the events surrounding the Russian default in August 1998. Again, many of those providing cover had themselves large exposed positions, so that it was precisely in those states of nature where they would be called upon to provide insurance that they would (with a high probability) be unable to do so.

*If* it were possible to have "good" risk adjustments for capital adequacy standards, it is clear why that would serve to put strong incentives for banks to have more conservative portfolios. Since it would be costly for banks to have a riskier portfolio – in the sense that the bank would have to have more "high-cost" capital – they would take these extra costs into account when making decisions about whether to have a riskier portfolio. In a sense, appropriate risk adjusted capital adequacy standards would enable the regulator to close the gap between the marginal social risk and the marginal private risk (e.g. arising from deposit insurance.) In fact, not only is this not possible, but in recent years, there have even been instances in which risk adjustment seemed to have exacerbated risk taking. Risk weights for short-term lending to emerging markets has been lower than for longer-term lending, presumably because the bank has more flexibility in pulling back its short-term loans. This has encouraged short-term lending. (It implied, for instance, that foreign banks could make short-term loans available at more favorable terms than they otherwise would.) But it is short-term foreign denominated lending which gives rise to economic volatility in emerging markets.[27] The excessive short-term lending (in the aggregate, relative to reserves) has been identified as one of the key factors responsible for the economic crisis in the East Asian countries.[28]

Another reform intended to improve incentives (as well as information) is a requirement of a publicly traded tranche of uninsured capital.[29] The interest rate paid on that tranche would provide information about the riskiness of the bank: if the price of the bonds fall, it indicates a perception of increased risk on the part of market participants. If a fraction of the bonds has to be rolled over at frequent intervals, then there will be a high cost

---

[27] See Furman and Stiglitz (1999); Rodrik and Velasco (1999).
[28] More fundamentally, financial and capital market liberalization enabled these short-term foreign denominated debts to occur; and inadequate bank supervision meant that banks could undertake the implied high level of risk.
[29] See the discussion above, Calomoris and Kahn (1991), and Stiglitz (1992b).

to the bank of engaging in risky lending. The bank thus faces enhanced incentives to avoid excessive risk taking.[30]

Most of the regulations – both those designed to enhance incentives for prudential behavior and to impose constraints which reduce the opportunity for excessive risk taking – are aimed at the bank as an organization. But increasingly, there has been a recognition that decisions are made by individuals, and what matters is the incentives that the individuals within the organization face. To be sure, organizational incentives typically do get translated into incentives facing individual decision makers, but the translation is at best imperfect. Hence, some regulators have deliberately provided incentives for decision makers, both carrots and sticks, making them more accountable for the decisions which they make, e.g. by making them pay all or part of the deficiencies arising from non-payment of loans for which they are responsible.[31] It is, however, extremely difficult to calibrate these incentives. It is particularly problematic for longer-term loans, where repayment may depend on events that happened subsequent to the loan being issued and which would have been difficult, if not impossible, to anticipate. (For instance, it would not have been reasonable for lending officers to be held accountable for the failure of loans made just prior to the huge run up in oil prices in 1973 for projects entailing heavy inputs of oil.)[32]

---

[30] One criticism of these proposals is that the market in these bonds is often thin, and easily manipulated. Thus, the owners of the bank can obfuscate the signal being sent (though to the extent that they buy the bonds, they have more of their own capital at risk, and the tranche of uninsured capital acts much like a standard increase in capital adequacy requirements).

[31] It appeared, for instance, that many of those responsible for the bad Latin American loans of the 1970s were not fired, but actually progressed up within the organization: their ability to push these loans demonstrated their prowess. If the loans failed, how were they to blame? Their judgments were no more faulty than those of almost all the other players. Implicitly, compensation is based on relative performance, see e.g. Nalebuff and Stiglitz (1983a, 1983b), and such incentive schemes can lead to herd behavior, and exacerbate economic fluctuations.

[32] One can make this point somewhat more precisely. Optimal incentive schemes for risk averse managers in situations where output provides a very weak signal concerning effort entail relatively little weight being put on output. Matters here are even more difficult, because of the ambiguity in ascertaining whether (or when) a loan goes sour that we noted earlier. Would the loan eventually have been repaid if it were rolled over? Or would rolling over a loan simply compound the losses? If the loan is not rolled over, the original lending officer may say the blame for non-repayment lies not with him, but with the decision not to roll over.

## Concluding remarks

The portfolio approach to regulation focuses on the limitations of each of these mechanisms for regulatory control. Each is imperfect, and all of them can be used to complement each other. As we have noted, there are costs associated with imposing capital adequacy standards, capital is often very imperfectly measured, and the risk adjustments are imperfect. There are costs associated with each of the other constraints, and none of them by itself can prevent all instances of banks engaging in excessive risk taking (where social risks exceed private risks.) That is why, in general, a *portfolio* approach is required, with the emphasis on different elements depending on the stage of development of the economy, its regulatory capacities, and the nature of the risks which it faces.

## The theory of financial restraint

We have argued that constraints can play an important role in sound prudential regulation; regulators should not, in general, just rely on rigid enforcement of capital adequacy standards.

Murdoch and Stiglitz (1993) have argued more broadly that financial restraints[33] played a positive role in East Asia's rapid growth. (Financial restraint should not be confused with financial repression, which led to highly negative real interest rates, and had adverse effects on economic growth[34]; under financial restraint, interest rates remain positive, though often low.) Financial

---

[33] Financial restraints entail not only the constraints discussed in the previous section of this chapter, but also entry restrictions, discussed more fully in chapter 10. These entry restraints are important, because without them, the restraints on, say, deposit rates will not translate into higher profits, but will be dissipated in excess entry. As we noted earlier, the importance of franchise value poses a difficult policy choice: more competition, even as it provides a spur to innovation and efficiency, leads to lower profits, less franchise value, and therefore a higher chance of bad lending practices. Note that having a large number of banks need not ensure competition in the market on which we focus in this book, the supply of credit, so that there need not be a simple relationship between the *number* of banks and the effectiveness of competition. It may be possible to design policies which, while they restrain the number of banks, increase the effectiveness of competition. Pursuing this issue would take us beyond the scope of this book.

[34] See Shaw (1973); McKinnon (1973, 1988a, 1988b).

restraint not only entailed restrictions on interest rates, but also on entry. Financial restraint thus enhanced profitability – increasing franchise value *and* net worth – on both accounts leading to more prudential lending (banks had more resources with which to lend, and stronger incentives not to engage in excessive risk taking, because they had more at risk.)[35] Financial restraint arguably led to increased aggregate savings (since the adverse effect of the lower deposit rates on household savings was negligible, while there was a large positive effect from redistributing income from the household sector to the corporate sector, where the marginal propensity to invest, and thus to save was very high), and since financial restraint resulted in lower borrowing costs for firms, it led to higher levels of net worth, an enhanced ability to bear risk, and increased levels of investment and growth.

Critics of financial restraint simply failed to note the limitations on alternative ways of increasing firm and bank equity,[36] they under-emphasized the distinction between debt and equity,[37] underplaying the advantages that equity provided. They over-emphasized the significance of household interest elasticity of savings, under-emphasized the importance of *security* of deposits,[38] and perhaps under-emphasized the impact of the redistributive consequences of financial constraints on aggregate savings and investment.

### Concluding remarks

The essential point of this extensive discussion of the design of bank regulations is to show the richness of the equity-constrained theory of banking, its ability to provide guidance not

---

[35] Other restraints (such as on real-estate lending) presumably had adverse effects on franchise value.

[36] That is, they ignored the limitations on the ability to raise equity that were the focal point of our discussions in chapter 2.

[37] To be sure, the governments might have improved equity markets, e.g. through legal reforms, but even in most industrialized countries, as we have noted, little new capital is raised through equity markets, partly because even today, relatively few countries have adequate protections for minority shareholders.

[38] By enhancing bank net worth, they reduced the likelihood of default. Government deposit insurance was, of course, an alternative way of enhancing security.

only in the design of monetary policy, but also regulatory policy. Changes in regulatory regimes – both in regulations and in the manner in which they are implemented – have had marked impacts on the supply of loanable funds. For instance, we saw earlier how tightening capital adequacy standards can (and normally would) result in a reduction in the supply of loans at each interest rate. In several instances (such as the recession that occurred in 1991), these changes in regulatory regime have played a major role in contributing to an economic downturn or inhibiting a quick recovery. The 1991 downturn was not only related to the deterioration of banks' balance sheets that had occurred over the previous decade, but to the tightening of regulations and their implementation that followed the 1989 bail-out.

# TEN

# Financial market liberalization

One important form of regulation in many developing countries is entry restrictions, especially for foreign banks. These seemingly protectionist measures have been widely criticized, and the WTO has recently been involved in liberalizing the market for financial services. In our earlier discussion, we decomposed a change in the regulatory environment into impacts on constraints (including resource constraints) and incentives. We can approach this aspect of financial services liberalization from the same perspective. Here, we want to use the framework of part I to assay the impact of these measures on both the flow of credit to domestic firms and the stability of the financial system, and hence the economy.

One of the advantages of such opening up is presumably that it creates credit institutions which can make use of foreign expertise to provide credit more efficiently and effectively. On the other hand, the foreigners' information base is often markedly weaker, at least with respect to small and medium-sized domestic firms, than is that of domestic banks. Foreign banks lend disproportionately to foreign firms, where they are likely to have an informational advantage (that is, they are likely to be better informed about such firms than are domestic banks, which are likely to be better informed about small and medium-sized domestic firms).

In the model of restrictive banking, we saw how a change in the supply of deposits to any bank affects its lending activity. The opening up of new foreign banks which are capable of taking deposits changes the supply of credit. It might – if the enhanced competition leads to an increased deposit rate – lead to overall increased credit (unless such increases are offset by monetary authorities). But some groups of borrowers (foreign firms) might get more and others (small and medium-sized domestic firms) might get less. In a world of monopolistic competition, the additional entry may not lead to more savings, or at least sufficiently large increases in savings to compensate for the disadvantages which will be shortly described. The questions are: What is the elasticity of savings? And how much will the deposit rate increase?[1] Aggregate savings in financial institutions could decrease, even if there were a slight increase in the real interest rate, because of a more than offsetting reduction in the security of deposits as a result of the lower net worth of domestic banks (as competition lowered profit margins and diverted some high-profit customers).[2]

The reduced deposits in domestic banks would (at least in the model of restrictive banking) lead not only to fewer resources available to those banks to lend to domestic firms, but also (as a result of a wealth effect) could lead them to invest a smaller proportion of their reduced wealth in risky domestic loans.[3] And to repeat what we said earlier, foreign lending and domestic lending are *not* perfect substitutes, since the two sets of institutions have different information bases, and therefore are likely to lend to different kinds of firms. It is possible that even if overall lending increased, domestic firms could be worse off. And because they have less access to resources, growth would be retarded.

---

[1] It is even possible that the deposit rate could fall. Hoff and Stiglitz (1997) show that in reasonable models of monopolistically competitive banking, seemingly perverse behaviors can arise quite naturally.

[2] One of the reasons that it is argued that financial restraint may have promoted economic growth in East Asia was that it led to stronger banks, and given their increased strength, those in the country had more confidence in them, and thus entrusted their savings to them.

[3] As we shall see below, there is a countervailing effect, arising from the decreased franchise value, which typically is not strong enough to undo the effects just described.

The predictions of the critics have been borne out, at least to some extent, in the developing country which has perhaps gone the furthest in opening up its financial markets to foreign banks, Argentina. Medium-sized and small domestic enterprises have found themselves starved for funds, so much so that the Menem government set up a special ministry to try to find ways of enhancing the flow of credit to them; and the lack of credit flow is generally viewed as playing a major role in the persistence of high (double-digit) unemployment, since 1995.[4]

Ironically, similar issues were of central concern in the development of the banking system in the United States. There was a worry that with national banks, money would flow into the money centers, such as New York; that the money-center banks would disproportionately concentrate their lending near their home bases,[5] thus arresting growth elsewhere in the country. It was only in the mid-1990s – well after the United States had pushed for financial market liberalization abroad – that the United States finally eliminated the restrictions on national banking, and only because the banking system had found ways of circumventing many of the regulations.

But perhaps an equally serious consequence of liberalization may be the *incentives* generated for excessive risk taking. As we have noted earlier, incentives to avoid *excessive* risk taking (essentially taking advantage of the government guarantees) or looting[6] depend on the bank's wealth, both its physical capital (net

---

[4] The argument that the root cause of the unemployment problem is labor market rigidities has become increasingly unconvincing, as an increasing fraction of the labor force and production has moved into the informal, unregulated and non-unionized sectors (by some estimates, up to 50 percent or more). In standard theory, so long as there is a substantial sector with flexible wages, that sector should be able to absorb all the labor; the rigidities should result only in wage differentials, not unemployment.

[5] To be sure, in the political discussions of the time, the information-theoretic base to these worries was not well articulated.

[6] In this chapter, we have focused primarily on the former rather than the latter, and, as we discussed earlier, the line between the two may be thin and difficult to distinguish in practice. A risky loan to a business partner may be the result of the lack of incentives for prudential behavior, and/or it may represent an attempt to use the banks' assets for private gain. In either case, however, interest rates charged are not commensurate with the risks incurred, either because of the implicit government guarantee or because of agency problems. For a discussion of looting, see Akerlof and Romer (1993).

worth) and its franchise value. Increased foreign competition will erode the franchise value of domestic banks, inducing them to undertake greater risk. If this were simply a matter of increasing their loans to domestic small and medium-sized enterprises (a movement to the right along the *RR* curves of part I) then this might be all to the good: it could at least partially offset the erosion of credit to domestic firms as a result of the new foreign entry. It is even conceivable that overall lending to both domestic and foreign firms increases. But the reduction in franchise value is likely not only to induce greater willingness to lend, it is also likely to shift the lending portfolio to high-risk loans. Indeed, banks may be willing to make such loans, even if they have lower over-all social returns.

It is thus not surprising that empirical studies confirm an association between opening up capital markets or financial market liberalization more generally and a later crisis in the financial sector.[7] To be sure, these adverse effects can be avoided, or at least mitigated, by a strengthening of other aspects of regulation, for instance by imposing additional restrictions on real-estate lending. But typically, governments, swept up in the spirit of liberalization, have enhanced opportunities for exces-sive risk taking, just as they should have been tightening them. And, as we have already noted, typically in the process of liber-alization, the regulatory institutions are weakened, as the new foreign banks bid away the most qualified personnel.

### Correcting the bias in lending

Many countries have already moved well down the road to opening up their economies to foreign banks, and others are contemplating doing so. A question which needs to be asked is: are there ways by which the possible adverse effects on lending parterres can be mitigated? A possible answer is provided by the Community Reinvestment Act (CRA) in the United States, which

---

[7] See, for instance, Caprio (1997, 1999); Demirgüç-Kunt and Caprio (1997); Demirgüç-Kunt and Detragiache (1998a, 1998b, 1998c).

in effect imposes a mandate on banks to devote a certain percentage of their lending to within the community. Though CRA requirements have been highly controversial (some arguing that they are an important instrument not only for social purposes – reducing discrimination in lending[8] to communities which have not had access to capital – others that they represent another intrusion of government in the market) the banking community more broadly has come to accept these restrictions, as they have found that CRA lending has encouraged them to develop untapped markets, with reasonable returns.[9] By the same token, developing countries that open up their financial markets to banks from developed countries and elsewhere should consider insisting on CRA requirements, for instance that a large fraction of loans be made to domestic enterprises. Such requirements could be imposed uniformly on domestic and foreign banks, and thus would, in this sense, be non-discriminatory, though to be sure, their impact would largely be on the foreign banks.

---

[8] Some forms of seeming discrimination, e.g. red-lining, in which banks refuse to make any loans within a particular geographical area, can themselves be explained by imperfections of information; given these informational imperfections, there is no interest rate at which loans in the red-line region can yield as high an expected return as loans elsewhere. As we have repeatedly noted, with imperfect information, market allocation processes may not be (constrained) Pareto-efficient, and this may be particularly so in the case of red-lining.

[9] See Canner and Passmore (1997); Schwartz (1998); Seidman (1999).

# ELEVEN

# Restructuring the banking sector

All too often, countries faced the difficult task of restructuring their banking sector. Mounting non-performing loans result in liabilities in excess of assets; banks cannot fulfill their promise to their depositors, let alone continue to perform their central role in providing credit. Inevitably, the recriminations – against politicians who have allowed lax regulation, possibly under the influence of corruption, and pursued misguided macro-economic and structural policies – are followed by bail-outs and bank closures, accompanied by high-minded speeches about never allowing such a state of affairs to arise again. Occasionally, a natural citizen outrage at the very notion of bail-outs has slowed down the process; but the countries that have postponed the bail-out, such as Japan, have suffered, as the contraction of credit inevitably has led to contraction of the economy, or at least stagnation.

Unfortunately, many of the doctors that have been called in to nurse the banking sector back to health have too little understanding either of the role of finance and credit in the economy or of the micro-economic foundations of banking. Thus, all too often, the prescription of the visiting medics entails the following recipe: first, a triage – dividing the banks into three categories, those that are healthy, those that are so sick that they should simply be shut down, and those in between, where a good dose

239

of new equity would restore the patient to health. "Health" is typically measured by the extent to which the bank meets the capital adequacy requirements. The middle category of banks are those that are slightly deficient; they are told to quickly meet those requirements by raising new capital – and if they cannot they scale back their level of operations. The final step in restructuring entails taking out the bad loans from the good banks, putting them into a separate entity to be "resolved" (like the RTC, the Resolution Trust Corporation[1]). Part of the resolution involves, of course, bankruptcy proceedings, which are carried out through conventional bankruptcy law.

The record of those following this prescription has not been stellar, as exemplified by Thailand and Mexico. Four years after the crisis, non-performing loans in Thailand remained at a high level – between 30 percent and 40 percent of total outstanding loans; and the lack of availability of credit has played an important role in that country's slow recovery. Mexico's banks, having been restructured once according to this standard prescription, failed again, and a half decade after the Mexican Tequila crisis, estimates of the cost of bail-out ranged as high as 20 percent of GDP or more. The banks were still not providing adequate credit, especially to the non-traded goods sector, appeals were being made to the World Bank to provide additional support, and the country would have been in a disastrous shape, were it not for the fact that credit to finance its export-led recovery could be obtained through American banks and American trading partners. Meanwhile, Korea and Malaysia, which followed a markedly different course, experienced relatively quick recoveries (see chapter 13).

Many of the premises underlying these policies are the same as those underlying the regulatory policies discussed in chapter 10 – and they have failed for many of the same reasons for which we criticized those policies.

We are concerned in this chapter with systemic bank failures – not the failure of an isolated bank in a well-functioning economy, but the massive failures of financial institutions that are associated with financial crises, and have led to so many major economic

---

[1] Typically, these are called "Asset Management Corporations," AMC for short.

downturns of capitalist economies. The failure to appreciate the difference between these two situations has also played an important role in the failure of some IMF restructuring strategies.

Given the systemic nature of the problem, we take it that one of the central concerns of policy should be the quick restoration of strength to the economy, and that requires the maintenance and restoration of credit flows. Thus, in evaluating alternative strategies, we first need to ask, what is the short-run impact on credit flows.

Restructuring often costs money – typically public money – and often plenty of it. The US bail-out amounted to less than 2 percent of GDP, but other countries' restructuring programs were typically much more expensive in relation to their GDP.[2] But the expenditures on restructuring are often markedly different from other categories of expenditure. It is not that so much resources are actually used in the restructuring (to be sure, there are often considerable administrative expenditures, but these seldom amount to more than a fraction of a percent of GDP), but that money goes from one set of individuals (taxpayers) to others (to pay off depositors, and to recapitalize the banking system). The money that goes to pay off depositors can be thought of as a transfer payment, the money that goes to recapitalize the banking system as an investment. But it is a *financial* investment, not a *real* investment, that is, it does not use real resources – it is not as if a new bank building is constructed. On both accounts, the impacts on the level of aggregate economic activity are markedly different from, say, the impacts associated with building a new school or road. The transfer payments are simply movements of money from one pocket to another – movements which can still have real consequences. The recapitalization expenditures should be part of the capital budget, not treated as part of current expenditures. But typically, national budgets do not differentiate these different categories of expenditures, and a government deficit to finance an investment receives the same opprobrium as any other deficit. Thus, a second desideration of restructuring is to minimize the

[2] In the early 1990s, the Scandinavian countries Norway, Sweden, and Finland found themselves in a banking crisis, with bail-out costs ranging from 4 to 11 percent of GDP. The bailout costs in the Mexican crisis of 1994/95 were 20 percent of GDP. See Mishkin (2000).

budgetary cost to the government, with a clear understanding of the different consequences of different "kinds" of deficits.

Finally, restructurings (bankruptcies) typically involve changes in management and control. The objective of these changes is to ensure that those who control and manage assets are those who can, and have the incentive to, do so best. A third criterion for evaluating restructurings is thus the extent to which they succeed in doing so.

With these criteria in mind, we can evaluate the process of restructurings, as advocated and implemented by the IMF, e.g. in East Asia, and contrast it with alternatives.

Since credit *information* is highly specific, not easily transferable, it is important not to lose the information embedded within institutions. This is especially true since typically each borrower, especially SMEs, has only one or two lenders. (In part I we explained the reason for this.) The general principle of *corporate reorganization* applies here as well: how to preserve as much of the value (here largely reflected in *informational capital*). While wholesale *liquidation* should be a relatively rare event in corporate bankruptcy – since it implies that the value of the organizational (including informational) capital of the firm is zero or negative – it should be even rarer in the context of bank reorganization, for there is virtually no asset *other* than the organizational/informational capital. To be sure, there are banks that are so badly managed (or where the management is so corrupt) that the best solution is shutting down the bank. But when the cause of the financial stress facing a bank is a macroeconomic event – particularly a macro-economic event of the magnitude of the global financial crisis of 1997–1998, a once-in-a-life-time event – then many of the financial institutions that are in distress are there through little fault of their own; even prudent lending policies would have led to distress. The *presumption* that bad management is the cause of the problem is certainly changed. The restructuring of the US S & L institutions is telling in this regard: relatively few banks were shut down; most were taken over by other banks, in ways which preserved much of the organizational and informational capital. Wholesale shutting down banks *on the basis of their current asset positions* simply does not make sense, particularly when the country is already facing severe macro-economic problems.

It may, or may not, make sense to consolidate banks. Merging two weak banks together does not make one strong bank – except if the reduced competition increases the franchise value, or if one weak bank has good management, the other does not. But for a strong bank to take over a weak bank may make sense, if the strong bank achieved its position as a result of good management, not just as a result of luck (and it may be difficult to distinguish the two).

Taking out the bad assets of the banks and putting them into a special "firm" to resolve the bad loans should be viewed from the same perspective. The US RTC was remarkably successful in disposing of its assets relatively quickly, and on reasonably good terms. But the assets were of a specialized nature – real estate. There is no reason to believe that a new government corporation entrusted with the restructuring of the debts, let alone the management, of say, a major automobile company, should that company have defaulted on its loans, would have done a particularly good job. And the history of such asset resolution companies has been, to say the least, mixed. The major argument in favor of taking out the assets from the banks is that it then allows the banks to focus on new lending, and not be distracted with the management problems of the old loans; moreover, it allows a better assessment of the performance of the bank – it is as if it starts with a clean slate. To be sure, there are less noble motives that often underlie the strategy: the bank may be compensated for the loans which the government agency takes over at a value in excess of the true value – it becomes a hidden way of subsidizing the bank, and of injecting new capital into it, when outright "investments" would be frowned upon, given the mantra against government ownership of banks. Alternatively, the country can brag that the level of non-performing loans *within the banking system* has been reduced enormously (as one sometimes hears both for Mexico and Thailand); but the level of non-performing loans within the economy may be little improved. It is all a matter of public appearances. Presumably, relatively few people should be fooled by this charade.

The central issue should be, who can manage the bad loan portfolio best – the bank, which has detailed knowledge of the borrower, or a new institution? If the loan portfolio is bad because of, say, connected lending, then a new institution may well be more effective, but if the loan portfolio is bad because of an unprecedented macro-economic shock, and the bank management has had a two-decade-long success in making good loans, then the case for a new institution is less compelling. In practice, the two issues are often blended together. There was some connected lending in Korea. But Western banks were the *marginal* lenders to many of the Korean conglomerates; they were under no political pressure to make loans to the *chaebol*, and when they made the loans, they were fully aware of the high indebtedness and the highly cyclical nature of many of their businesses. They even seemed less prudent than the Korean banks, not insisting on collateral. If Western banks are *presumed* to be well managed, then the fact that Korean banks had made more secure loans than the Western banks (and had, in many cases, even obtained some cover for the foreign exchange risk) should be evidence of good management; the presumption that new management is required *in general* seems questionable at best.

The general point is one that has been emphasized elsewhere.[3] Strategies for restructuring when there is a single weak bank or corporation should be markedly different than when there are systemic problems, for several reasons:

(1) The inferences about the *quality of management* are different.

(2) The consequences of *delay in restructuring are greater* – when a single firm or bank has a problem, and it is small, then it makes little difference whether it takes six months or six years to restructure; but if a significant fraction of the economy is in distress, then there will be macro-economic consequences from delay – production and employment will be adversely affected; and the individual participants in the restructuring bargaining will not

---

[3] See Miller and Stiglitz (1999); Stiglitz (1999, 2000b); Bhattacharya and Stiglitz (2000).

take into account these macro-economic externalities.[4] That is why it is a mistake simply to leave the resolution to the individual participants. This is particularly the case when there is hope of some kind of bail-out, if the macro-economic problems persist. Some creditors may hold out, thinking that more favorable terms may be obtained.

(3) The *difficulties of restructuring* are greater. If the management of one firm or bank needs to be replaced, there are presumably a large number of alternative candidates; but when most of the firms (or banks) in the country are in distress, where is the new management to come from? There is no reason to believe that the mistakes were made only by top management. And there is little reason to believe that foreign management will be more effective, especially in banking, where informational capital is of such importance. Certainly, the track record of American banks – excessive lending to Latin America in the 1970s, bad real-estate lending in Texas and the Southwest in the 1980s, the S & L *débâcle* that was brought to a head in 1989 – does not inspire confidence that they can simply step in. As many commentators have noted, one of the impressive aspects of the East Asia miracle is that the countries were able to invest at such high levels with such high returns for so long, and this success in part has to do with the banking system.

(4) But most importantly, there is a real specter of the *fallacy of composition:*[5] if each bank tries to increase its capital adequacy, the capital adequacy of the banking system as a whole can actually deteriorate. As each bank tries to meet the requirements, it either has to raise new capital or reduce its lending. But a recession is hardly the best time to raise new capital, and this is especially

---

[4] More generally, bargaining with imperfect information often results in inefficiencies, e.g. strikes. See Farrell (1987).

[5] Samuelson (1948) discussed the fallacy of composition in the context of savings: in an unemployment equilibrium, if all individuals increase their savings (at each level of income), it does not mean that aggregate savings will increase; on the contrary, if investment is fixed, aggregate savings will remain unchanged; aggregate income will simply fall.

the case if the recession has been partially precipitated by weaknesses in the banking system. If new capital is not forthcoming (or if it is forthcoming only on highly unfavorable terms) and if the government is unwilling to put in additional capital into the banking system, the banks must contract their lending. But as each contracts its lending, more firms find they cannot find finance; production is cut back, the economic downturn is exacerbated, and more loans become non-performing.

The recognition of the difference between isolated and systemic distress (bankruptcies) implies that there should be different approaches to restructuring (both corporations and financial institutions). When there is systemic distress, there should be a greater *presumption* for maintaining existing management (the likelihood that the problem is caused by bad management is lower, the likelihood of finding good alternative management is also lower, and the cost of any disruptions associated with the change in management is higher); and there should be greater emphasis on *fast* resolution – the macro-economic consequences of delay take on a first-order importance. Elsewhere, in the context of corporate restructuring, we have argued for, in effect, a strengthening of Chapter 11 provisions of the US bankruptcy code to reflect these principles – a super-Chapter 11.[6] Similar principles need to be developed for the resolution of distress in the financial system.

Recognizing the importance of maintaining financial flows and the difficulties of raising new capital privately, some countries have made the wise decision to inject more capital into the banking system. The question is, how to do this in ways which entail the least cost. A couple of countries have tried an ingenious approach which limits the cost. The government, in effect, borrows money from banks at a low (say, zero) interest cost, and uses the proceeds to buy equity in the banks. Given the increase in the equity of the bank, the bank can increase its lending. To be sure, the usual bank multiplier is attenuated by the fact that the bank has already lent out some money to the government, but that is all.

---

[6] See Miller and Stiglitz (1999); Stiglitz (1999).

There are three criticisms of this approach, only one of which has some validity. The first is that it interferes with the efficiency of the capital market to charge different interest rates to different borrowers. This argument is sheer nonsense: we have already pointed out that the credit market is not an auction market, with credit allocated on the basis of price; and in any case, prices are relevant only at the margin, and the refinancing of the banking system is inframarginal. There are however large distributional consequences of paying zero (or low) vs. high interest rates; in particular, it puts large strains on the public, forcing the government either to borrow more, increase taxes, or reduce expenditures. To be sure, if capital markets worked well, presumably the markets would be unfazed by the additional borrowing, since it finances an asset (the equity shares of the bank) which presumably is of value at least equal to the amounts borrowed. But capital markets are far from perfect and do pay attention to the *apparent* deficit, and no wonder: major international financial institutions, like the IMF, focus on the *apparent* deficit, paying scant attention to the underlying balance sheets, and scare off investors from countries who have large deficits regardless of the reason. The alternatives to increased borrowing, increased taxes or reduced expenditures, do have *real* consequences.

A second objection is that what we have done is nothing but smoke and mirrors; there has been no real strengthening of the banking system. But contrast this low-cost strategy with what normally happens. The government issues bonds to finance the recapitalization at market interest rates. The banks buy the bonds. The new *equilibrium* looks just like the one just described, except that the government is making large interest payments to the banks. In what sense is one a more "smoke and mirrors" equilibrium than the other?

This can be looked at in another way, recalling the discussion at the beginning of this chapter. There is a sense in which relatively little *real* has happened. The government had an implicit liability, picking up the pieces if the bank goes under. It has a quasi-equity position: it shares in the losses, but not the gains. With the equity injection, the government has made its commitment explicit; it put its money "up front," and in return for this receives a fraction of the profits of the bank, should there be profits. A full accounting would show that the value of the *implicit* liability has decreased, at the same time that the assets of the government (its equity holdings) have increased. The government's financial position may have increased, if it has "bargained" well with the bank, i.e. obtained a "fair" equity share for its equity position.

The one argument that has some merit is that the low or zero interest rate paid on the bank borrowing weakens the banks, and certainly that is the case *relative* to what would have happened if the government paid the bank a high interest rate. But the new equity injection itself benefits the bank – the observed increase in its capital adequacy ratio enhances confidence in the bank. And the lower interest payments of the government may increase confidence in the government and in the economy more broadly, and this too redounds to the benefit of the banking system. In the end, the government needs to balance off the benefits and costs of various ways of helping the banking system. In earlier chapters, for instance, we described how financial restraint (restricting deposit rates) can enhance the franchise value of banks. One of the advantages is that it does so without *direct* budgetary cost to the government. Alternatively, the government can contribute bonds to the banks, as its equity investment, with reduced interest rates and with interest deferred, even at the reduced interest rate. The deferral, one might argue, only helps the cash flow of the government, not its *real* position. But we have already repeatedly emphasized the deficiencies in the public accounting systems and the imperfections of the capital markets: as a result, public cash flows do seem to matter.

The final restructuring issue concerns the relationship between corporate and financial sector restructuring. In the context of East Asia, some argued that one should be given precedence over the other. In practice, they must occur simultaneously. If the problems of the corporate sector are not resolved, injecting more money into the banking system will be only a temporary palliative, as corporations will still not be able to start producing until their problems are addressed, and as a result, there will continue to be problems with non-performing loans. But unless corporations can have access to credit at reasonable terms, their problems cannot be addressed. So corporate distress can be resolved only if there is a functioning banking system.

Some have argued that resolving the corporate distress problems simultaneously with the problems posed by the banking system will cost too much, and so priorities have to be established, and the first *public* priority is restructuring the banking system. But this misses an essential point: one does not need – and one should not have – a public bail-out to restructure the corporate sector. Corporate restructuring entails only a restructuring of claims on existing assets, and possibly a change of management. Bankruptcy does not entail the *disappearance* of assets, only the rearrangement of rights to income and control. Beyond limited transactions costs, no real expenditures are required for these rearrangements. There is no public commitment to pay off shareholders, or even bondholders, of corporations, in the way there is a public commitment to pay off depositors. Once those rearrangements have occurred, any viable corporation should be able to obtain whatever funds it needs from private markets, *if the financial system is functioning.* The private sector may not, by itself, efficiently restructure (private participants fail to take into account the social costs of delay), and that is why there may need to be a large role for government in facilitating restructuring; but that role does not require the expenditure of funds.

It is remarkable the extent to which much of the advice by the IMF, the US Treasury, and other outside advisers concerning restructuring in East Asia missed these elementary principles. Countries were told to shut down quickly banks that were undercapitalized, and the way that the banks were shut down in Indonesia – with sixteen banks shut down, an announcement that there would be further bank shut downs, but that depositors would not be covered – precipitated a run that led to the further collapse of the private banking system. As a result, there was massive interruption of credit flows. Countries were told not to interfere with the private restructuring of distressed corporations, advice that Korea and Malaysia studiously ignored, but which Thailand took to heart. Korea and Malaysia made quick progress – with concomitantly quick recoveries; in Thailand, four years after the crisis, very few firms had gone through the bankruptcy process, and non-performing loans remained a massive problem. But while governments should have taken a large role in *financial restructuring*, once firms are on a firm footing, allocative decisions should be left to the private sector. Ironically, the IMF advisers had strong views concerning this *real* restructuring – selling off assets, such as excess capacity in the chip industry – which should have been left to the private sector. Again, fortunately, Korea ignored this advice – its subsequent recovery was led by the profits in the chip industry, as the cyclical downturn in that industry came to an end.[8] And while we have argued that the financial restructuring of corporations should not involve public money, some senior US Treasury officials argued vehemently that a substantial part of the funds being provided by the Japanese (under the so-called Miyazawa initiative) be reserved for financing such restructuring. Again, ironically, this discussion served to delay the restructuring: the hope of outside funds provided further impetus for delay by creditors, especially foreign creditors – in their mind, they saw no reason that the bail-out of foreign lenders to governments and financial institutions should not be extended more broadly.[9]

Finally, there are important interrelationships between macroeconomic policy, regulatory policy, and restructuring: the high interest rate policy advocated by the IMF led to high levels of bankruptcy, thus increasing both the magnitude and the costs of the requisite restructuring. Restrictions on capital markets in Malaysia allowed the country to maintain its interest rates at a lower level without further depreciation of the exchange rate, and thus lowered the extent and cost of the requisite restructuring.

---

[8] While the IMF may have *claimed* competency in macro-economics (a competency which the critics strongly dispute), even the IMF did not claim competency in substantive matters of industrial policy, and indeed, in other contexts, argued that government bureaucrats should not be involved. But that did not seem to prevent it from pronouncing on whether there was excess capacity, e.g. in the chip industry, a judgment which presumably required detailed knowledge about the future evolution of that industry. (To be sure, it was easy to see, given the downturn, that there was *currently* excess capacity, but that has only limited bearing for longer-term decisions.)

[9] It was, of course, not clear whether US Treasury officials were confused in their economics, or simply trying to have the money spent in ways which would be of benefit to US creditors.

# TWELVE

# Regional downturns and development and monetary policy

The increasing liberalization and integration of world capital markets and the establishment of the European Monetary Union (EMU) have raised questions about the ability to use monetary policy to offset an economic downturn (or to limit overheating) in a single country, especially one within a currency union.[1] It is unlikely, for instance, that the European Central Bank (ECB) will lower interest rates, simply to offset an economic downturn in Portugal. Indeed, the fact that governments would have to give up this seemingly powerful instrument is often cited as one of the reasons for not joining a currency union. The counterargument is that with open financial markets, governments really have little discretion in any case; any discrepancy between interest rates in the country and those elsewhere (adjusted for expectations concerning exchange rate changes) will lead to huge capital flows.

The analysis of this book helps us to understand both why regional fluctuations remain important, even in highly integrated economies like the United States, and why national governments still may have some ability to use monetary policy, or more precisely, to affect the flow of credit. It explains why there is still a

---

[1] This chapter is based on joint work with J. Levinson. See Greenwald, Levinson and Stiglitz (1993).

role for central banks in countries, like Ecuador, that dollarize: for them, there is, after all, life after dollarization.

Credit, as we have repeatedly said, is based on information, and information – especially about small and medium-sized enterprises (SMEs) – is local. Credit does not flow freely from one area to another. Banks play a central role in providing credit, and at least in an era where banks are local (or national) changes in the net worth of banks in a given locale (region, nation) are not immediately offset either by a movement of new banks into a region or new capital into existing banks. The theories of equity rationing provide an explanation for why this is so. The significance of this is highlighted by the fact that, while perfect information theories would suggest that capital is more mobile than labor, and that capital would accordingly flow into regions or countries facing a relative scarcity of capital, in practice, however, adjustment often occurs through the migration of labor. Such regions (countries) are often characterized by weak financial institutions – unable to screen between good or bad projects, or to monitor projects well enough to ensure that funds are used well. Hence, while in principle there may exist some good investment opportunities (that is the implication of the fact that there is capital scarcity), outsiders cannot find these opportunities, and hence capital (credit) cannot flow in.

By the same token, an adverse event in one region – an oil price shock in Texas, a cutback in military expenditures in California – has a direct and immediate effect on the net worth of the local banks, in terms of increases in the number of non-performing loans. This, as we have seen, results in reduced lending, and a reduced level of economic activity (both through the ordinary multiplier processes, and through the credit multipliers). If linkages throughout the economy were equally strong, the second- and further-round effects would be dissipated uniformly throughout the national economy. But this is not the case: linkages are stronger within the region in which the original shock occurs, leading as a result to regional recessions.

Such regional linkages and their accompanying recessions are evidenced even in a highly integrated economy such as the United States (though admittedly, until recently, there were restrictions on national banking, which probably served to concentrate the economic impacts). One way of ascertaining the importance of these regional effects is to ask to what extent is the growth in employment in any industry in any state related to local (i.e. state) economic conditions, as reflected in the state rate of growth of employment. "Local" variables can affect local industry employment growth in "traded" goods through several channels. The first is labor supply conditions, which should affect all industries but should be relatively stable over time. Thus, if local supply and other variables are measured as deviations from local trends, the impact of these variables should disappear, since they should be absorbed by the local trends. The second are local "demand" and financial variables. These may vary quite rapidly with local business cycles. Poor local economic conditions should lead to a deterioration of local bank equity positions (as loan defaults rise) and to a decline in non-manufacturing employment (i.e. in industries serving local customers). However, poor local economic conditions should lead to a strengthening in manufacturing employment *if local financial markets are not important.* Lower local service employment demand should reduce local wages and stimulate manufacturing output and employment. However, if local financial markets are important, lower local activity, leading to a deterioration in local bank equity positions (as loan defaults rise), should cause a decrease in loan availability to all local borrowers, and lower manufacturing output and employment.

Thus, estimation of a model

$$N_{jkt} - \overline{N}_t = a + b(N_{kt} - \overline{N}_t) + c(N_{jt} - \overline{N}_j) \qquad (12.1)$$

should discriminate between a model of information-based, regional capital market segmentation and a more traditional competitive model, where

> $N_{jkt}$ = Employment in region $j$ in industry $k$ at time $t$ (used as a surrogate for output)
> $\overline{N}_t$ = Total national employment in period $t$
> $N_{kt}$ = National employment in industry $k$ in period $t$
> $N_{jt}$ = Local employment in region $j$ in period $t$ (used as a surrogate for local economic activity),
> $\overline{N}_j$ = Average local employment in region $j$.

As discussed above, all the variables are measured in terms of percentage deviation from their trend values. In a traditional model, the coefficient on regional employment, $c$, should be negative and that on national industry employment should be positive. Only in an imperfect information model should the coefficient $c$ on regional employment be positive. Hence, in order to test the appropriateness of the theoretical model of the previous section we have estimated a variant of (12.1).

### Estimation

The variant of (12.1) that we estimated used log-differences as the basic variables, essentially regressing percentage employment growth in industry $k$ in region $j$ on national percentage employment growth, national percentage employment growth in industry $k$, and percentage employment growth in region $j$. The data used are for the United States with each region corresponding to a particular state. Industries were identified by 2-digit SIC code with only manufacturing industries used, and the effects of industry conditions were allowed to differ by industry. The data are for the years from 1972–1982. The results are presented in table 12.1.

The signs of the industry variables are generally positive (as expected) and where negative (in two cases) are insignificant. The national economic activity variable is strongly positive, suggesting that positive capital market (or traditional Keynesian) effects on the national market are large and significant (both statistically and economically). More importantly the local activity variable is also strongly positive and statistically significant, suggesting that there are strong local economic spillovers among industries and that, since these are positive, some form of the capital market imperfections model seems to apply.

Note that if the coefficient on the state growth rate of employment had been negative, it would have implied only that improved local supply conditions as a result of a downturn are stronger than the financial market effects. Those may still have the predicted sign. By contrast, when the coefficient on the state growth rate of employment is positive, it suggests that the local

Table 12.1  *Regression results, industry percentage growth in employment by state in each year (dependent variable)*

| $R^2 = 0.0876$ | | |
|---|---|---|
| Variable | Coefficient | $T$-statistic |
| National growth rate of employment | 0.885 | 32.01 |
| State growth rate of employment | 0.673 | 17.39 |
| National growth rate of employment in industries: | | |
| SIC22 | −0.034 | 0.27 |
| SIC23 | −0.019 | 0.71 |
| SIC24 | 0.005 | 0.26 |
| SIC25 | 0.024 | 1.20 |
| SIC26 | 0.005 | 0.20 |
| SIC27 | 0.045 | 2.02 |
| SIC28 | 0.068 | 3.26 |
| SIC29 | 0.039 | 1.62 |
| SIC210 | 0.017 | 0.37 |
| SIC211 | 0.113 | 2.58 |
| SIC212 | 0.054 | 1.31 |
| SIC213 | 0.020 | 0.94 |
| SIC214 | 0.029 | 1.15 |
| SIC215 | 0.032 | 1.80 |
| SIC216 | 0.049 | 2.60 |
| SIC217 | 0.046 | 1.93 |
| SIC218 | 0.106 | 2.70 |
| SIC219 | 0.067 | 2.26 |

capital market effects are very large indeed – significantly larger than the offsetting labor market effects.

The only disturbing element in the regression is the relatively small magnitude of the industry effects, but this may well be attributable to definitional problems in allocating firms to SIC codes and the resulting errors in variables. Nevertheless, the empirical results provide relatively strong support for the basic hypothesis of capital market imperfections.

There is a flip side to the fact that financial institutions are, at least to some degree, local: with highly integrated capital markets, capital flows freely, so that one cannot use subsidies (direct or indirect) to local financial institutions to encourage local lending, and thereby local economic activity. Strengthening local institutions may indeed lead to more lending, but the money will find its way to the highest return investments; if a local economy is facing a downturn, it is unlikely that much of it will remain in the locality. But if information is highly local, then at least a large fraction of the increased lending capacity (or desire to lend) will be reflected in local lending activity. Similar results hold for other policies (such as changes in regulations) that might affect total lending activity: a disproportionate amount of the induced lending will remain local.

Thus, in a standard neo-classical model, one might have expected that the huge disparity in capital per worker between the newly freed economies in Eastern Europe and the economies of the West would be easily addressed, as capital flowed from the latter to the former, until returns were equalized. In fact, relatively little capital flows, and much of the adjustment has been through labor migration.

In such situations, a compelling case can be made for the development of appropriate mechanisms for the allocation of capital; providing subsides to the institutions involved can certainly be justified in terms of the kinds of informational failures which this book has addressed (provided that the country has advanced along enough to have put into place an effective regulatory structure for financial institutions).

In simple welfare terms, lending in these models is always suboptimal. It is constrained, on the one hand, by imperfect information concerning borrowers and on the other by the reluctance of banks to lend when they cannot diversify the risks of their lending by selling new equity. It is the second difficulty that is most easily addressed. Providing financial institutions with equity capital (especially if all institutions are forced to accept the funds so that they do not individually suffer from the adverse signal of doing so) on a subsidized basis should yield a net welfare gain. The question then arises what form such subsidies might most effectively take. Here history suggests that the seigniorage associated with the power to issue money (on favorable interest terms) is a valuable subsidy mechanism. Money creation has almost universally been associated in developed economies with lending institutions that support critical social institutions (government debt issue in the early days of banking and commercial and industry lending more recently). To be sure, like any powerful instrument it can be, and has been, abused. Strong prudential bank regulations, and even the independence of the central bank (with all of its drawbacks in a democratic society[2]) are ways that have been devised for limiting these abuses. The *advantages* of this subsidy mechanism (recognizing the dangers) are several: First, the subsidy directly passes to the institutions (i.e. the banks) with the information and incentives to use it effectively as a basis for greatly amplified amounts of lending activity.[3] Second, when there are constraints on bank interest payments (either formal or informal), the seigniorage effectively takes the form of equity capital which is the form most difficult to raise in financial markets.

To see the importance of just these two factors, consider first the likely impact on economic activity of a $25 billion increase in household wealth. This might stimulate some increase in consumption – by standard estimates less than $2 billion. In a $10 trillion economy, this is likely to have a trivial effect. However, an equal increase in bank capital could, if the banks were constrained by their capital in their lending activity, generate a multiple increase in investment, e.g. a tenfold, or more, increase.[4] A $250 billion increase in investment can have a significant effect, even on a $10 trillion economy. In an economy

---

[2] For a more extensive discussion of these, see Stiglitz (1998a).

[3] The word "effectively," while vague, should be emphasized. Because banks look only to the returns which they appropriate, which do not include the "profits" of the entrepreneurs to whom they lend, in general bank lending decisions may not be Pareto-optimal. But the distortions arising from ignoring these returns may be small compared to the advantages arising from the use of dispersed information and the incentives that banks have (when properly regulated) to make loans that at least repay what has been lent, with interest.

[4] The amount by which lending could or would increase would depend on which of several constraints are binding, e.g. if the capital adequacy requirements constraint is binding, and the country has an 8 percent capital requirement, an increase in capital can support a twelve fold increase in lending. A risk averse bank, however, might not decide to allocate all the additional portfolio to lending; it might, for instance, decide to buy some long-term government bonds. If the reserve requirement is binding, then we have to look at how the particular action of the government affects the base money supply.

in which deposit rates are equal to zero, an increase in the money supply by \$25 billion increases its annual seigniorage by \$2.5 billion, if the interest rate is 10 percent, and if the change is expected to be permanent (e.g. if short-term interest rates follow a random walk), the present discounted value of that is (approximately) \$25 billion.[5]

"Seigniorage" subsidies have one further advantage – flexibility. They can be supplied more or less continuously (as opposed to tax subsidies which are usually constrained by annual budget cycles). They can even be targeted. For example, central banking authorities may directly subsidize regional banks by cutting their reserve requirements either directly or by lending through the discount window against reserves at very low rates of interest. Comparable flexibility in fiscal programs is rare.

The analysis also raises an important caveat to recent policy changes through much of the developed world, a note we have already sounded several times: the deregulation of bank interest rates has gone a long way to eliminating seigniorage profits in the United States; not only does this necessitate a tightening of prudential standards (since the franchise value of the bank is reduced), but it also means that the ability of the government to use monetary policy in the effective way that it has been used in the past may be reduced. It may be that the government has no choice: modern technologies have limited the ability of the government to restrict competition in the banking sector (without strong adverse consequences). While more flexible and competitive markets *may* reduce the need for government intervention to stabilize the economy (that is one interpretation of the observation that the United States had an expansion for almost two decades before the recession in 2001, with only a short, and

---

[5] The manner of increasing the bank's net worth just described may not directly translate into the large increase in lending described earlier; it is not net worth but "capital on hand" that matters for the capital adequacy requirements. But on the basis of the increased net worth, the bank might be able to raise additional outside capital. Alternatively, if the bank had limited its lending because of its risk aversion, the increased net worth may make it willing to lend more (lending will typically be a multiple of net worth).

by some accounts moderate,[6] downturn in 1990–1991, but there will still be fluctuations, times at which government would like to stimulate the economy. This may be especially so for particular regions, and our analysis suggests that monetary policy may prove an increasingly ineffective instrument for doing so.

## Regional banking and regional development: the importance of institutions

The models presented here argue for the efficacy of institutional (e.g. banks, insurance companies, venture capital firms) rather than public market mechanisms for allocating capital (e.g. the New York Stock Exchange, NYSE). Among these, industrial companies are perhaps the most important, through their power to direct their retained earnings. The greater mobility of within-firm capital (as opposed to public financial market capital) suggests that investment decisions of large multinational or national corporations are efficient means of funding regional development. Similarly, the existence of national as opposed to regional financial institutions might, in principle, help to offset regional imbalances in capital availability.[7]

However, there is an important limit to this, related to the central themes of this book. Information is imperfect, and does not flow freely *even within firms, whether they are financial or non-financial*; and indeed, we have argued that these informational imperfections lie at the root of the immobility of capital. If the individuals within a national firm or bank who are responsible for investment decisions are located in and thus well

---

[6] There is some debate about how severe the downturn was. As measured by the increase in unemployment from where the unemployment rate had been before, the 1990–1991 downturn appears moderate. But, elsewhere we have argued that the size of the recession should be measured relative to the economy's potential, and there is evidence that NAIRU (the unemployment rate at which the inflation rate starts to increase) had, by 1990, declined substantially (Braun 1984; Stiglitz 1997), implying that the economy's potential output was substantially greater. By this reckoning, the 1990–1991 recession was of average size. (See Stiglitz 1998a.)

[7] Moreover, national banks allow greater diversification of risk, and thereby greater risk taking by banks.

informed about one region of a national economy, then investment funds will tend to be concentrated in that region. The
resulting imbalance in the allocation of funds can be more severe than that under a regime of local banks or firms. In the case
of local banking, local firms in the favored region would be constrained in their access to funds (particularly equity) and this
would limit any bias in favor of that region. National banks or
firms would, in contrast, have access to national sources of
funds and the investment imbalance would then not be limited
by barriers to capital mobility. Mechanisms of this kind may account for the relative lack of success in regional development
in the United Kingdom, France, and Italy as opposed to the
striking success of the locally based banking system in the
United States in promoting growth in the formerly depressed
Southeastern United States. By the same token, local banks (and
local venture firms) have taken a central role in financing Sili-
con Valley's expansion. The United States has been rapidly moving towards a system of national banks. The good news is that,
so far, the headquarters of these national banks have been dispersed throughout the country. Maintaining this diversity – and
working towards the national collection of investment opportunity information, not just the pooling of national funds – is
essential if the strong basis of geographical dispersed growth is
to be maintained.

These considerations play out on an even grander scale at the
global level. There remains a real risk that financial market deregulation in less developed countries – if not attentive to the institutional and informational issues stressed here – will work to
impede the balanced development of those countries.[8]

---

[8] As we emphasized in chapter 10.

# THIRTEEN

# The East Asia crisis

The East Asia crisis has provided a wonderful – yet unfortunate – opportunity for testing many of the ideas presented here. The crisis demonstrated powerfully the dangers of misguided monetary theories; the alternative paradigm presented here, while it clearly could not have forestalled the downturn,[1] might have led to policies that would have resulted in recessions that were less deep and less prolonged. The basic story of that crisis is now well known. During the 1970s and 1980s, the countries of East Asia experienced rapid economic growth – by most accounts the most rapid development any region of the world had experienced. The growth brought with it improvements in social indicators (health, education) and marked reductions in poverty. While there was some controversy over the "model" that they had pursued, it combined a strong role for government with market oriented policies. Governments had helped create financial institutions, and they were highly regulated. In the early 1990s, largely under the influence of outsiders (the US Treasury and the IMF), policies of financial and capital market liberalization were put into place. This resulted in a flood of capital coming into the countries in the

---

[1] Though the theories presented here would have discouraged the rapid financial market liberalization which played such an important role in creating the preconditions for the crises.

region – and then a sudden reversal, a huge outflow. The magnitude of these changes in flows was enormous. In the case of Thailand, the change in flows amounted to 14 percent of GDP and in the case of South Korea 9 percent of GDP. In the case of East Asia as a whole, the turnaround in capital flow between 1996 and 1997 amounted to $105 billion, more than 10 percent of the GDP of these combined economies.[2] In 1990, long-term net resource flows to East Asian and Pacific countries were over 26 billion USD. By 1997, they reached over 100 billion USD.[3] While much of the flow of funds was foreign direct investment (FDI), there was a substantial amount of short-term funds, such as bank loans. Given the high savings rate, the countries hardly needed the additional funds; they would have been hard pressed to invest what savings they had well. Indeed, some view their sustained ability to invest their high level of savings reasonably well to be the real "East Asia miracle."

The ideologues pushing capital market liberalization argued that it would allow a greater diversification of sources of funding, and that would enhance economic stability. In making this argument, they did not look either to the theory or evidence of short-term capital flows. In fact, such flows typically are pro-cyclical: as the old adage goes, bankers are willing to lend to those who do not need their funds. Accordingly, when a crisis appeared on the offing (and note that the model in chapter 7 argues that such crises need not be related to weak fundamentals, but simply to changes in sentiment[4]) they pulled their money out of the country – and their expectations were self-fulfilling.

The IMF responded with its usual prescription, fiscal and monetary contraction, though the circumstances in East Asia were markedly different from those in Latin America (and even there, their record of success might be viewed as questionable in terms of the long-run impacts – a lost decade of growth). The East Asian countries (in contrast to the Latin American countries at the time of their crisis) were initially in rough macro-economic balance,

---

[2] See Rodrik (1999).
[3] See Global Development Finance (1998).
[4] And research supports the view that most of the disturbances to developing countries have been exogenous. See Calvo and Reinhart (2000).

with fiscal surpluses, and little inflation.[5] The falling stock market prices and declining exchange rates, as well as overall pessimistic expectations, had the predictable effect of lowering domestic consumption and investment; the latter was especially significant in countries like Thailand where the real-estate bubble that had been feeding the economy burst. Thus, even without the contractionary monetary and fiscal policies, the economies were headed into a recession. The Fund compounded these problems by excessively tight monetary and fiscal policies. This is not the place to analyze the sources of these marked policy failures on the part of the IMF: to what extent they were the result of faulty models, and to what extent they were the consequence of the fact that the objectives of the Fund may differ markedly from those of the particular country.[6]

Here, we want to focus on how a set of monetary theories led to consistently wrong policies, which converted what might have been ordinary recessions into deep recessions and depressions. The essential failure related to the failure to recognize the central role of credit and the institutions that provide credit.

### Raising interest rates

The governments were told to raise interest rates – and not just by twenty-five or fifty basis points. Before the crisis, Korea's real interest rates were reasonable – around 9 percent with an inflation rate of 4 percent. It was told to raise its interest rates to 25 percent – but then it was decided that that was not enough; they should be allowed to float up to 40 percent! For highly leveraged firms (and, as was well known, many Korean firms were very highly leveraged with short-term debt) in competitive industries, such increases in interest rates, even if held for

---

[5] Indeed, many observers believed that part of the problem facing the East Asian countries was "excess capacity" – in effect a situation of excess *supply*, not demand.

[6] That is, some critics of the IMF believe that the Fund was more concerned with ensuring that creditors got repaid than with ensuring that GDP in the affected countries remained high. (The fact that they may have failed on both accounts may shed little light into their *objectives*.)

only a short period of time, were devastating. It was not certain how long those interest rates would be held. Not surprisingly, the wealth effect of this policy was enormous. These high-interest policies interacted with other policies (some of which are described below) which led to a contraction in the availability of credit. In some cases, even firms that were willing to pay the high interest rates could not get credit.

It was not only that as a result of these monetary policies firms cut back on their investment and liquidated their inventories, but they also cut back on production, even for exports. It was exporters' failure to respond to the huge exchange rate reduction[7] – which should have stimulated demand – which makes it clear that the economy was not just responding to a fall in aggregate demand. Such consequences were inevitable, unless the producer could obtain cheaper sources of credit elsewhere (as some exporters could) or unless wage and price adjustments were sufficiently large to compensate for the huge increase in capital costs. In practice, even reductions in real wages of 20 percent or more did not suffice. Thus, monetary policy had the usual effects on aggregate demand (amplified by the adverse effects of increased bankruptcy probabilities on firm demands) which have been the subject of traditional discussions, but they also had huge effects on aggregate supply.[8]

While the first-round effects may have occurred through reduced availability of credit, higher interest rates, and the resulting increases in cost of capital and lower firm net worth, a second set of effects quickly came to dominate: bankruptcy. The credit interlinkages emphasized in chapter 7 took center stage. Firm bankruptcies weakened banks, which led to reduced credit and less favorable terms, contributing to the downward spiral.

While the negative effects were thus far greater than traditional theory might have suggested, the benefits that advocates of these policies had touted did not materialize. The argument put forward by the advocates of these policies was a simple one. It is

---

[7] In some cases, though dollar exports were stagnant or down, export *volumes* were up; but the increases in aggregate export volumes were far less than one would have expected, given the magnitude of the devaluation, especially given the downward adjustment in real wages.

[8] See Greenwald (1998).

based on a simple portfolio theory. Individuals allocate their wealth among different assets. If one increases the return on one asset, the demand for that asset will go up – hardly rocket science. There was a simple diagnosis of the countries' problem: markets had lost confidence in these countries; funds had to be attracted back in, and the way to do so was to increase the return to holding funds in the country. Meanwhile, reforms would be undertaken in the country, and as the effect of those reforms could be seen, confidence would be restored, so the need for high interest rates would diminish.

There was a single, crucial variable that was omitted from the analysis: the probability of bankruptcy, the variable which we have argued, is at the center of all monetary analysis. If everyone always repaid their loans, then there would be little role for financial institutions. Credit would be a trivial matter. It was understandable, perhaps, for economists who had been trained in macro-economics a quarter of a century ago to have failed to pay adequate attention to that variable. Even today, the term "bankruptcy" does not appear in the indices of most macro-economics textbooks. Yet, for policymakers the mistake is unforgivable. Why was it that the banks were refusing to roll over their loans to Korea? Simply because they believed that the probability of bankruptcy had increased, and presumably, in accordance with the Stiglitz–Weiss model, they were unconvinced that there was any interest rate at which they could obtain the required return in risk-adjusted terms.

Worries about bankruptcy were at the heart of the crisis, and accordingly, worries about how policies would affect those bankruptcy probabilities – which were clearly endogenous – should have been at the heart of the policy discussions. But they were not. Not only were they not at the heart of the discussion, they were not seldom if ever even raised.[9]

---

[9] Stiglitz (who was then Chief Economist of the World Bank) cannot recall a single instance in which the impact on the probability of bankruptcy was discussed by IMF officials (other than when he raised the issue), not a single study of the IMF which attempted to estimate the impact, nor a single study in which the effect of the increased bankruptcy probabilities on the aggregate level of economic activity in East Asia was taken into account in a serious way.

Both the policies pursued and the words spoken by the IMF contributed to the perception of an increased bankruptcy probability. We have already noted the adverse effects of the increase in interest rates. The policies concerning shutting down banks exacerbated these problems – many firms found that the banks upon which they had relied for credit were shut down. Under the circumstances, it is not surprising that other banks were unwilling to take them on as new customers.[10]

Sachs has emphasized the adverse effect of the public rhetoric.[11] He described it as like calling "fire" in a crowded theater. It was the policy panic, as much as anything else, that caused the damage. In earlier crises (say, in Latin America), countries were identified as facing severe problems of macro-management, budget deficits, and loose monetary policy. An agreement with the IMF that stipulated the size of the deficit and the pace of monetary expansion could address these problems quickly; and as investors saw these problems being addressed, their willingness to put money into the country returned (though often slowly). Here, however, the situation was entirely different. There were no complaints or anxieties about the countries' ability to pursue sound monetary and fiscal policies; that had been a hallmark of the region for three decades. Indeed, in many respects, they put to shame the supposedly more advanced countries of the OECD. The IMF, the US Treasury and other critics focused on another set of variables – from weak financial institutions to crony capitalism. The difficulty was that these problems cannot be dealt with overnight, with a stroke of the pen, in the way that fiscal deficits and monetary constraints can be imposed. Indeed, for outsiders, it may take years to tell whether governments have adequately dealt with a problem in, say, the weaknesses of financial institutions. Ronald Reagan papered over the problems in the US S & L well enough to satisfy many of those in the market for years (though not well enough to satisfy academic critics); it was several years before it became recognized that his seeming solution simply provided more room for the problem to fester, so that when it was finally addressed in 1989,

---

[10] In some instances, IMF policies made this impossible.
[11] Radelet and Sachs (1998).

it was far worse than it would have been had it been addressed earlier.

To be sure, governments could sign programs affirming their commitment to undertake strategies for strengthening financial institutions and reducing the extent of crony capitalism, and such programs will help. But will they be fully believed, until the fruits of those programs are realized? That may take a long time. Given the mismatch between the depth of the structural–political problems described and the time allowed for correcting the problems, it is not surprising that most investors outside the country did not restore their credit at the signing of the IMF programs. There was, in effect, nothing the governments could have done that could have (in the relevant time span) fully allayed those concerns.

Even more dramatic was the impact on sentiment of those within the country. As economic conditions within the country worsened, given the open capital markets, it made perfect sense for these individuals to diversify their portfolios, taking money out of the country. Indeed, one could have anticipated that this effect might be large: analysis of portfolio holdings in the region suggested that many held portfolios that were too concentrated within the region. Their portfolios were disproportionally concentrated in East Asia because they felt returns were high, sufficiently high to compensate them for the risk. But the high interest rate/large fiscal contraction policy increased the risk and reduced the return; the optimal portfolio reallocation entailed huge flows abroad, which would have been only partially alleviated under the most optimistic scenarios even if the government had complied fully with the IMF programs. Making matters still worse, many in the region were rightly convinced that, given the misguided nature of those policies, "full compliance" likely would have worsened the situation – and even the IMF eventually came to agree that its excessively contractionary fiscal policies had done so.

Anyone who looked at the problems through these lenses would have had a markedly different reaction to the increase in interest rates than that the IMF rhetoric suggested should happen. *They* said it would "restore confidence" – though the details of why it should do so were never made clear. The explanations they put forward were simple, but hardly convincing.[12] The high interest rates, they asserted, would strengthen the exchange rate (though in the past they frequently did not).[13] Seeing the strengthened exchange rate, confidence would be restored – but why this should be so, if the only reason that the exchange rate is strengthened is that there is a high interest rate which will be maintained for only a temporary period, is also not clear. The same argument holds for the massive bail-outs which were supposed to support the exchange rate. In effect, the IMF was claiming that a temporary intervention, resulting in a movement along the demand curve for foreign exchange, could have long-term effects, shifting the demand curve. The only explanation of this proffered by the IMF was an appeal to the mystical concept of "confidence." The IMF and its friends played the role of market psychologist, dangerous grounds for anyone, but especially for bureaucrats who are not betting their own money. Their ability to predict market reactions was dismal. But what was particularly disturbing was the lack of a theoretical framework with which to assess the *consistency* of the assumptions about *expectations*. For instance, one of the few models which are consistent with a temporary increase in interest

---

[12] For a more extended discussion of this point, see Stiglitz (1999).

[13] See Furman and Stiglitz (1998); Kraay (1998a, 1998b). Equally disturbing was the absence of a discussion – let alone a substantive theoretical and empirical analysis – of the incidence of interest rate increases vs. exchange rate decreases. It was simply asserted that the failure to support the exchange rate would have disastrous effects, far worse than the high interest rates that were imposed in the (failed) attempt to support the exchange rate. Even at the time, it should have been clear that further declines in the exchange rate might have had only limited *further* adverse effects, especially in Malaysia (where firms had very limited foreign indebtedness) and Thailand, where the foreign denominated debt was held by real-estate firms and the financial institutions which had lent to them (both of which were, in effect, already in bankruptcy as a result of the bursting of the real-estate boom) and exporters, who would have stood to gain as much or more from the depreciation of the exchange rate as they stood to lose from the increased Baht value of their indebtedness; and even the limited adverse effects could have been mitigated had effective policies of systemic bankruptcy (standstills) been put in place. To be sure, such policies might have adversely affected foreign creditors; and within the countries, such policies would have more adversely affected those who had gambled, borrowing short-term abroad without adequate cover. The IMF seemed to be putting the interests of these parties ahead of the innocent bystanders, small and medium-sized businesses, who had not only engaged in reasonable borrowing to fund the natural growth of their firms, a growth which had underlain the East Asia miracle, but had engaged in neither imprudent foreign borrowing nor lending.

rates having a permanent effect on exchange rates (even after interest rates are reduced) is based on a *signaling model* in which the actions (the high interest rates) are used to convey a message (that the central bank is willing to deal with the problems in a serious way, by constraining the supply of credit). But in the context of East Asia, few informed outsiders doubted the commitment of the central banks and the finance ministries to deal effectively with those issues. More problematic was the ability of the central banks to deal with the subtleties associated with restructuring highly levered firms and financial institutions. The high interest rate signal, as effective as it may have been in conveying information concerning the willingness to deal with the problems of excessive monetary expansion and large (non-cyclical) budget deficits, may actually have been counterproductive in dealing with the problems facing East Asia. Following the same or similar recipes might well have suggested to investors that the IMF and the countries' monetary authorities were simply unaware of the important differences in the circumstances. Thus the high interest rate policy, rather than restoring confidence to the economy, may actually have served to undermine it.

Indeed, the high interest rate policies exacerbated what were often identified as the underlying problems facing the countries. In Korea, for instance, the problem of excessive leverage was exacerbated; firms with short-term debts had to pay out an increasing fraction of their income to their creditors, and many had to borrow more simply to stay alive — they had actually to increase their indebtedness, when the long-term solution for increasing stability required a reduction in indebtedness. Throughout the region, the increased bankruptcies and corporate distress that the high interest policy (and the macro-economic contraction to which fiscal tightening also contributed) induced increased the level of non-performing loans, further weakening the banking system – again cited throughout the region as an underlying source of weakness.

Lack of transparency – lack of information about the financial position of firms – was also cited as an underlying source of the region's difficulty. But the huge increases in interest rates had correspondingly huge impacts on asset values, and would have greatly increased the uncertainty about the value of different firms' net worth. One would have had to have detailed information about precisely which assets were held to make even a rough estimate, and with the turmoil in asset markets only increased by the huge increases in interest rates, even knowledge about today's market values of particular assets provided an unreliable guide to future market values.

The analysis of this book thus helps explain why it was that the rescue packages, with their large bail-outs and contractionary fiscal and monetary policies, failed in every respect – failed to arrest the decline in the exchange rate, failed to maintain the economic strength of the region, failed to prevent defaults against the foreign creditors (the objective which seemed to be high in the IMF's mind), failed to restore confidence; but on the contrary may well have exacerbated each of these problems. The IMF has now ceded that it made mistakes in pushing excessively contractionary fiscal policies, in under-estimating the strength of the trade linkages, in the strategy of bank restructuring in Indonesia. But it continues to maintain that it was correct in its monetary policies. Our analysis suggests, on the contrary, that once the adverse effects on bankruptcy probabilities are taken into account (which the IMF ignored), the cost-benefit analysis of raising interest rates is completely changed. Given the prevailing high levels of short-term leverage, it almost surely made it less, not more, attractive to put funds into the countries and thus contributed to a fall in exchange rates, with all the adverse effects associated with that decline that the IMF had pointed to. But even if the increase in bankruptcy probabilities did not fully offset the direct gains from the higher nominal interest rate, the net increase in expected returns would have been small, so that little capital would have been attracted; and the high interest rates imposed huge costs on large sectors of the economy – costs which were especially high given the high short-term leverage. Assessing the balance of costs and benefits required looking at the micro-economic underpinnings – how firms, households, and financial institutions would be affected by changes in exchange rates and interest rates. While the standard monetarist approach (and the methodologies prevalent in the IMF) suggest that such micro-economic detail is irrelevant, our credit-based paradigm moves such micro-economic analyses to center stage. It especially focuses on the role of banking institutions.

## Banking institutions

A central theme of this book is the importance of credit in the functioning of a modern economy, and that the provision of credit depends on specific institutions within a society, e.g. banks and firms, in their role of credit suppliers. The provision of credit entails specific information contained within specific institutions about each specific firm. Credit, in this respect, is very different from money. Money is perhaps the most homogeneous of commodities. One dollar bill is identical to another. Each loan, however, is markedly different from any other loan. We argued, too, that because there are specific, sunk costs associated with the acquisition of this highly specific information, there are likely to be one, or at most, only a few banks in the market for supplying loans to any particular firm, especially if that firm is small or medium-sized. Closures of any bank or firm entail the destruction of organizational and informational capital, the value of which is often summarized in the "goodwill" of the firm. The specific information required for a group of individuals to know how to react and interact with each other typically takes time and is costly to develop; once the organization is destroyed, that capital is destroyed, and to recreate it will be expensive and time-consuming. In most competitive markets, however, there are other firms who have the knowledge, e.g. how to produce pencils, and so their organizational/informational capital provides a base for the expansion of production, if the demand for pencils warrants it. The information which is relevant to an increase in credit is, however, highly specific. To be sure, other banks know the process, how to go about screening and monitoring. But they do not have the specific information base relating to the particular borrower. Replacing that information base is costly; it is an investment, which may or may not pay off.

The East Asia crisis – like other economic downturns – was a situation where firms typically engaged in disinvestment, in liquification of their assets (reducing inventories), not expansion. We have already seen why banks contract their lending: typically, their net worth decreases as loans go sour; their perceptions of risk have (rightly) increased; and in many cases, they face the threat either of bankruptcy or regulatory constraints. Thus, when one bank shuts down, there is a good chance that other banks will not pick up that bank's clients as new customers.

Many of the banks in East Asia were weak. They had made bad loans. Even if they had made only good loans, they might have been in trouble. As any economy goes into a deep recession or depression, many firms go into distress. This is especially the case when the firms are highly leveraged. It is inevitably the case when these firms with high short-term leverage face usurious interest rates of the kind that the IMF demanded. Research at the World Bank even suggests that bankruptcy performed no sorting function, that is, firms which had previously been performing well were as likely to go bankrupt as firms whose performance previously had been weak.[14]

The question of the best way to deal with weak banks has engendered considerable controversy, especially during this crisis. *The central mistake of the IMF – beyond failing to recognize that high interest rates increase the probability of default and thereby increase the flow of capital out of a country, rather than entice a flow of capital into the country – was that their programs failed to realize the importance of trying to preserve the credit system.* This was a failure borne of focusing on the old monetarist approach. Thus, in Indonesia, when they closed sixteen banks, they failed not only to take into account the direct effect of those closures (they focused on the forward-looking effect that they believed such closures would have on *future* incentives, not on the effect that the closures would have on the *current* supply of credit), they failed to take into account how those closures, combined with statements that deposits beyond a minimum amount in other private banks would not be insured, would lead

---

[14] See Ferri and Kang (1999).

to a run on other private banks, greatly undermining the entire credit system. Their focus on monetarist models had led them to look at *total liquidity* of the banking system. If that was all right, they presumed there was nothing to worry about. But as we have said, information is highly specific. Those firms that relied on the banks that were closed or forced to cut back on their lending as a result of the bank runs could not immediately (or possibly ever) go to the banks that had excess liquidity to obtain funds. The latter banks were not necessarily interested in or willing to bear the risk of opening new accounts and expanding lending to new, highly risky customers, who might well return to their original banks, should those banks recover. (Nor would banks with excess liquidity lend these funds to banks with a shortage for exactly the same reason – a lack of confidence in the loans being repaid.)

Remarkably, in the midst of this massive contraction of credit in the Indonesian and Thai economies, some economists at the IMF began to focus on the excess liquidity – the amounts which banks could have lent had they chosen to do so. They became worried about a potential inflationary threat. What would happen if the banks all of a sudden decided to lend to their limit? Aggregate demand might increase. Inflation might break out. An economist versed in traditional (or common-sense) economics might have thought that an increase in aggregate demand would be all to the good: the economies might recover from their deep recession, but the IMF economists thought the economies might experience inflation. They argued for tightening monetary targets, mopping up the liquidity, in the jargon employed. But it seemed to me that while *their* fears were greatly exaggerated, there was another danger which was far more serious: the very imperfect mops might not just mop up the excess liquidity in the "good" banks with high capital that decided not to lend. Their instruments were far more blunt, and typically affected banks which were already at their lending limits. So while the aggregate statistics still showed an excess of "liquidity" – the banking system was not fully loaned up – the process of mopping up liquidity reduced credit, in a situation where many firms were already credit starved.

The monetarist approach particularly lends itself to these policy failures. For it focuses on a variable which is not of intrinsic interest – the money supply – and whose relationship to the variables that should be of concern – like credit – changes markedly when an economy faces a financial crisis, with large number of financial institutions in distress. Money and credit may typically move in tandem; since data on money is easier to collect than data on credit, it may make sense for economists *in normal times* to focus on the money supply. However, when structural relations are changing dramatically, as they are when an economy is going through a crisis, focusing on money and reduced-form relationships which held in another period is not only foolish, it can also be dangerous.

Interestingly, economists and government officials in the affected countries were much more sensitive to these nuances than were many of the outside advisers, including those imposing "conditions" for the rescue packages. They intuitively grasped the fact that behind the aggregate statistics there was a wealth of micro-economic data, and that one could not, or at least should not, ignore the micro-economics. They argued that there was a change in the structure, which implied a change in the reduced-form relationships, which therefore should have implied a change in policy. In case after the case, their pleas fell on deaf ears.

These are only the most egregious examples of how the old monetary theories led to policies which had such an adverse effect on the countries in the region. We have already noted how the large changes in interest rates led to huge changes in asset values, thus contributing to the uncertainty about firm net worth (that was quickly being eroded directly in any case by the high interest rates). These uncertainties simply compounded the increased risk associated with lending that would, in any case, have accompanied the economic downturn – an economic downturn that the monetary and fiscal policies of the IMF had only made deeper and more uncertain. (The model of part I explains why such increased uncertainty, by itself, would have led to less lending; why did the IMF need to aid and abet this natural market response?)

The strategy for restructuring, discussed in greater length in chapter 11, was based on similarly inadequate models of the banking system, paying insufficient attention to the role and nature of credit, and also exacerbated the problems of those countries that followed the IMF prescriptions.

## Concluding remarks

*Economic theories do matter.* Policies inevitably are guided by theories, especially when there is a lacuna of experience and evidence. The world had not had a crisis that was exactly like the East Asia crisis before; there had not been a crisis of this magnitude for almost three-quarters of a century, and much had changed in the intervening years. But while there had not been a crisis of this magnitude, there have been an unfortunate multitude of crises, both more recently, in the developing countries, and throughout the history of capitalism. One can make inferences from these experiences, about the structure of the economy, and about the consequences of alternative policies. Surely, models which assume away bankruptcy can be of little relevance in a crisis in which bankruptcy and corporate distress are at the center. Models which ignore the details of credit and financial markets can be of little relevance in a crisis in which weaknesses in financial institutions are at the center. We began this book by emphasizing the inadequacies of traditional monetary models. Yet, remarkably, those models continue to be relied upon by policymaking institutions – with disastrous consequences, as we have seen. Had alternative theories not been available, or had the mismatch between the models and the situations been confronted not been so obvious, these mistakes might have been more forgivable. One can only ask: what were the other forces at play?

# FOURTEEN

# The 1991 US recession and the recovery

The 1991 US recession and recovery illustrate in several ways the relevance of the issues upon which we have focused. We want to argue that the recession, though from some perspectives shallow[1] and short, could have been even shorter and shallower, if the Fed had correctly understood the role and behavior of financial institutions – and banks in particular. This is, of course, a remarkable criticism, since, if the Fed is an expert on anything, it surely is on the nature of the US financial system. But the Fed relied on (implicitly or explicitly) over-simplistic models, including modern developments of the standard *IS–LM* curves, which did not adequately take into account the nature of financial markets. As a result, the Fed was taken by surprise at the inefficacy of its policies.

The recovery itself represents somewhat a puzzle. The standard mantra put forward, not only by the Clinton Administration, which wished to claim credit for it, but also by the popular press, was that the deficit reduction allowed the Fed to lower interest rates, and this provided the needed stimulation of the economy. But this explanation, while widely accepted both within the economics profession and by pundits more generally, was deeply disturbing. In spite of all of the rhetoric, the connection between

---

[1] But see Stiglitz (1997).

deficit reduction and economic recovery remained somewhat of a puzzle: Shouldn't the Fed be able to manage monetary policy to maintain the economy at full employment, that is, at the NAIRU (non-accelerating inflation rate of unemployment)? Nothing in the modern theory of monetary policy suggested that the Fed's ability to do that should be affected in any way by deficits or deficit reduction, so long as the changes were appropriately anticipated and offsetting actions undertaken. If the government ran a slightly larger deficit, then the Fed would have to run a slightly tighter monetary policy; the short-run macroeconomic performance would be the same, but the composition of output would shift from private investment to government spending, potentially impairing long-run growth. Was there a suggestion that the Fed was holding the US economy hostage: that so long as deficits were too high, it would refuse to maintain the economy at full employment? Was it trying to impose Wall Street's preferences, to which the Fed is often thought to be closely allied, over those of the elected representatives? In the discussion below, we suggest that deficit reduction did play an important role in the US recovery, but for quite different reasons from those provided by the standard answers. Ironically, it turns out that just as the failure of the Fed to understand the nature of financial markets lay beneath its inability to stem the 1991 recession, a similar failure lies beneath the failure to squash the strong recovery that began in 1993 – which it might have done had it followed the dictates of its own models.

To understand the origins of the 1991 crisis, we need to go back almost a decade, to the Fed's attempt to bring inflation under control by letting interest rates soar. While the *real* interest rate levels may have been moderate, the change in interest rates imposed a huge strain on the S & Ls, the Savings and Loan institutions, whose major asset was long-term fixed interest rate mortgages. They faced an impossible dilemma: if deposit rates were not increased, funds would flow out; if they raised deposit rates, the return on their mortgages would be less than what they paid depositors. In short, raising interest rates had not only diminished their net worth, in many cases net worth had become negative. Regulators, and the Reagan Administration, tried to stave off the crisis, by regulatory forbearance, by allowing the

S & Ls to engage in higher-risk (and presumably higher-return) activities, and by allowing them to include some of their "goodwill" – the value of the S & Ls' organizational capital, its market niche, etc. – as part of their capital. At the time, critics, such as Kane (1990), saw the strategy as a disaster: the negative net worth institutions (Kane called these Zombie institutions – dead institutions that remained among the living) had every incentive to undertake high-risk lending (as Kane put it, to gamble on resurrection). If the gambles paid off, the bank might survive; if they failed, the bank was, in any case, dead. To put it more forcefully, by putting their money only in safe investments, there was no way that they could survive. The gambles did not pay off, and by the late 1980s, a massive bail-out was required. It was recognized that the strategy had had a high cost – forbearance for half a decade or more had greatly increased the cost to the public of the eventual resolution of the problem. The regulatory response was a natural one – a tightening of lending standards.

While banks had not been hit so hard, they had suffered large negative net worth shocks. In both cases, the institutions' net worth had also been adversely affected by a large number of non-performing loans – loans to Latin America that went sour in the debt crisis of the early 1980s, oil and gas loans that went sour in the mid-1980s as the price of oil and gas fell, real-estate loans in Texas and Oklahoma, as the falling oil prices had its repercussions throughout the region, real-estate loans in California, as the downscaling of military expenditures in the aftermath of the Cold War helped burst the real-estate bubble, and finally real-estate loans in the Northeast. (The tax reforms of 1986, which had reduced or eliminated many of the special tax provisions for real estate, probably contributed in an important way to these real-estate crashes.) The theory presented here explains why, given these large net worth shocks, those institutions which remained viable would nonetheless retrench on lending. Tightened regulatory standards exacerbated the effects, and may have even played a more important role in limiting lending. Expectations also played a role: Having been badly burned by real-estate lending, they were reluctant to re-enter the market.

Our model suggests that under these circumstances, lower interest rates may not lead to a large increase in lending activity. Traditional analyses focus on the demand for funds. Here, however, the problem was more on the supply. At lower interest rates, more "safe" borrowers might be willing to borrow. But lower interest rates also reduced banks' seigniorage. While demand for funds might thus have increased, the supply of funds might actually have decreased.[2] If there was credit rationing (of at least some categories of borrowers) then the increased demand would not result directly in increased lending; and it is possible that because of the supply effects, lending could actually decrease.

The Fed was caught off guard; it did not see the critical role that the credit contraction would have on the economy. As a result, its forecasts about where the economy was going were consistently wrong. In July 1991, even as the National Bureau of Economic Research (NBER) was about to declare that the economy was in recession, the Fed Chairman's Humphrey–Hawkins testimony (which he is required to give before Congress twice a year) did not indicate that the Fed was worried about recession. In his prepared testimony, he asserted that "on balance, the economy still appears to be growing, and the likelihood of a near-term recession seems low."

To be fair, economic forecasters have almost always missed recessions. (Also, we should add parenthetically that one of the responsibilities of Fed officials is to maintain confidence in the economy. Private views may be more pessimistic than public pronouncements. Still, in this particular case, policy seemed to conform remarkably closely to the public pronouncements. Moreover, the Fed Chairman is a master of Fedspeak – some say a modern version of a Delphic oracle – which is designed to carefully calibrate what information is revealed and what is obscured rather than to provide complete enlightenment. This provides plenty of opportunity for him to make announcements

---

[2] Even if lower interest rates had a substitution effect shifting bank portfolios towards risky assets, the magnitude of the effect was insufficient to offset the decreases in supply of loans arising from the other effects; moreover, as noted below, even a shift towards risky assets did not imply increased lending – the banks could (and did) decide to hold more long-term government bonds.

that bolster confidence in the economy while being sufficiently vague so that in retrospect they seem to provide keen insights into the workings of the economy *regardless of what happens.*)

As the downturn persisted, the Fed continued to see it as an unexpected shock leading to a "normal" cyclical downturn that would respond to standard policies. This viewpoint is evident in the Humphrey–Hawkins testimony from February 1992, which reads "nonetheless, the balance of forces does appear to suggest that this downturn could well prove shorter and shallower than most prior post-war recessions. An important reason for this assessment is that one of the most negative economic impacts of the Gulf war – the run-up in oil prices – has been reversed. Another is that the substantial decline in interest rates over the past year and a half – especially over the past several months – should ameliorate the contractionary effects of the crisis in the Gulf and of tighter credit availability."

Indeed, as the nature of the problem became clearer, and as the political pressure to do something mounted, monetary policy was eased twenty-four times. It was clear that monetary easing was not having the predicted effect. It was not until the economy was on its way to recovery, in February 1993, that the Fed finally recognized the "economy has been held back by a variety of *structural factors*" (emphasis added), most notably fundamental weaknesses in the financial system. Within the Fed itself, there were those who recognized the important role that credit constraints, and changes in the financial institutions, can play, including its Vice-Chair, David Mullins, who had made important contributions to understanding of how information imperfections translated into financial market imperfections. But they were evidently in a minority, and the Fed seemed to stick with its "basic model."

Ironically, the same misunderstandings that made the Fed ineffective in addressing the 1991 recession were important in allowing the subsequent boom to occur. There is a tendency to think of mistakes as one-sided – always working to the detriment of the economy. But mistakes, by their nature, should be random, and in at least some cases should work to the benefit of the economy. In this case, there were in fact two errors on the part of the Fed, and both lay at the basis of the economy's strong recovery.

Throughout the earlier 1990s, the Fed continued to have an overly pessimistic view concerning the NAIRU, and the economy's potential for reducing unemployment without inflation increasing. But they also continued to under-appreciate the role of financial markets and continued to fail to understand key aspects of banking behavior. As a result, the Fed underestimated the basis for, and strength of, the recovery when it occurred, and thus the economy was allowed to show that it could operate at much lower unemployment rates without inflation accelerating.

To understand what happened – and why the Fed failed (fortunately) to see the strength of the recovery – we need to return to the early days of the Clinton Administration. When the President took office in February 1993, he moved quickly to introduce a deficit-cutting budget. Eventually the Congress enacted a plan to reduce the deficit by $500 billion over five years (in contrast, the 1997 balanced budget legislation only cut the deficit by $200 billion over five years). Old-style Keynesians warned that deficit reduction would undermine the fragile recovery. Those who believed that the markets were forward looking argued that a credible, pre-announced deficit reduction would lower interest rates and thus stimulate the economy. What took even the optimists by surprise was just how much it was stimulated.

Parsing out how credit for the deficit reduction should be divided up became a preoccupation. To be sure, the strong economy played a role, but this just leads to the further question of how much of the strong economy was attributable to deficit reduction. But as we have already noted, there was – at least in the traditional theory – no connection between deficit reduction and strengthened economic activity. (If the deficit reduction was based on expenditure cuts that were quickly implemented, then the adverse contractionary effects of fiscal policy would be felt before positive effects of the loosening of monetary policy; even if the Fed were quickly to react to the new budgetary situation, it would take six months or more before the effects of the monetary expansion were felt.)

There is a connection, but it is subtle and captured only in models, such as those presented in this book, based on the link between financial markets and economic activity. It is an interesting story, and illustrates that while two wrongs do not make a right, in economic policy two mistakes can more than offset each other, and result in an economic boom.

In the early 1990s, banks had significant holdings of long-term T-bonds. This represented a gamble on falling interest rates. Banks were allowed to take this gamble because accountants valued these bonds at face value and regulators judged risk by the chance of default – which was zero in this case – not by the likely volatility of asset prices (interest rate risk). The Fed made a mistake in the way that risk was assessed. If one believed in well-functioning markets, the higher interest rate paid on these long-term government bonds just compensated for the higher risk of a fall in asset value; the excess of interest over the short-term interest should have been used to provision against the fall in the value of the bonds. But no provisioning was required, and the higher interest was treated just like any other source of income. The strong cash flow helped recapitalize the banks – or would do so long as bond prices remained high.

The mistaken nature of this regulatory policy was widely recognized by, among others, members of the first Bush Administration, including its chair, Michael Boskin, who argued with the Fed, but to no avail. But the misguided regulation allowed banks to gamble. In this case, the gamble paid off. The 1993 deficit reduction, which barely made it through Congress, resulted in lower interest rates, and higher prices for long-term bonds. In a sense, the lower interest rates were undoing the damage that had been created a little more than a decade before with high interest rates. When interest rates rose in the early 1980s, the value of bank assets fell, setting off a process that culminated in the S & L bail-outs. Subsequently, with the 1993 deficit reduction and the lowered inflationary expectations, interest rates declined. The result was a major revaluation of bank assets – in effect a bank recapitalization, an unintended by-product of deficit reduction. Given their increased net worth and cash flow, banks were both willing and able to increase their lending. And this is precisely what they did.[3]

While in this case, the gamble paid off, the gamble could just as well have failed (after all, the market was paying high interest rates on long-term bonds, largely because the market anticipated higher interest rates in the future). And had it failed, the banking system would have been in a disastrous shape.

We now come to the second critical mistake of the Fed – and again it was a mistake with strikingly positive consequences. Had the Fed understood what was going on, how the financial system was being recapitalized and with it, lending was likely to pick up quickly, they would have acted quickly to stifle the expansion. Had they better understood these factors, given their beliefs about the NAIRU and given their strong aversion to inflation, they would have prevented the unemployment rate from declining below 6.0 percent to 6.2 percent. It might have been a long time – possibly never – before we learned about the economy's real potential.[4] It was our good fortune that they did not see accurately where the economy was going! As the expression goes, "the rest is history." As the expansion continued, the economy demonstrated that it was possible to run at a much lower unemployment rate without inflation increasing. The wisdom of the Fed's economic policy was that it was pragmatic – as the economy demonstrated that the NAIRU was lowered, the Fed resisted the calls of the inflation hawks (including recommendations from the OECD and the IMF) to raise interest rates.

---

[3] This story is exactly the counterplay to that of the East Asia crisis, where IMF policies of high interest rates decapitalized the already weak banks, exacerbating the crisis.

[4] Indeed, we have argued that there is a "reverse hysterisis effect": as the unemployment rate is reduced, previously marginalized workers are drawn into the labor market, develop and maintain worker and job search skills that might otherwise have atrophied, and the economy's NAIRU is thereby actually lowered. If this is the case, then the "mistake" of allowing the unemployment rate to fall below 6 percent was actually crucial in the economy's longer-term improved performance. See Stiglitz (1997).

# FIFTEEN

# The new paradigm and the "new economy"

Much has been written in recent years about the "new economy," the changes in technology, and the pace of technological change. The new economy has also been marked by globalization, a closer integration of capital, labor, and product markets, a freer flow of ideas and knowledge, as a result of technological innovations which have reduced transportation and communication costs as well as of changes in global policies which have brought down man-made barriers. These changes have had an impact on the overall structure of the economy and on macro-economic performance. While the downturn that set in in the United States in late 2000 demonstrated that even the new economy could be subjected to fluctuations (at least in the pace of economic growth), it does appear that economic expansions (at least in the United States) are markedly longer than was previously the case. Similarly, downturns since the Second World War are far shorter than they were previously.

The credit paradigm helps us focus on the consequences of these changes in the economy, and leads to markedly different predictions concerning, for instance, the future efficacy of monetary policy than those that might be derived from the transactions-based approach. Changes in the financial sector have played a pivotal role in the new economy – the financial sector has been among the sectors which have been most changed, and it has, at the same time, induced the most change in the overall performance of the economy. It was the evolution of information technologies which finally laid to rest the notion that money was required for transactions. Individuals always used credit extensively in dealing with those who they knew well; but when they engaged in exchanges that went beyond this narrow circle, money was required, except in those circumstances where the magnitude of transactions was large, when letters of credit would be drawn up, drawn on those whose reputation was well established. But the new technologies allowed information to be transmitted instantaneously anywhere in the world. A store in Malaysia could instantaneously verify that a purchase by one of the authors was within the credit limits set by his bank, and his bank could similarly instantaneously make note of how much of the credit line he had used up. Credit cards have increasingly replaced money as a "medium of exchange."

There have been other changes in the economy on which we have focused in this book. Increased competition within the banking sector, and even more importantly from non-banking financial institutions (NBFIs) – and the reduction in certain artificial regulatory constraints, in particular on the interest rates paid[1] – combined with increased efficiency in the banking sector (largely from the new technologies) has resulted in deposit rates that differ little from T-bill rates. This has fundamentally altered the ways that monetary policy impacts the credit supply (and thus the economy). We have argued that its effects today are largely realized through substitution effects and regulatory constraints, and that these channels may well be weaker than the traditional effects which operated through the level of deposits and the profits banks garnered from the difference between the lending rate and the (artificially suppressed) deposit rate. In this perspective, monetary policy today, and even more so in the future, may be less effective, particularly in stimulating the economy in recessions.[2] But before addressing this issue at greater

---

[1] The elimination of these constraints should, of course, be viewed as endogenous: given the competition from the non-banking sector, which would have been very hard to control, regulators had no choice.

[2] The caveat is relevant, because at such times banks may have excess liquidity, so that lowering reserve requirements or capital adequacy requirements may not lead to increased lending.

length, we wish to touch on certain other ways in which the "new economy" may affect the effectiveness of monetary policy.

First, monetary policy has always exerted its influence (in the short run) largely because of imperfect substitutability: as a borrower's bank reduces the credit it makes available (or makes it available only at much less favorable terms), the borrower cannot easily turn to sources of credit *outside the banking system* of the country. The analysis of chapter 7 where we explored credit linkages explained, in part, why other lenders *within the country* would be affected in a similar way. But globalization may have increased, at least to some extent, the extent of substitutability on the supply side. While the direct beneficiaries of this substitutability are the large, multinational corporations (MNCs), who can get capital anywhere in the world, and almost costlessly move it from place to place, all borrowers are potential beneficiaries; for as these multinationals reduce their borrowing within a country (when banks contract the availability of credit or make it available only at less favorable terms), more funds are made available to other firms. In the limit, of course, the demand curve for loanable funds within a country would be horizontal; but exchange rate risks imply that borrowing in one currency is not a perfect substitute for borrowing in another[3] (and hedging is at best imperfect, and in many cases costly), and information asymmetries combined with risk aversion mean that even large borrowers face upward sloping supply curves for funds abroad.

More broadly, our theory is based on the hypothesis that banks are risk averse and that information is imperfect. We can ask, how will changes in technology and the associated changes in market structures affect the extent of risk aversion and the magnitude and importance of information asymmetries? For instance, new technologies allow easier (less costly) verification of credit histories and aggregation of amounts of outstanding credit, information that previously might have been hard to come by. New technologies and product innovations have allowed for broader diversification

---

[3] And even if the firm borrows abroad in its domestic currency, someone has to bear the exchange rate risk; it will be reflected in the terms at which credit is made available in that currency.

and sharing of risks (e.g. through securitization). Better asset markets facilitate collaterization, which lowers the risk borne by lenders. (And there have been important interactions among these innovations: better collaterization has supported more extensive securitization.) Better statistical techniques have resulted in better credit scoring methodologies. All of these innovations should have the effect of extending the scope for the provision of credit.

At the same time, however, many of these innovations may reduce the incentive to invest in screening and monitoring. For instance, the risk borne by the bank may be lowered if loans are largely collateralized. By the same token, as risk associated with any particular loan or set of loans gets reduced, the bank will shift its portfolio towards riskier loans, e.g. to loans that cannot be collateralized, such as to finance investment in intangibles.

Because of both the portfolio shift effect and the screening/monitoring effect, the *net* risk borne by the bank, as it were, will not be reduced by as much as the innovations associated with the new economy might suggest.

Moreover, several of the changes associated with the "new economy" may enhance the risks facing lenders. To be sure, some of the traditional sources of macro-economic instability have taken on less importance: the changing structure of the economy has meant that inventories play a less important role, and the better control and production technologies (just-in-time (JIT) production) imply that inventories will be smaller in relationship to production and less likely to become substantially out of line with production and consumption needs. Thus, inventories will be a less important source of fluctuations. But there are many other sources of fluctuations – like excessive real-estate construction, or even excessive investment in certain types of equipment, and, perhaps most importantly, over-zealous reactions to the threat of inflation by monetary authorities. Some sources of volatility may even increase: The 1998 global financial crisis brought home the fact that capital market liberalization can be associated with massive movements of capital, bringing about large macro-economic disturbances. There are standard arguments to the effect that better information may lead to increased asset price volatility[4]; and whether that is the reason or not, there is increasing attention focused on asset price volatility.[5] Assets with high price volatility do not provide as effective collateralization as assets with low price volatility.

It is important to recognize that many of the changes associated with the "new economy", and especially those associated with lowering transactions costs and facilitating the faster processing of information, do not necessarily lead to better resource allocations or greater stability. The following example illustrates the point.[6] Assume $100 bills were suddenly to float down from the ceiling of a lecture hall, one to the foot of each student. Assume that initially there was some restraint that prevented each student from picking up the $100 dollar bill until after the end of the lecture. Now assume that that constraint was removed. Each student would instantly move to pick up his $100 bill, and if his neighbor had not done so, his neighbor's. The Nash equilibrium, of course, would entail each getting his own $100 bill. No one has gained from picking up the $100 faster. Indeed, one can argue that social welfare is lowered – as the flow of knowledge of the lecture has been interrupted. Many financial innovations are precisely of that nature: *if* no one else responded, they would enable you to gain at the expense of others; but when they all respond, no one gains – and if the new technologies use up some resources, overall welfare may be lowered. Even if the financial innovations resulted in more accurate pricing of the value of assets within the day, no changes in *real* investments will be made as a result of better intraday price discovery.

On balance, we suspect that changes associated with the "new economy" will facilitate the provision of credit, will reduce the extent and significance of information asymmetries, and will enhance the ability of banks to bear, transfer, and diversify risk. But they will also enhance the ability of NBFIs to do similarly. Indeed, one of the structural changes in our economy may be the enhanced role of NBFIs in the provision of credit. This has

---

[4]  See e.g. Furman and Stiglitz (1998) and the references cited there.
[5]  See, in particular, Shiller's (2000) discussion of market irrationality.
[6]  See Hirschleifer (1971); Stiglitz (1975a, 1975b, 1980).

important implications, for it limits the extent to which government can impose regulatory constraints on banks. There are costs associated with these constraints. Before, depository institutions had a marked advantage over other financial institutions, e.g. in the interest rates that they had to pay to acquire deposits. Moreover, because of government provided deposit insurance, they were perceived as being far safer. Improvements in capital markets may reduce the risk premium that other financial institutions have to pay to acquire funds, and greater competition has increased the interest rate that banks have to pay on deposits. Banks must compare these much-reduced advantages with the costs resulting from regulatory constraints, and regulators are well aware that their regulations act as a tax on banks: as the tax is increased, more lending activity shifts to other financial institutions.

Our concern, however, is not just with the *size* of banks, or the level of bank credit, but with the effectiveness of monetary policy. There is the possibility that as the share of bank lending in the overall economy diminishes, the effectiveness of monetary policy may as well diminish, while its distortionary impact may increase. Monetary policy, as we have noted, works directly on only one part of the financial system, the banking sector, though it has ripple effects (e.g. through credit interlinkages) throughout the economy. The effectiveness will depend not only on the strength of response of the banking sector, but also on the absence of close substitutes. But for reasons which we have explained repeatedly, even if NBFIs are effective long-run substitutes, there may be significant short-run impacts. Still, as the NBFI sector grows, even the short-run impacts are likely to be attenuated. And to the extent that there are not substitutes, and the banking sector lending is focused, e.g. on small business loans, that part of the economy will bear the brunt of monetary policy.

To be sure, under current financial arrangements, tighter monetary policy does seem to have large effects on some parts of the economy that are heavily dependent on credit which is not mediated through the banking system – particularly mortgages. This seems largely due to certain imperfections in the capital market, which one could envisage becoming less important in the future. As we noted earlier, variations in nominal interest rates – even when they simply offset changes in inflation rates – seem to have real effects, partially because of the resulting liquidity impacts (cash flow effects) *under current mortgage arrangements.* But one can certainly envisage innovations in the mortgage market (entailing variable rate mortgages with negative amortization, payment levels that are indexed to the rate of inflation, and variable maturities) which reduce the impact of these cash flow effects.

But even apart from this, there are questions about the extent to which and the mechanisms through which monetary policy affects the *relevant* interest rates paid by borrowers. How do open market operations affect *other* interest rates: after all, an open market operation is simply an exchange between a government guaranteed deposit and a government T-bill, both of which yield approximately the same interest rate. When such operations lead to changed lending behavior by banks, e.g. when they change the constraints facing banks, then they can have large and predictable effects through their impact on bank lending. But when, for one reason or another, banks do not change their lending behavior, what is the channel through which impacts are realized?

One channel, often hypothesized, is through the information *signal* conveyed by the central bank's action. But in the "new economy," it is becoming increasingly clear that the central bank may have little if any informational advantage over private agents, and thus the informational value of its actions may be minimal.

More broadly, there is a view that central banks have effects because market participants believe that they have effects. They have an effect through *information/coordination.* If all believe that the loosening of monetary policy is going to lead to economic expansion, and they respond accordingly by increasing their investment and hiring, it becomes a self-fulfilling prophecy. But there is, in this, an element of a confidence game, and like all confidence games, there is a high level of fragility. If market participants believe that the central bank is ineffective, then it will in fact be ineffective. In this interpretation, the "credibility" of the central bank, and the central banker, are critical – and certainly central bankers' statements seem to give some credence to this interpretation. Keynes emphasized that it was virtually impossible to fathom the determinants of market expectations – they were like animal spirits.[7] Credibility is very much of the same ilk: for credibility is nothing more than beliefs about the individual's or institution's competence and information. Market participants gave enormous credence to Greenspan's credibility as the market expanded during the Clinton years, though there was little evidence that the boom was of his making (as we saw in chapter 14); all that could be said was that he had not mismanaged monetary policy grossly, as monetary policy had been mismanaged before, in bringing to a halt prematurely an expansion. But with the economic slowdown towards the end of 2000, questions of credibility were raised: Had the Fed tightened excessively, at a time when rates that corporations faced in borrowing were already significantly up? As these questions were raised, the mistakes of 1991 – which had been all but forgotten during the Clinton Boom – were recalled. When Greenspan seemed to support Bush's tax proposals, questions were raised not only about his economic judgment, but also his political judgment, and the arguments he gave (the notion that *eventually* the surpluses would eliminate the supply of government debt, which would have adverse effects on the conduct of monetary policy) did little to help.

If monetary policy must rely on the credibility of the central bank and the central banker, then it is indeed a fragile instrument. For it may increasingly be the case that this particular emperor has no clothes, or is, at the very least, scantily clothed, and while such assertions are seldom made in polite circles, there is already a growing suspicion that this may indeed be the case.

To mix our metaphors: Central bank governors will continue to assert that they are indeed driving the car; they will continue to make grave speeches, to maintain appearances they are in charge. They will continue to adjust the steering wheel, sometimes to the left, sometimes to the right: a steady hand, never swerving too far to one side or the other. They are clever not to disclose the secret to their success: the steering wheel is only loosely connected to the wheels, and the wheels have a self-adjusting gyroscope, that works *most of the time*. Intuitively, they grasp the fact that if they follow the direction that the wheels

---

[7] See Keynes (1936).

have taken quickly enough, all will believe that they are controlling the wheels, not the other way around.

The fiction is a harmless one – except when the driver becomes too cocky, and, believing that he can drive the economy better than he can, slams on the brakes too hard or swerves too far in one direction or the other; for while the steering wheel may be loosely connected, it is not unconnected: the central bank still has the power to derail the economy. There is one other circumstance when the fiction is not harmless: when the economy truly faces a crisis. It is then that all available tools will have to be called upon. There is no reason to believe that in the "new economy", monetary policy will be any more effective in bringing an economy out of a deep recession than in the old, and some reasons to believe that it may be less effective. If the over-confidence in monetary policy leads to a reluctance to use other instruments, then the economy may well suffer – the downturn or slowdown may be longer than it otherwise would have been.

# SIXTEEN

# Concluding remarks

We have developed here an alternative paradigm for monetary economics, based on credit, rather than the transactions demand for money. While the intellectual foundations of the latter theory have perhaps always been questionable, the new transactions technologies make the need for an alternative paradigm imperative.

In these concluding remarks, we want to highlight some of the relationships – and distinctions – between credit and money, some of the key ways in which a credit-based monetary theory differs from a transactions-demand-for-money theory, including implications for policy, and end with some final observations about the nature of decentralization.

## Money and credit

Money can be thought of as a particularly simple way of keeping accounts. Recall those childhood games, in which individuals began the game with a certain amount of play money. As the game progressed, points were scored, and lost, which were translated into gains and losses in individuals' holdings of money. At the end of the game, the individual who had the most money won. One could have kept score in a quite different way, simply by having a central banker keep track of the points as they were scored, and adding up the result. Money is a convenient way of keeping score, but that is all. It is hardly essential. To be sure, it is absolutely essential within a market system for there to be some way of keeping score, some way of ascertaining who has claims on resources.

Even in modern economies, money provides a way of keeping score, but one which has increasingly been found to be inconvenient. (In a world in which there is no way of peering into the future, to see whether individuals will be receiving income, and hence will be able to meet any promises, money might be required for transactions (other than barter) to occur.[1] The fact that the individual has money ensures that the individual is not attempting to commandeer more resources than his life-time budget constraint[2] allows.) Conventional macro-economic models, relying on the cash-in-advance constraint, are not only ad hoc in not explaining the source of this constraint, but plainly wrong.

The growth of CMAs, in which the individual can write checks (on bank accounts in which funds are instantaneously deposited and withdrawn, generating an infinite velocity) against the value of their portfolio, has simply verified that what is crucial for facilitating economic transactions is not money, but *credit*. In those circumstances in which there has been an inadequate supply of currency, alternatives have easily been found.

Indeed, it is surprising that the *LM* curve has remained such a focal point of macro-economic analysis for so long. As we noted, if money were required to engage in transactions, then the relationship between money and output would necessarily be unstable, since only a small fraction of all transactions are those directly related to income generation: most transactions are exchanges of assets and these exchanges can exhibit great volatility, much greater volatility than is exhibited by national income, or the interest rate, or any other macro-economic variable.

---

[1] Even then, it assumes that there are no credit enforcement mechanisms, or that such enforcement mechanisms are prohibitively expensive, or that the adverse selection problem operates with such vengeance that Akerlof's (1970) equilibrium with no trade arises. (In general, even with adverse selection, there will be some trade.)

[2] Assuming no implicit or explicit credit obligations.

How then can we explain the central role that money has come to play in modern macro-economic theory? This, we suspect, has to do with the close link between the creation of money and credit. When a bank extends a loan, it creates a deposit account, increasing the supply of money. Firms do not borrow unless they wish to make a purchase: otherwise, having a credit line will suffice. Thus, the creation of money and the creation of credit occur together. When banks are restricted in the amounts which they can lend, they are simultaneously restricted in the amount of money they can create. Increasing reserve requirements, for instance, reduces the amount that banks can lend, at the same time that it reduces the money supply.

What difference then does it make whether we focus our attention on money or on credit? There are several differences. First, while in the past, there may have been a close relationship between the creation of money and the creation of credit, the relationship is by no means a firm and fast one. There are other institutional arrangements by which credit can and is provided. Attempts to restrict banks may simply divert more of the credit creation activities to non-bank sources of credit. *The relationship between money and credit is an endogenous one, and affected by economic policy (including monetary policy).*

Secondly, interest rates, and interest rate adjustments, do not play the central role that they do in traditional monetary theories. This is not to say that they are irrelevant, but only to suggest, as we have argued above, that credit is not primarily allocated via an auction market. Rather, credit is largely allocated by a system in which potential lenders make judgements about the risk associated with various borrowers. They then, in effect, bid to be the lender, aware, as they bid, of the winner's curse: that they are likely to win precisely in those circumstances where they have been overly optimistic concerning the lender's prospects. Because of the sunk costs associated with the acquisition of information, these loans markets are inherently imperfectly competitive. Only a few lenders (banks) will have information relevant to judging the riskiness of any particular borrower.

It thus becomes apparent why bank failures can have such a disastrous effect on the economy. For the failure of banks results in the destruction of *informational* and *organizational* capital, information with which to make judgements concerning the terms upon which loans sold can be made.

This simply exacerbates a problem already present in recessions: making a loan is like making an investment decision; to judge whether a loan should be made uses up valuable organizational resources. Financial constraints result in an increase in the shadow interest rate as an economy goes into a recession and banks find their net worth decreasing, making investments less attractive, including the investments required to ascertain to whom to lend. The investment costs associated with a new lender acquiring information about a potential borrower are even greater. Accordingly, borrowers whose bank from which they traditionally borrow has ceased lending will find it difficult to find alternative sources of credit. In effect, firms that might have been classified as "good borrowers" because of the information already available to their now defunct bank become classified with the "ungrouped" borrowers. They may be credit constrained (because of the adverse selection problem) when they otherwise would not have been; or they may be charged more than they otherwise would have been. In either case the amount borrowed will be reduced.

There is a third important difference upon which we have focused, arising from the method by which credit is allocated. How is one to be sure that the value of the certifications of credit worthiness, the magnitude of the loans which banks are willing to make (guarantee), is just sufficient to ensure full employment? Each borrower treats his certification as the right to a claim on current resources. If too many individuals have been granted certifications, a situation with excess demands will result.

Traditional theory has a well-formulated theory of adjustment: interest rates equilibrate demand and supply of funds (presumably, in neo-classical theory, at full employment). In fact, interest rates are not a primary part of the adjustment mechanism. Real interest rates, rather than falling in recessionary periods to restore investment to equality with full-employment savings, remain either relatively unchanged, or, as in the Great Depression and in the Reagan recession, actually rise. Indeed, an argument can be made that, in the absence of government intervention, the dynamics may well be unstable: if too many certifications (loans) are made, prices increase, increasing profitability of past investments; this reduces the bankruptcy rate, increasing banks' willingness to lend[3]; and it increases firm's equity, increasing firms' willingness to borrow. Thus, the amount of credit extended may be further increased, exacerbating the problem.

In the absence of price (interest rate) adjustments to serve as coordinating devices to attain a full-employment equilibrium, the burden rests on the monetary authorities. In those cases where the credit constraints are binding and where banks have no free reserves, they can at least partially control the level of credit extended. In those cases, such as the Great Depression, where there are free reserves, and/or where it is firms' willingness to borrow that is the operative constraint on the amount of loans outstanding, monetary authorities may be relatively impotent. This is, of course, a long-standing view concerning the efficacy of monetary policy; but while no persuasive basis for these asymmetries of responses can be found in the traditional *LM* theory, it is a natural consequence of our credit theory.

Finally, and perhaps most importantly, the credit nexus is an extremely complicated one, with different firms being simultaneously borrowers and lenders. This gives rise to an important kind of interdependence, quite different from that stressed in traditional Walrasian theory, an interdependence which leaves the system resilient to small shocks, but quite fragile in the face of large shocks. That is, with traditional loan contracts, small shocks to the profits of any particular firm are absorbed by the equity owners of that firm. (These equity shocks have small further ramifications, particularly for the investment and employment decisions of the affected firms in subsequent periods.) But the consequences of large shocks can be quite disastrous. The default of

---

[3] Though, as we have noted, inflation reduces the real value of the repayments, and this effect, by itself, leads to lower bank net worth, and thus reduced lending. As a practical matter, as long as inflation remains moderate and relatively stable, the net effect seems to be positive: the *observed* reduction in the probability of bankruptcy combined with the associated *beliefs* in reduced prospects for bankruptcy more than offset the reduced real value of the amounts repaid.

one firm can cascade into the breakdown of the entire system, as we demonstrated in chapter 7 of this book. Centering attention on bankruptcy leads us to think about these non-linearities and the associated irreversibilities. This formulation also forces us to go beyond the traditional focus on aggregate demand to look at the simultaneous effects on aggregate supply.

Thus, we have criticized traditional monetary theory, derived from the transactions-based demand for money, not just because its theoretical underpinnings are unpersuasive, but because it leads to misguided approaches to monetary policy: to policies which focus on the wrong variables (like money supply, or the T-bill interest rate, which may, at times, or even frequently, be highly correlated with the variables of ultimate interest, but for which the correlations may weaken, or even disappear, at certain critical junctures, such as when an economy is entering a crisis) and which ignore other considerations that should be front and center.

## Policy implications

There are a host of specific policy implications that have been raised in these chapters – ways in which monetary policies derived from the credit paradigm differ from those that naturally emanate from the transactions-demand-for-money paradigm. Here, we summarize a few of these key issues:

(1) The tightness of monetary policy may not be well measured by real interest rates; credit availability may be important; under credit rationing, loan demand is not relevant; it is only *loan supply*.

(2) The relevant real interest rate for economic activity is the *loan rate*, and there may be marked changes in interest rate spreads – the difference between T-bill rates and loan rates.

(3) *Banks* are central in the provision of credit, and it is therefore imperative to understand how various policies impact them; static efficiency effects may be overwhelmed by a variety of other effects (e.g. effects on franchise value); one cannot simply use the standard

competitive paradigm to analyze, for instance, the effects of deregulation and liberalization.

(4) Monetary authorities have to be particularly attentive to retaining the *informational and organizational capital* within the banking system as the economy goes into a downturn; failing to do so may exacerbate the depth and duration of the recession.

(5) Credit is by its nature *heterogeneous*; aggregates may accordingly be highly misleading: the excess liquidity in one bank is no substitute for the shortage of funds at another.

(6) *Regulatory policy* (e.g. capital adequacy standards, including the risk adjustments and the vigorousness with which they are enforced) can have as much of an impact on credit availability (and thus on the economy) as traditional monetary instruments. Accordingly, even if separate agencies are given responsibilities for supervision and monetary policy, there needs to be close coordination; attempts by the monetary authority to stimulate the economy can be completely vitiated by offsetting changes in regulatory policy.

(7) Regulatory policy, like monetary policy, needs to be based on a theory of *bank behavior*; simplistic approaches, such as reliance on (even risk-adjusted) capital adequacy requirements are not only not (Pareto-) efficient, but may well be counterproductive, leading to increased risk taking of banks at certain times. We have presented an alternative approach, called the *portfolio* approach to regulation, which identifies an array of measures through which regulatory authorities can affect both bank incentives and opportunity sets.

(8) Monetary (and regulatory) policy exercises its effects not just through aggregate demand, but through *aggregate supply*; and indeed aggregate demand and aggregate supply are intertwined.

(9) Because credit is not, in general, allocated through auction processes, and because the market allocations of credit are not in general (constrained) Pareto-efficient, it

is a shibboleth that any intervention in financial markets is welfare-reducing. Governments have played a key role in creating credit institutions, which have filled important lacunae in the previous market situation. By the same token, while changes in prices always have allocative *and* redistributive effects, given the role of banks and financial institutions in allocating credit, the redistributive effects may predominate over the *traditional* allocative effects; nevertheless, the allocative effects associated with the redistributions may take on a first-order importance. Accordingly, monetary authorities need to be particularly sensitive to the consequences of large changes in interest rates, and governments generally need to be open to ensuring a *supply of credit at reasonable terms* to particular groups that may be particularly adversely affected in periods of marked credit tightening.

(10) *Bankruptcy* is a variable of first-order importance, and monetary policy accordingly has to take into account impacts on the likelihood of bankruptcy. Tightened monetary policy may lead to an increase in bankruptcy, thus driving capital out of a country rather than attracting capital into it, and thus leading to lower exchange rates. While it is has long been recognized that there are long and variable lags associated with monetary policy, especially because of bankruptcy, there may be important non-linearities and irreversibilities (hysteresis effects). Large increases in interest rates may lead to high levels of bankruptcy, and subsequently lowering interest rates does not unbankrupt the firms who have been forced into bankruptcy.

(11) In confronting a crisis, and especially in restructuring financial systems, governments need to take into account the impacts on the *flow of credit*; there are ways of restructuring which exacerbate those impacts, and ways which reduce it. Governments too need to be sensitive to the general equilibrium consequences – which may differ markedly from the partial equilibrium

consequences – both through credit interlinkages and through bankruptcy impacts.

(12) Because monetary policy affects the economy through impacts on the credit supply, there is a role for central banks even in countries which have dollarized.

(13) Because monetary policy disproportionately affects certain sectors of the economy (and in the future, this may be even more so), excessive reliance on monetary policy may be distortionary; and may induce institutional adjustments (e.g. less reliance on the bank) which, over time, attenuate the effectiveness of monetary policy.

(14) Changes in transaction and information technologies may, in the future, have marked effects on the efficacy of monetary policy.

### Remarks on decentralization

A central aspect of the market economy is its decentralization; we often praise the fact that no one has to co-ordinate, no one has to know the preferences of all the consumers or the technologies of all the firms – the price system does all that. It is, in this sense, highly informationally efficient. In this book, we have been concerned about a quite different set of information problems information about a particular borrower's credit worthiness, the likelihood that she will repay a loan. That information is highly specific and it too is widely dispersed in a modern market economy. But it is not codified in simple variables, like a "price," which serves as a sufficient statistic for a wide range of purposes. As we have noted, one individual's judgments may differ from those of another (there is not "common knowledge").

Modern technologies have had a marked impact on the economy's ability to use this dispersed information efficiently: a seller in any store in the world can, through the credit card system, ascertain in seconds whether one of the credit card companies has ascertained that the individual is "credit worthy." When such information was not available, individuals had to have money – direct claims on resources – to engage in transactions with "strangers," those that were not in a position to judge their credit worthiness and/or to use reputation mechanisms to enforce promises.

These new technologies allow for the quick exchange of information, e.g. about whether individuals are late in making some payments, and on that account the asymmetries of information may be reduced. Still, for most lending, e.g. in the corporate sector, highly detailed information is relevant; particular lenders know particular things about particular borrowers. The central thesis of this book is that, accordingly, changes that impact particular lenders will affect their ability and willingness to supply credit to particular borrowers; a reduction in lending by one lender will often not be fully offset by increased lending by others. The decentralization entails complex interlinkages in the flow of credit within an economy, with firms being both lenders and borrowers, but with banks playing a pivotal role. It is hard to conceive how this information could ever be centralized.

We have explored how such a credit economy works today – and how it might work in the future, as banking becomes more competitive. It should be clear that simple models, which treat the capital market like any other market, are likely to go seriously awry. The recent global financial crisis provides the strongest testimony for the importance of the perspectives argued for here. It was simple-minded theories (in conjunction possibly with vested interests) that led to the deregulation of financial and capital markets, which in turn contributed so strongly to these economies' vulnerability. It was models that were insufficiently attuned to the credit mechanisms (including impacts on and of defaults) that led to the vast under-estimate of the depth of the downturns, and that led to policy prescriptions that made those downturns deeper and more prolonged than they needed to have been.

The theories developed here are far from complete, but it is our hope that we have sketched them in sufficient detail that they will provide the basis of a research program amplifying the theory and testing its empirical implications. We also hope that these new perspectives will provide the basis for policies that will better mitigate the fluctuations in economic activity that have plagued capitalism for the past 200 years.

# Bibliography

Abel, A. B. and O. J. Blanchard, 1989. "Investment and Sales: Some Empirical Evidence." In W. A. Barnett, E. Berndt and H. White, eds., *Dynamic Econometric Modeling: Proceedings of the Third International Symposium in Economic Theory and Econometrics*. New York: Cambridge University Press

Akerlof, G. A., 1970. "The Market for 'Lemons': Quality Uncertainty and the Market Mechanism," *Quarterly Journal of Economics*, 84, 3, pp. 488–500

Akerlof, G. A. and P. Romer, 1993. "Looting: The Economic Underworld of Bankruptcy for Profit," *Brookings Papers on Economic Activity*, 2, pp. 1–60

Akerlof, G. A. and J. Yellen, 1990. "The Fair Wage–Effort Hypothesis and Unemployment," *Quarterly Journal of Economics*, 105, 2, pp. 255–283

Allen, F. and D. Gale, 2000. *Comparing Financial Systems.* Cambridge, Mass.: MIT Press

Alvarez, F. and U. J. Jermann, 2000. "Efficiency, Equilibrium, and Asset Pricing with Risk of Default," *Econometrica*, 68, 4, pp. 775–797

Arnott, R. and J. E. Stiglitz, 1991. "Price Equilibrium, Efficiency, and Decentralizability in Insurance Markets," *NBER Working Paper*, 3642

Asquith, P. and D. W. Mullins, 1983. "The Impact of Initiating Dividend Payments on Shareholders' Wealth," *Journal of Business*, 56, 1, pp. 77–96

 1986. "Equity Issues and Offering Dilution," *Journal of Financial Economics*, 15, 1–2, pp. 61–89

Bardhan, P., ed., 1989. *The Economic Theory of Agrarian Institutions.* Oxford: Clarendon Press

Barro, R. J., 1974. "Are Government Bonds Net Wealth?" *Journal of Political Economy*, 82, pp. 1095–1118

Barth, J., G. Caprio and R. Levine, 2001a. "Banking Regulations Around the Globe: Do Regulations and Ownership Affect Performance and Stability?" In F. Mishkin, ed., *Prudential Regulation and Supervision: Why It Is Important and What Are the Issues?* Cambridge, Mass.: National Bureau of Economic Research

2001b. "Prudential Regulation and Supervision: What Works Best," *Policy Research Working Paper*, World Bank, Development Research Group, Washington, DC

Bartholomew, P. and B. Gup, 1999. "A Survey of Bank Failures in Non-US G-10 Countries Since 1980." In I. Finel–Honigman, ed., *European Union Banking Issues: Historical and Contemporary Perspectives.* Greenwich, Conn.: JAI Press

Bartolini, L. and A. Drazen, 1997. "Capital Account Liberalization as a Signal," *American Economic Review*, 87, 1, pp. 138–154

Beckeni, S. and C. Morris, 1992. "Are Bank Loans Still Special?" *Economic Review*, Federal Reserve Bank of Kansas City (third quarter), pp. 71–84

Bernanke, B. S., 1983. "Nonmonetary Effects of the Financial Crisis in the Propagation of the Great Depression," *American Economic Review*, 73, 3, pp. 257–276

Bernanke, B. S. and A. S. Blinder, 1992. "The Federal Funds Rate and the Channels of Monetary Transmission," *American Economic Review*, 82, 4, pp. 901–922

Bester, H., 1985. "Screening vs. Rationing in Credit Markets with Incomplete Information," *American Economic Review*, 75, 4, pp. 850–855

Bhattacharya, A. and J. E. Stiglitz, 2000. "The Underpinnings of a Stable and Equitable Global Financial System: From Old Debates to a New Paradigm." In B. Pleskovic and J. E. Stiglitz, eds., *Annual World Bank Conference on Development Economics 1999.* Washington, DC: World Bank

Blinder, A. S. and L. J. Maccini, 1991. "Taking Stock: A Critical Assessment of Recent Research on Inventories," *Journal of Economic Perspectives*, 5, 1, pp. 73–96

Blinder, A. S. and J. E. Stiglitz, 1983. "Money, Credit Constraints and Economic Activity," *American Economic Review*, 73, 2, pp. 297–302

Board of Governors of the Federal Reserve System, 1999. "Using Subordinated Debt as an Instrument of Market Discipline," *Staff Study*, 172, Washington, DC

Braun, S., 1984. "Productivity and the NAIRU (and Other Phillips Curve Issues)," United States Board of Governors of the Federal Reserve System. Division of Research and Statistics. National Income Section, Wages, Prices and Productivity Section, 34:1–21, February

Braverman A. K. Hoff and J. E. Stiglitz, eds., 1993. *The Economics of Rural Organization: Theory, Practice, and Policy.* New York: Oxford University Press

Braverman, A. and J. E. Stiglitz, 1982. "Sharecropping and the Interlinking of Agrarian Markets," *American Economic Review,* 72, 4, pp. 695–715

1986. "Cost Sharing Arrangement Under Sharecropping: Moral Hazard, Incentive Flexibility and Risk," *Journal of Agricultural Economics,* 68, 3, pp. 642–652

Burki, S. J. and G. E. Perry, 1998. *Beyond the Washington Consensus: Institutions Matter.* Washington, DC: World Bank

Calomiris, C. W. and G. Hubbard, 1989. "Price Flexibility, Credit Availability, and Economic Fluctuations: Evidence from the United States, 1894–1909," *Quarterly Journal of Economics* 104, pp. 429–452

Calomiris, C. W. and G. Hubbard, 1990. "Firm Heterogeneity, Internal Finance, and 'Credit Rationing'," *Economic Journal,* 100, pp. 90 104

Calomoris, C. W. and C. Kahn, 1991. "The Rule of Demandable Debt in Structuring Optimal Banking Arrangements," *American Economic Review,* 81, 3, pp. 497–513

Calomiris, C. W. and A. Powell, 2000. "Can Emerging Market Bank Regulators Establish Credible Discipline? The Case of Argentina," Washington, DC: World Bank

Calvo, G. A. and C. M. Reinhart, 2000. "When Capital Flows Come to a Sudden Stop: Consequences and Policy Options." In P. Kenen, M. Mussa and A. Swoboda, eds., *Key Issues in Reform of the International Monetary Systems.* Washington, DC: International Monetary Fund

Canner, G. and W. Passmore, 1997. "The Community Reinvestment Act and the Profitability of Mortgage-Oriented Banks," *Finance and Economics Discussion Series,* 1997-7

Caprio, G., 1996. "Bank Regulation: The Case of the Missing Model," *Policy Research Working Paper,* 1574, presented at a Brookings, KPMG conference on "The Sequencing of Financial Reform,"

1997. "Safe and Sound Banking in Developing Countries: We're Not in Kansas Anymore," *Research in Financial Services: Private and Public Policy,* 9, pp. 79–97

1999. "Banking on Crises: Expensive Lessons of Financial Crises." In George Kaufman, ed., *Research in Financial Services, 10.* Greenwich, Conn.: JAI Press

Caprio, G., I. Atiyas and J. A. Hanson, eds., 1994. *Financial Reform: Theory and Experience.* Cambridge: Cambridge University Press

Caprio, G. and P. Honohan, 1999. "Restoring Banking Stability: Beyond Supervised Capital Requirements," *Journal of Economic Perspectives,* 13, 4, pp. 43–64

    2000. "Reducing the Cost of Bank Crises: Is Basel Enough?" In David Dickinson, ed., *Managing Money in the Economy.* London: Routledge

Caprio, G., P. Honohan, and J. E. Stiglitz, eds., 2001. *Financial Liberalization: How Far, How Fast?* Cambridge: Cambridge University Press

Caprio, G. and D. Klingebiel, 1999. "Episodes of Systemic and Borderline Financial Crises." Washington, DC: World Bank

Caprio, G. and M. S. Martinez-Peria, 2000. "Avoiding Disaster: Policies to Reduce the Risk of Banking Crises," *Discussion Paper,* Egyptian Center for Econmic Studies, Cairo, Egypt, http://www.eces.org.eg

Cass, D. and J. E. Stiglitz, 1970. "The Structure of Investor Preferences and Asset Returns, and Separability in Portfolio Allocation: A Contribution to the Pure Theory of Mutual Funds," *Journal of Economic Theory,* 1, pp. 122–160

    1972. "Risk Aversion and Wealth Effects on Portfolios with Many Assets," *Review of Economic Studies,* 39, pp. 331–354

Cavalcanti, R. de O., A. Erosa and T. Temzelides, 1999. "Private Money and Reserve Management in a Random-Matching Model," *Journal of Political Economy,* 107, 5, pp. 929–945

Cavalcanti, R. de O. and N. Wallace, 1999. "Inside and Outside Money as Alternative Media of Exchange," *Journal of Money, Credit and Banking,* 31, 3, part 2, pp. 443–457

Cho, Y. J., 2001. "Korea's Financial Crisis: A Consequence of Uneven Liberalization." In G. Caprio, P. Honohan and J. E. Stiglitz, eds., *Financial Market Liberalization. How Far, How Fast?* Cambridge: Cambridge University Press

Choe, H., B. Kho and R. Stulz, 1999. "Do Foreign Investors Destabilize Stock Markets? The Korean Experience in 1997," *Journal of Financial Economics,* 54, pp. 227–264

Claessens, S. and M. Jansen, 2000. *The Internationalization of Financial Services: Issues and Lessons for Developing Countries.* Dordecht: Kluwer

Clay, K., B. Greenwald and J. E. Stiglitz, 1990. "Money Neutrality in a Model of Firm Adjustment," *Working Paper,* Stanford University

Cox, J. C., J. E. Ingersoll and S. Ross, 1985. "A Theory of the Term Structure of Interest Rates," *Econometrica,* 53, 2, pp. 385–407

Dasgupta, P. and J. E. Stiglitz, 1988. "Potential Competition, Actual Competition and Economic Welfare," *European Economic Review,* 32, pp. 569–577

Demirgüç-Kunt, A. and G. Caprio, 1997. "The Role of Long-Term Finance: Theory and Evidence," *World Bank Working Paper*, 1746

1999. "Financial Liberalization and Financial Fragility." In B.. Pleskovic and J. E. Stiglitz, eds., *Annual World Bank Conference on Development Economics 1998*. Washington, DC: World Bank.

Demirgüç-Kunt, A. and E. Detragiache, 1998a. "The Determinants of Banking Crises in Developing and Developed Countries," *International Monetary Fund Staff Papers*, 45, 1, pp. 81–109

1998b. "Financial Liberalization and Financial Fragility," *Proceedings of Annual Bank Conference on Development Economics*, Washington, DC, April 20–21

1998c. "Monitoring Banking Sector Fragility: A Multivariate Logit Approach with an Application to the 1996–97 Banking Crises," unpublished paper. World Bank and International Monetary Fund, June

Dewatripont, M. and J. Tirole, 1993. *The Prudential Regulation of Banks*. Cambridge, Mass.: MIT Press

Diaz-Alejandro, C., 1985. "Good-Bye Financial Repression, Hello Financial Crash." *Journal of Development Economics*, 19, 1–2, pp. 1–24

Dobell, R., 1968. "Optimization in Models of Economic Growth," address delivered at the 1968 National Meetings of the Society for Industrial and Applied Mathematics, Toronto, Institute for The Quantitative Analysis of Social and Economic Policy, University of Toronto, June

Dooley, M. P., 1996. "A Survey of Literature on Controls over International Capital Transactions," *International Monetary Fund Staff Papers*, 43, pp. 639–687

Duffie, D., 1996. *Dynamic Asset Pricing Theory*, 2nd edn. Princeton: Princeton University Press.

Duffie, D. and K. J. Singleton, 1997. "An Econometric Model of the Term Structure of Interest Rate Swap Yields," *Journal of Finance*, 52, pp. 1287–1323

Dyck, A., 1999. "Privatization and Corporate Governance: Principles, Evidence and Challenges for the Future," Washington, DC: World Bank, mimeo

Easterly, W. R., R. Islam, and J. E. Stiglitz 2000a. "Shaken and Stirred: Volatility and Macroeconomic Paradigms for Rich and Poor Countries," Michael Bruno Memorial Lecture. Washington, DC: World Bank

2000b. "Shaken and Stirred: Explaining Growth Volatility." In B. Pleskovic and J. E. Stiglitz, eds., *Annual Bank Conference on Development Economics 1998*. Washington, DC: World Bank

Eaton, J. and M. Gersowitz, M., 1981. "Debt with Potential Repudiation: Theoretical and Empirical Analysis," *Review of Economic Studies*, 48, pp. 289–309

Edlin, A. and J. E. Stiglitz, 1995. "Discouraging Rivals: Managerial Rent-Seeking and Economic Inefficiencies," *American Economic Review*, 85, 5, pp. 1301–1312

Englund, P., 1999. "The Swedish Banking Crisis: Roots and Consequences," *Oxford Review of Economic Policy*, 15, 3, pp. 80–97

Evanoff, D. and L. Wall, 2000. "Subordinated Debt and Bank Capital Reform," *Federal Reserve Bank of Chicago Working Paper*, WP 2000–07, August

Fair, R., 1987. "International Evidence on the Demand for Money," *Review of Economics and Statistics*, August, pp. 473–480

Fair, R. and R. Dominguez, 1991. "Effects of the Changing US Age Distribution on Macroeconomic Equations," *American Economic Review*, December, pp. 1276–1294

Farrell, J., 1986. "How Effective is Potential Competition?," *Economics Letters*, 20, pp. 67–70

1987. "Information and the Coase Theorem," *Journal of Economic Perspectives*, 1, 2, pp. 113–129; reprinted (in part) in S. Baker and C. Elliott, eds., *Economics of the Public Sector: Readings and Commentary*. Lexington, Mass.: Heath, 1989

Ferderer, P. J., 1993. "The Impact of Uncertainty on Aggregate Investment Spending: An Empirical Analysis," *Journal of Economic Literature*, 31, 4, pp. 1875–1911.

Ferri, G. and T. Kang, 1999. "The Credit Channel at Work: Lessons from the Republic of Korea's Financial Crisis," *World Bank Policy Research Working Paper*, 2190

Friedman, B. M. and K. N. Kuttner, 1993. "Economic Activity and the Short-Term Credit Markets: An Analysis of Prices and Quantities," *Brookings Papers on Economic Activity*, 2, pp. 193–283

Furman, J. and J. E. Stiglitz, 1998. "Economic Crises: Evidence and Insights from East Asia," *Brookings Papers on Economic Activity*, 2, presented at Brookings Panel on Economic Activity, Washington, DC, September 3, 1998, pp. 1–114

Gavin, M., R. Hausman, R. Perotti and E. Talvii, 1996. "Managing Fiscal Policy in Latin America and the Caribbean: Volatility, Procyclicality and Limited Creditworthiness," Inter-American Development Bank, Office of the Chief Economist, *Working Paper*, 326

Greenwald, B., 1986, "Adverse Selection in the Labour Market," *Review of Economic Studies*, 53, 3, pp. 325–347

1998. "International Adjustments in the Face of Imperfect Financial Markets," *Annual Bank Conference on Development Economics 1998*. Washington, DC: World Bank

Greenwald, B., M. Kohn and J. E. Stiglitz, 1990. "Financial Market Imperfections and Productivity Growth," *Journal of Economic Behavior and Organization*, 13, 3, pp. 321–345

Greenwald, B., A. Levinson and J. E. Stiglitz, 1993. "Capital Market Imperfections and Regional Economic Development." In A. Giovannini, ed., *Finance and Development: Issues and Experiences.* Cambridge: Cambridge University Press

Greenwald, B., M. Salinger and J. E. Stiglitz, 1990. "Imperfect Capital Markets and Productivity Growth," paper presented to NBER Conference in Vail, Colorado, April; revised March 1991, unpublished

Greenwald, B. and J. E. Stiglitz, 1986a. "Externalities in Economics with Imperfect Information and Incomplete Markets," *Quarterly Journal of Economics*, May, pp. 229–264

1986b. "Adverse Selection in the Labour Market," *Review of Economic Studies*, 53, 3, pp. 325–347

1987a. "Imperfect Information, Credit Markets and Unemployment," *European Economic Review*, 31, pp. 444–456

1987b. "Keynesian, New Keynesian and New Classical Economics," *Oxford Economic Papers*, 39, pp. 119–133

1987c. "Financial Structure and the Incidence of the Corporate Income Tax," unpublished

1988a. "Examining Alternative Macroeconomic Theories," *Brookings Papers on Economic Activity*, 1, pp. 207–270

1988b. "Imperfect Information, Finance Constraints and Business Fluctuations." In M. Kohn and S. C. Tsiang, eds., *Finance Constraints, Expectations, and Macroeconomics.* Oxford: Oxford University Press, pp. 103–140

1988c. "Information, Finance Constraints and Business Fluctuations," Proceedings of Taipei Symposium on Monetary Theory, Institute of Economics, Academia Sinica, pp. 299–336

1988d. "Money, Imperfect Information and Economic Fluctuations." In M. Kohn and S. C. Tsiang, eds., *Finance Constraints, Expectations and Macroeconomics.* Oxford: Oxford University Press, pp. 141–165

1988e. "Pareto Inefficiency of Market Economies: Search and Efficiency Wage Models," *American Economic Review*, 78, 2, pp. 351–355

1989a. "Impact of the Changing Tax Environment on Investments and Productivity," *Journal of Accounting, Auditing and Finance*, 4, 3, pp. 281–301

1989b. "Toward a Theory of Rigidities," *American Economic Review*, 79, 2, pp. 364–369

1990a. "Asymmetric Information and the New Theory of the Firm: Financial Constraints and Risk Behavior," *American Economic Review*, 80, 2, pp. 160–165

1990b. "Macroeconomic Models with Equity and Credit Rationing." In R. B. Hubbard, ed., *Asymmetric Information, Corporate Finance, and Investment.* Chicago: University of Chicago Press, pp. 15–42

1991a. "Monetary Policy and the Institutional Structure of Banking," June, unpublished

1991b. "Towards a Reformulation of Monetary Theory: Competitive Banking," *Economic and Social Review,* 23, 1, pp. 1–34

1991c. "Capital Market Imperfections and Labor Market Adjustments," paper presented to NBER/CEPR Conference on Labor Market Dynamics, Cambridge, Mass. October, unpublished

1991d. "Local Financing Alternative to the International Incidence of Corporate Income Taxes," paper presented to NBER Conference on International Aspects of Taxation, September, unpublished

1992. "Information, Finance and Markets: The Architecture of Allocative Mechanisms," *Industrial and Comporate Change,* 1, 1, pp. 37–63

1993a. "Financial Market Imperfections and Business Cycles," *Quarterly Journal of Economics,* 108, 1, pp. 77–114

1993b. "New and Old Keynesians," *Journal of Economic Perspectives,* 7, 1, pp. 23–44

1993c. "Monetary Policy and the Theory of the Risk-Averse Bank," Center for Economic Policy Research, Stanford University and Federal Reserve Bank of San Francisco, March 5

1995. "Labor Market Adjustments and the Persistence of Unemployment," *American Economic Review,* 85, 2, pp. 219–225

Greenwald, B., J. E. Stiglitz and A. Weiss, 1984. "Informational Imperfections in the Capital Markets and Macroeconomic Fluctuations," *American Economic Review,* 74, 2, pp. 194–199

Harris, M. and R. M. Townsend, 1981. "Resource Allocation under Asymmetric Information," *Econometrica,* 49, 1, pp. 33–64

1995. "Deposit Mobilisation through Financial Restraint," with T. Hellmann and K. Murdoch, *Stanford Graduate School of Business Reasearch Paper,* 1354, July; reprinted in *Banking and Financial Institutions,* 3, 5B, February 7, 1996

1996. "Deposit Mobilization Though Financial Restraint," With T. Hellmann and K. Murdoch. In N. Hermes and R. Lensink, eds., *Financial Development and Economic Growth.* London: Routledge, pp. 219–246

Hellmann, T., 2000. "Franchise Value and the Dynamics of Financial Liberalization: The Use of Capital Requirements and Deposit Rate Controls for Prudential Regulation." In A. Meyendorff and A. Thakor, eds., *Financial Systems in Transition: The Design of Financial Systems in Central Europe.* Cambridge, Mass.: MIT Press

Hellmann, T., K. Murdoch and J. E. Stiglitz, 2000. "Liberalization, Moral Hazard in Banking and Prudential Regulation: Are Capital Requirements Enough?," *American Economic Review*, 90, 1, pp. 147–165

Hellmann, T. and J. E. Stiglitz, 2000. "Credit and Equity Rationing in Markets with Adverse Selection," *European Economic Review*, 44, 2, pp. 281–304

Hicks, J. R., 1937. "Mr. Keynes and the 'Classics': A Suggested Interpretation," *Econometrica*, 5, 2, pp. 147–159

Hirschleifer, J., 1971. "The Private and Social Value of Information and the Reward to Inventive Activity," *American Economic Review*, 61, pp. 561–574

Hoff, K. and J. E. Stiglitz, 1997. "Moneylenders and Bankers: Price-Increasing Subsidies in a Monopolistically Competitive Market," *Journal of Development Economics*, 52, pp. 429–462

Holland , T. E., 1969. 'Operation Twist' and the Movement of Interest Rates and Related Economic Time Series," *International Economic Review* 10, 3, pp. 260–265

Honohan, P., 2000. "Banking System Failures in Developing and Transition Countries: Diagnosis and Prediction," *Economic Notes.*

2001a. "Perverse Effects of an External Ratings-Related Capital Adequacy System," *Economic Notes*, 30, 3

2001b. "Recapitalizing Banking Systems: Implications for Incentives, Fiscal and Monetary Policy," *Policy Research Working Paper*, 2540. Washington, DC: World Bank

Honohan, P. and D. Klingebiel, 2000. "Controlling the Fiscal Costs of Banking Crises," *Policy Research Working Paper*, 244a. Washington, DC: World Bank

Honohan, P. and J. E. Stiglitz, 2001. "Robust Financial Restraint." In G. Caprio, P. Honohan and J. E. Stiglitz, eds., *Financial Liberalization: How Far, How Fast?* Cambridge: Cambridge University Press

Hubbard, G., 1998. "Capital-Market Imperfections and Investment," *Journal of Economic Literature*, 36, pp. 193–225

Ingves, S. and G. Lind, 1996. "The Management of the Banking Crisis – in Retrospect," *Quarterly Review*, Sveriges Riksbank, 1, pp. 5–18

Islam, R., 1999. "Should Capital Flows be Regulated? A Look at the Issues and Policies," *Policy Research Working Paper*, 2293. Washington, DC: World Bank

Jaffee, D. and J. E. Stiglitz, 1990. "Credit Rationing." In B. Friedman and F. Hahn, eds., *Handbook of Monetary Economics*. Amsterdam: Elsevier, pp. 837–888

Jensen, M. and W. Meckling, 1976. "Theory of the Firm: Managerial Behavior, Agency Costs and Ownership Structure," *Journal of Financial Economics*, 3, pp. 305–360

Jones, C. P. and Wilson, J. W., 1997. "Long Term Returns and Risk for Bonds," *Journal of Portfolio Management*, Spring, pp. 15–28

Kaminsky, G., S. Linzondo and C. M. Reinhart, 1998. "Leading Indicators of Currency Crises," *IMF Staff Papers*, 45, pp. 1–48

Kaminsky, G. and S. Schmukler, 2001. "On Financial Booms and Crashes: Regional Patterns, Time Patterns, and Financial Liberalization," *Policy Research Working Paper*, Development Research Group. Washington, DC: World Bank, forthcoming

Kane, E., 1985. *The Gathering Crisis in Federal Deposit Insurance.* Cambridge, Mass. MIT Press

1987. "Dangers of Capital Forbearance: The Case of the FSLIC and 'Zombie' S & Ls," *Contemporary Policy Issues*, 5, 1, pp. 77–83

1990. "Incentive Conflict in the International Regulatory Agreement on Risk-Based Capital," *National Bureau of Economic Research Working Paper*, 3308

2000a. "The Dialectical Role of Information and Disinformation in Regulation-Induced Banking Crises," *Pacific Basin Finance Journal*, 8, pp. 285–308

2000b. "Architecture of Supra-National Financial Regulation," *Journal of Financial Services Research*, 18, 2/3, pp. 301–318

Keeton, W., 1984. "Deposit Insurance and the Deregulation of Deposit Rates," *Economic Review of the Federal Reserve Bank of Kansas City*, April, pp. 28–46

1992. "The Reconstruction Finance Corporation: Would it Work Today?" *Federal Reserve Bank of Kansas City, Economic Review*

Kehoe, T. and Levine, D. K., 1993. "Debt-Constrained Asset Markets," *Review of Economic Studies*, 60, pp. 868–888

Keynes, J. M., 1936. *The General Theory of Unemployment, Interest and Money.* London: Macmillan; reprinted New York: Harcourt Brace 1964

Kindleberger, Charles, P., 1978. *Manias, Panics, and Crashes: A History of Financial Crises.* New York: John Wiley; reprinted 1996

King, R. G. and R. Levine. 1993a. "Finance and Growth: Schumpeter Might be Right," *Quarterly Journal of Economics*, 108, 3, pp. 717–737

1993b. "Finance, Entrepreneurship, and Growth," *Journal of Monetary Economics*, 32, 3, pp. 13–43

Kishan, R. P. and T. P. Opiela, 2000. "Bank Size, Bank Capital, and the Bank Lending Channel," *Journal of Money, Credit, and Banking*, 32, pp. 121–141

Kiyotaki, N. and R. Wright, 1989. "On Money as a Medium of Exchange," *Journal of Political Economy*, 97, 4, pp. 927–954

Klingebiel, D., 2000. "The Use of Asset Management Companies in the Resolution of Banking Crises: Cross Country Experiences," *Policy Research Working Paper*, 2284. Washington, DC: World Bank

Kocherlakota, N. R., 1996. "Implications of Efficient Risk Sharing without Commitment," *Review of Economic Studies*, 63, pp. 595–609

Kose, J., A. Saunders and L. Senbet, 2000. "A Theory of Bank Regulation and Management Compensation," *Review of Financial Studies*, 13, 1, pp. 95–125

Kraay, A., 1998a. "Do High Interest Rates Defend Currencies Against Speculative Attacks?," World Bank, August, unpublished

1998b. "In Search of the Macroeconomic Effects of Capital Account Liberalization," World Bank, Development Research Group

Kydland, F. E. and T. Cooley, 1995."Economic Growth and Business Cycles." In T. Cooley, ed., *Frontiers of Business Cycle Research*. Princeton: Princeton University Press, pp. 1–38

Kydland, F. E. and E. C. Prescott, 1990. "Business Cycles: Real Facts and a Monetary Myth." In F. E. Kydland, ed., *Business Cycle Theory*, Elgar Reference Collection, International Library of Critical Writings in Economics, 58. Cheltenham: Edward Elgar, pp. 67–82

Lustig, N., 1999 "Crises and the Poor: Socially Responsive Macroeconomics," Presidential Address at the Fourth Annual Meeting of the Latin American and Caribbean Economic Association, Santiago, Chile, October 22

MaCurdy, T. E. and J. B. Shoven, 1992. "Stocks, Bonds, and Pension Wealth." In D. E. Wise, ed., *Topics in the Economics of Aging*, A National Bureau of Economic Research Project Report. Chicago: University of Chicago Press

Mayer, C., 1988. "New Issues in Corporate Finance," *European Economic Review*, 32, pp. 1167–1189

1990."Financial Systems, Corporate Finance, and Economic Development." In R. G. Hubbard, ed., *Asymmetric Information, Corporate Finance, and Investment*. Chicago: University of Chicago Press, pp. 307–332

McKinnon, R., 1973. "Money and Capital in Economic Development." Washington, DC: Brookings Institution.

1988a. "Financial Liberalization and Economic Development: A Reassessment of Interest Rate Policies in Asia and Latin America." San Francisco: International Center for Economic Growth

1988b. "Financial Liberalization in Retrospect: Interest Rate Policies in LDCs." In G. Ranis and T. R. Schultz, eds. *The State of Development Economics*. New York: Basil Blackwell

Mehra, Y. P., 1978. "Is Money Exogenous in Money-Demand Equations?" *Journal of Political Economy*, 86, 2, pp. 211–228

Meiselman, D., 1962. *The Term Structure of Interest Rates*. Englewood Cliffs, NJ: Prentice-Hall

Miller, M. and J. E. Stiglitz, 1999. "Bankruptcy Protection against Macroeconomic Shocks: The Case for a 'Super Chapter 11',"

Conference on Capital Flows, Financial Crises, and Policies, World Bank, April 15–16

Mishkin, F., 2000. "Securing a safety net against economic free fall," *Financial Times*, June 6, 2000.

Modigliani, F. and M. H. Miller, 1958. "The Cost of Capital, Corporation Finance and the Theory of Investment," *American Economic Review*, 48, 3, pp. 261–297

Myers, S. C. and N. Majluf, 1984. "Corporate Financing and Investment Decisions When Firms Have Information that Investors Do Not Have," *Journal of Financial Economics*, 13, pp. 187–221

Nalebuff, B., A. Rodriguez and J. E. Stiglitz, 1993. "Equilibrium Unemployment as a Worker Screening Device," *NBER Working Paper*, 4557; originally paper presented to NBER/CEPR Conference on Unemployment and Wage Determination, Boston, October 1991

Nalebuff, B. and J. E. Stiglitz, 1983a. "Information, Competition and Markets," *American Economic Review*, 73, 2, pp. 278–284

1983b. "Prizes and Incentives: Toward a General Theory of Compensation and Competition," *Bell Journal*, 14, 1, pp. 21–43

Newberry, D. and J. E. Stiglitz, 1976. "Sharecropping: Risk Sharing and the Importance of Imperfect Information." In J. A. Roumasset *et al.*, eds., *Risk Uncertainty and Development*. SEARCA, A/D/C, pp. 311–341

Obstfeld, M., 1998. "The Global Capital Market: Benefactor or Menace?" *Journal of Economic Perspectives*, 12, 4, pp. 9–30

Orszag, P. and J. E. Stiglitz, 1999. "Bankruptcy, Credit Constraints, and Economic Policy," unpublished draft, July

Phelps, E., 1986. "The Significance of Customer Markets for the Effects of Budgetary Policy in Open Economies," *IIES Seminar Paper*, 315, University of Stockholm; *Annales d' Economie et de Statistique*, 1, 3, September, IIES Reprint Series, 330

Phelps, E. S. and S. G. Winter Jr., 1970. "Optimal Price Policy under Atomistic Competition." In E.S. Phelps et al., eds., *Microeconomic Foundations of Employment and Inflation Theory*, New York, Norton

Radelet, S. and J. Sachs, 1998. "The East Asian Financial Crisis: Diagnosis, Remedies, Prospects," *Brookings Papers on Economic Activity*, 1, pp. 1–74

Rey, P. and J. E. Stiglitz, 1993. "Short-Term Contracts as a Monitoring Device," *NBER Working Paper*, 4514

Robertson, D. H., 1922. *Money*. New York: Harcourt, Brace

Rodriguez, A. and J. E. Stiglitz, 1991a. "Equilibrium Unemployment, Testing, and the Pure Theory of Selection," paper presented to NBER/CEPR Conference on Unemployment and Wage Determination, Boston, October

1991b. "Unemployment and Efficiency Wages: The Adverse Selection Model," paper presented to NBER/CEPR Conference on Unemployment and Wage Determination, Boston, October

Rodrik, D., 1998a. "Globalization, Social Conflict, and Economic Growth," Prebish Lecture, *The World Economy*, 21, 2

1998b. "Symposium on Globalization in Perspective: An Introduction," *Journal of Economic Perspectives*, 12, 4, pp. 3–8

1998c. "Who Needs Capital Account Convertibility?" In S. Fischer *et al.*, *Should the IMF Pursue Capital-Account Convertibility? Essays in International Finance*, 207. International Finance Section, Department of Economics, Princeton University, May

1999. "The New Global Economy and Developing Countries: Making Openness Work," US Overseas Development Council, *Policy Essay*, 24

Rodrik, D., and A. Velasco, 1999. "Short Term Capital Flows," *Annual Bank Conference on Development Economics 1998*. Washington, DC: World Bank; *NBER Working Paper*, W7364

Ross, S., 1973, "The Economic Theory of Agency: The Principal's Problem," *American Economic Review*, 63, 2, pp. 134–139

Rothschild, M. and J. E. Stiglitz, 1970. "Increasing Risk: I. A Definition," *Journal of Economic Theory*, 2, 3, pp. 225–243

Sah, R. and J. E. Stiglitz, 1985. "Human Fallibility and Economic Organization," *American Economic Review*, 75, 2, pp. 292–296

1986. "The Architecture of Economic Systems: Hierarchies and Polyarchies," *American Economic Review*, 76, 4, pp. 716–727

1988. "Committees, Hierarchies and Polyarchies," *Economic Journal*, 98, 391, pp. 451–470

Samuelson, P., 1948. *Economics*. New York: McGraw-Hill

Schiller, R., 2000. *Irrational Exuberance*. Princeton: Princeton University Press

Schwartz, A., 1998. "From Confrontation to Collaboration? Banks, Community Groups, and the Implementation of Community Reinvestment Agreements." *Housing Policy Debate*, 9, 3, pp. 631–662

Seidman, E., 1999. "CRA in the 21st Century," *Mortgage Banking*. Washington, DC, October

Shaw, E. 1973. *Financial Deepening in Economic Development*. New York: Oxford University Press

Singleton, K. J., 1980. "Expectation Models of the Term Structure and Implied Variance Bounds," *Journal of Political Economy*, 88, pp. 1159–1176

1988. "Modeling the Term Structure of Interest Rates in General Equilibrium." In S. Bhattacharya and G. Constantinides, eds., *Theory of Valuation – Frontiers of Modern Financial Theory*, 1. Totowa, NJ: Rowan & Allenheld

Stigler, G., 1967. "Imperfections in the Capital Market," *Journal of Political Economy*, pp. 287–292

Stiglitz, J. E., 1969. "A Re-Examination of the Modigliani–Miller Theorem," *American Economic Review*, 59, 5, pp. 784–793

1970. "A Consumption Oriented Theory of the Demand for Financial Assets and the Term Structure of Interest Rates," *Review of Economic Studies*, 37, pp. 321–351

1972a. "Four Lectures on Portfolio Allocation with Many Risky Assets." In Szege, and Shell, eds., *Mathematical Methods in Investment and Finance*. Amsterdam: North-Holland, pp. 76–108

1972b. "On the Optimality of the Stock Market Allocation of Investment," *Quarterly Journal of Economics*, 86, 1, pp. 25–60

1972c. "Some Aspects of the Pure Theory of Corporate Finance: Bankruptcies and Take-Overs," *Bell Journal of Economics*, 3, 2, pp. 458–482

1973. "Taxation, Corporate Financial Policy and the Cost of Capital," *Journal of Public Economics*, 2, pp. 1–34

1974a. "On the Irrelevance of Corporate Financial Policy," *American Economic Review*, 64, 6, pp. 851–866

1974b. "Incentives and Risk Sharing in Sharecropping," *Review of Economic Studies*, 41, pp. 219–255

1974c. "Alternative Theories of Wage Determination and Unemployment in LDCs: The Labor Turnover Model," *Quarterly Journal of Economics*, 88, 2, pp. 194–227; subsequently published in D. Lal, ed., *Development Economics, 1*. Cheltenham: Edward Elgar, 1992, pp. 288–321

1975a. "The Theory of 'Screening', Education and the Distribution of Income," *American Economic Review*, 65, 3, pp. 283–300

1975b. "Information and Economic Analysis." In J. M. Parkin and A. R. Nobay, eds., *Current Economic Problems*. Cambridge: Cambridge University Press, pp. 27–52; Proceedings of the Association of University Teachers of Economics, Manchester, April 1974

1975c. "Incentives, Risk, and Information: Notes Towards a Theory of Hierarchy," *Bell Journal of Economics*, 6, 2, pp. 552–579

1982a. "Ownership, Control and Efficient Markets: Some Paradoxes in the Theory of Capital Markets." In K. D. Boyer and W. G. Shepherd, eds., *Economic Regulation: Essays in Honor of James R. Nelson*. Last Lansing: Michigan State University Press, pp. 311–341

1982b. "Information and Capital Markets." In W. F. Sharpe and C. Cootner, eds., *Financial Economics: Essays in Honor of Paul Cootner*. Englewood Cliffs, NJ: Prentice-Hall, pp. 118–158; see also *NBER Working Paper*, 678

1983a. "On the Relevance or Irrelevance or Public Financial Policy: Indexation, Price Rigidities and Optimal Monetary Policy"

In R. Dornbusch and M. Simonsen, eds., *Inflation, Debt and Indexation.* Cambridge, Mass.: MIT Press, pp. 183–222

1983b. "Some Aspects of the Taxation of Capital Gains," *Journal of Public Economics,* 21, pp. 257–294

1987a. "The New Keynesian Economics: Money and Credit," Fisher–Schultz Lecture presented at the Meetings of the Econometric Society, Copenhagen, August

1987b. "Sharecropping." In J. Eatwell et al., eds., *The New Palgrave: A Dictionary of Economics.* New York: St. Martin's Press; subsequently reprinted in J. Eatwell, *et al.,* eds., *The New Palgrave: Economic Development.* New York: St. Martin's Press, 1989, pp. 308–315

1988a. "On the Relevance or Irrelevance of Public Financial Policy." In K. J. Arrow and M. J. Boskin, eds., *The Economics of Public Debt.* New York: St. Martin's Press, pp. 4–76

1988b. "Money, Credit, and Business Fluctuations," *Economic Record,* 64, 187, pp. 62–72

1988c. "Technological Change, Sunk Costs, and Competition," *Brookings Papers on Economic Activity,* 3, 1987; Special issue of *Microeconomics,* M. N. Baily and C. Winston, eds., 1988, pp. 883–947

1989a. "Financial Markets and Development," *Oxford Review of Economic Policy,* 5, 4, pp. 55–68

1989b. "Mutual Funds, Capital Structure, and Economic Efficiency." In S. Bhattacharya and G. Constantinides, eds., *Theory of Valuation – Frontiers of Modern Financial Theory, 1.* Totowa, NJ: Rowman & Allenheld, pp. 342–356

1989c. "Imperfect Information in the Product Market." In *Handbook of Industrial Organization, 1.* Amsterdam: Elsevier, pp. 769–847

1989d. "Using Tax Policy to Curb Speculative Short-Term Trading," *Journal of Financial Services Research,* 3, 2/3, pp. 101–115

1990. "Credit Rationing," with D. Jaffee. In B. Friedman and F. Hahn, eds., *Handbook of Monetary Economics.* Amsterdam: Elsevier, pp. 837–888

1991. Federico Caffè Lectures presented to the University of Rome and the Bank of Italy, Rome, April; *NBER Working Paper,* 4117

1992a. "S & L Bailout." In J. Barth and R. Brumbaugh, Jr., eds., *The Reform of Federal Deposit Insurance: Disciplining the Government and Protecting Taxpayers.* New York: HarperCollins, pp. 1–12

1992b. "The Role of the State in Financial Markets," Proceedings of the Annual Conference on Development Economics. Washington, DC: World Bank

1992c. "Banks versus Markets as Mechanisms for Allocating and Coordinating Investment." In J. A. Roumasset and S. Barr, eds.,

*The Economics of Cooperation: East Asian Development and the Case for Pro-Market Intervention.* Boulder, Col.: Westview Press, pp. 15–38

1993a. "The Role of the State in Financial Markets," Proceedings of the Annual Conference on Development Economics. Washington, DC: World Bank, pp. 19–52

1993b. "Perspectives on the Role of Government Risk-Bearing within the Financial Sector." In M. Sniderman, ed., *Government Risk-Bearing.* Norwell, Mass: Kluwer Academic, pp. 109–30

1995. "Interest Rate Puzzles, Competitive Theory and Capital Constraints." In Jean-Paul, Fitoussi, ed., *Economics in a Changing World,* Proceedings of the Tenth World Congress of the International Economic Association, 5, Economic Growth and Capital and Labour Markets, Moscow, IEA Conference Volume, 111. New York: St. Martin's Press, pp. 145–175

1997. "Reflections on the Natural Rate Hypothesis," *Journal of Economic Perspectives,* 11, pp. 3–10

1998a. "Central Banking in a Democratic Society," *De Economist* (Netherlands), 146, 2, pp. 199–226

1998b. "Lessons from East Asia," paper prepared for the American Economic Association Annual Meetings. New York, January 4, 1999; *Journal of Policy Modeling*

1998c. "Lessons from the Global Financial Crisis." In J. R. Bisignano, W. C. Hunter and G. G Kaufman, eds., *Global Financial Crises: Lessons from Recent Events,* Bank for International Settlements/ Federal Reserve Bank of Chicago; Boston: Kluwer Academic, 2000, pp. 89–109

1999. "Knowledge for Development: Economic Science, Economic Policy, and Economic Advice," Opening address, Proceedings of the Annual Bank Conference on Development Economics, 1998. Washington, DC: World Bank

2000a. "Capital Market Liberalization, Economic Growth, and Instability," *World Development,* 28, 6, pp. 1075–1086

2000b. "Scan Globally, Reinvent Locally: Knowledge Infrastructure and the Localization of Knowledge." In D. Stone, ed., *Banking on Knowledge.* London: Routledge, pp. 24–43

2000c. "The Contributions of the Economics of Information to Twentieth- Century Economics," *Quarterly Journal of Economics,* 115, 4, pp. 1441–1478

2001. "Principles of Financial Regulation: A Dynamic Approach," *The World Bank Observer,* 16, 1, pp. 1–18

Stiglitz, J. E. and C. Walsh, 2002. *Economics.* New York: W. W. Norton

Stiglitz, J. E. and A. Weiss, 1981. "Credit Rationing in Markets with Imperfect Information," *American Economic Review,* 71, 3, pp. 333–421

1983. "Incentive Effects of Termination: Applications to the Credit and Labor Markets," *American Economic Review*, 73, 5, pp. 912–927

1986. "Credit Rationing and Collateral." In J. Edwards, *et al.*, eds., *Recent Developments in Corporate Finance*. New York: Cambridge University Press, pp. 101–135

1987. "Credit Rationing: Reply," *American Economic Review*, 77, 1, pp. 228–231

1990. "Banks as Social Accountants and Screening Devices for the Allocation of Credit," *Greek Economic Review*, 12, Supplement, Autumn, pp. 85–118; reprinted in M. K. Lewis, ed., *Financial Intermediaries*. Aldershot: Edward Elgar, 1995, pp. 297–330; see also *NBER Working Paper*, 2710, September 1988

1991. "Asymmetric Information in Credit Markets and Its Implications for Macroeconomics," *Oxford Economic Papers*, 44, 4, pp. 694–724.

Tobin, J., 1958. "Liquidity Preference as Behavior Towards Risk," *Review of Economic Studies*, 67, pp. 65–86

1969. "A General Equilibrium Approach to Monetary Theory," *Journal of Money, Credit and Banking*, 1, pp. 15–29

Townsend, R., 1978. "Optimal Contracts and Competitive Markets with Costly State Verification", *Journal of Economic Theory*, 21, pp. 265–293

Van Horne, J., 1993. *Financial Market Rates and Flows*, 4th edn. Englewood Cliffs, NJ: Prentice-Hall

Williamson, O. E., 1979. "Transaction Cost Economics: The Governance of Contractual Relations," *Journal of Law and Economics*, ??, pp. 233–261

1985. *The Economic Institutions of Capitalism: Firms, Markets and Relational Contracting*. New York: Free Press

1999. "The Economics of Transaction Costs." In S. Masten, ed., *Critical Writings Readers*. American International Distribution Corporation, Vermont

World Bank, 1999. *The East Asia Miracle*. New York: Oxford University Press

2001 *Finance for Growth*. New York: Oxford University Press

# Index